"There is not one linear path to success as an artist. You have to first define what success means to you in order to accomplish what you want in your career."

- Alicia & Kat

The Complete Smartist Guide

Essential Business and Career Tips for Emerging Artists

Alicia Puig and Ekaterina Popova

TABLE OF CONTENTS

INTRODUCTION

When we first came up with the idea for the original version of The Smartist Guide, we were sitting in a small, local restaurant exchanging stories about our individual experiences in the art world (and probably sipping a glass of rosé or two!). Reflecting on the past decade of our respective careers, we realized the numerous instances where we taught ourselves how to overcome obstacles and achieve our goals. We were both able to identify simple tips and bits of advice that had made a major impact on our professional success. As much as we may have wished that we had learned these lessons in art school, having to figure things out along the way pushed us to persevere and be resilient. That being said, we also agreed that it shouldn't have to be that hard for anyone else—and we jokingly said that we should write a book!

Originally, Kat founded *Create! Magazine* to provide a platform to showcase the work of talented emerging artists and while that mission has not changed, shortly after Alicia joined the team, we slightly shifted our focus. After receiving questions from our readers about how to submit work for media features, apply for gallery representation, write an artist statement, and more, we recognized that artists not only needed a place for their art to be seen, but also a trusted resource for career advice. While we initially addressed these questions in the form of articles and podcast episodes, eventually we decided that our community would be better served by collating all of this information in one place, so we launched *The Smartist Guide* in January 2019.

Our first book was only eighty pages, but we received such an overwhelming amount of positive feedback and requests for more content that we were inspired to write a longer, more comprehensive version. Thus, *The Complete Smartist Guide* was born. We committed to writing for a full year in order to share all of the tools we learned along the way and help emerging artists get started in their careers. Although our world, and the art industry within it, is changing daily, and we can't always keep up with new technology, we believe that you can learn from our experiences and apply aspects of what worked for us to your unique situation. Keep an open mind as you make your way through the book and try not to discard seemingly simple advice, as it can often be the most effective.

You can read *The Complete Smartist Guide* in any order that you wish. We understand that you may already be knowledgeable in some areas, but still need more guidance in others. When you reach the end of each chapter, we encourage you to follow the action steps to get the most out of this book—that's where the magic happens!

In select chapters, you'll notice that we've asked members of our incredible community to offer additional insight on topics such as licensing, commissions, working with high-end brands, and more. Our willingness to ask questions, get help, and reach out to others with expertise is part of the reason why we were able to build our online businesses and develop a loyal audience over the past several years.

Above all, we want you to remember that your work as an artist is important. It can provide joy, inspiration, and healing to your viewers, give confidence to other artists, bring hope and beauty to society during uncertain times, and most importantly, serve as an outlet for expressing your unique experience.

We sincerely hope that *The Complete Smartist Guide* makes it a little easier for you to share your work, get paid for doing what you love, and inspire others to do the same. Thank you for giving us the opportunity to share this book with you.

Happy Reading!
Alicia and Kat

Business Basics

YOUR ARTIST WEBSITE

Your artist website is a powerful tool to help collectors, galleries, and media outlets who want to work with you access your portfolio, biography, resume, and contact information all in one place. Our best advice here is: don't overthink it. All you need is something simple and easy to navigate that contains a collection of your best work—both past and current—a link to your email, a mailing list sign-up, a section that specifies your available work, and perhaps a webshop or a contact listing for any galleries that represent you.

We prefer and recommend websites with a plain white background so that any featured art can stand out and doesn't have to compete with anything else. Other neutrals, such as off-white and light gray, can also work. These colors may not seem very exciting, but the benefit of using them is that they mimic how your artwork would look on most gallery walls, and even in some of the homes of your potential collectors. It's always a nice idea to proactively assist interested buyers with envisioning your work in their space.

If your work has a lot going on visually, you especially do not need additional colors and patterns present on your website. A clean and minimalist *"Create a user-friendly online experience that will not only allow them to see your talent, but also inspire them to exhibit your art, feature it, or buy it!"* design will ensure that your site visitors are focused on your art alone. A few accents and pops of color are acceptable to show off your style and personality, but anything more than that is usually a distraction. If you are design savvy, feel free to personalize your pages, as long as they flow seamlessly with your work and aesthetic. For the rest of us, less is more when it comes to any art website.

Take a few minutes to browse your favorite contemporary artists' sites before getting started on your own. Do some research to figure out where these pages are hosted and how they are designed. At the time of writing this book, there are numerous platforms available that will help even the least computer-literate individuals create beautiful sites by using templates and easy-to-follow guides. We've listed some of our favorites on page 18.

While we do stress the importance of having a proper website, we don't think it's wise to invest a ton of money into one that is custom-designed by a professional if you are just starting out (unless you have the budget to do so). Your money is definitely better spent on applying to opportunities that will promote your art and purchasing quality materials at this stage. If you have a lot of trouble figuring it out and want assistance, consider asking a friend who enjoys website building, or you can hire someone on a site like Upwork or Fiverr at a more affordable rate.

There are a few key elements you should include to make it easy for collectors, dealers, and other visitors to view and appreciate your work, which we'll go over next. Create a user-friendly online experience that will not only allow them to see your talent, but also inspire them to exhibit your art, feature it, or buy it!

Professional Domain Name

Unless you work under a pseudonym, purchase a domain that contains your name, or as close as you can get to it. There are many artists out there and many art websites, so don't worry if your name is already being used by someone else. Play around with it to come up with a domain that works, whether that means shortening your first name or last name or using a nickname. For example, when Kat's full name was not available she simply dropped the "e" at the beginning of her first name to come up with www.katerinapopova.com. If you modify the domain name, make sure to include your full name throughout the rest of your site so that it shows up when people try to find you via a search engine.

Search engines are the primary reason for using your name directly in your domain! We have both come across artists who we wanted to learn more about, but when we typed them into Google we didn't find their website and were not able to follow up. If you want to maintain a blog or second page with a more creative title, that's absolutely fine, but do include your name in the domain of your artist website that you share with clients and galleries.

Using your name also underscores the fact that you are the sole, unique maker of your art and that what you create is original. Part of what you're selling as an artist is your work, of course, but another big part is your ideas, your creativity, your talent, and your personal story. Help your audience better engage with you by decisively connecting your artwork with your name.

Another solution for coming up with a domain if your name is not available is to add "art" or "studio" at the end. You could also reference the medium you work in. For example: katpopovapaints.com or ekaterinapopovapainter.com. Just make sure that if you choose a medium, it is the primary one you will be working in for the long term. These are great alternatives that won't sacrifice your professionalism if you want to avoid altering or abbreviating your name.

Readable Font

Pick a modern and easy-to-read font for the majority of text on your website. Luckily, templated websites usually come with a few standard options that are integrated into the design, and those should work perfectly. If you want to jazz up your headlines, you can add personality by choosing something more creative. We can't stress legibility enough, so if you choose to use a more unique font, make sure it's not impossible to decipher on a screen. If people can't read what is on your site, they will immediately leave and you will lose your chance of making a great first impression. If you have doubts, test it out with a family member or friend—it's a good idea to have another set of eyes anyway to help find mistakes or typos you may have missed.

Tip:

More and more people view websites on their smartphones or tablets these days. When designing your website, look for templates or themes that are "responsive." This means that the website will detect the visitor's screen size and adjust the layout accordingly, so your site will look great, no matter what kind of device your visitors use to visit. It's also a good idea to view your design choices on your phone to make sure you can read all the fonts and headings and that your images don't get cropped or distorted.

WEBSITE ESSENTIALS

Organizing Your Artwork

Artists usually organize their work by year, but if you don't have much art from one year you can combine it with another. For example, your year categories could look something like this: 2015 & previous, 2016 & 2017, 2018, and 2019.

You should also separate each series into subcategory pages or galleries, which are available on most website hosting platforms. Similarly, if you work in multiple mediums, such as painting and sculpture, for example, you may want to create a different section for each so that viewers aren't confused when browsing through your images. An exception to this is if you have works in various media that are part of the same series. Your ultimate goal is to create a seamless experience in which visitors can easily find and view a cohesive body of your work.

If your oeuvre includes several series, or you work in a variety of mediums, you should find a platform or template that will allow you to build all the pages or galleries that you need. Think of this from the beginning, and don't start working on a site unless it has the capabilities you require or it will be frustrating and limiting in the long run, especially if you're paying for the site—you want the best fit to get your money's worth.

Working with Images

Make sure your images are of the highest quality possible (300 dpi, minimum), but do periodically check to see how quickly they load and if that is affecting your bounce rate (i.e. how fast people leave your site). If it becomes an issue and the site is incredibly slow, use web-resolution (72 dpi) photos instead. Slow websites can frustrate visitors and negatively affect your search rankings, so optimize your images if they are too large by using an image compression website, such as www.tinypng.com. You can also resize your images using Photoshop or any similar image-editing program. There are several options for free web applications, such as Pixlr, that allow you to edit and resize photos, so you don't need to invest in expensive photo-processing software.

FINDING YOUR WEBSITE'S SPEED

You can find your website's speed information by registering it with Google Analytics. This is an incredible tool that gives detailed insight into who is visiting your website, how they access your site, what pages they spend the most time on, and more. It can seem intimidating or overwhelming to use at first, but a wealth of tutorials exist online, some provided by Google itself. Focus your time on learning and going through the features in the audience, acquisition, and behavior sections. If you really get into it, you can use Google Analytics to run ads for your website so that it ranks higher in search engine results, but beware that this can get costly very quickly, so it is only worth investing in if they result in strong artwork sales.

For each work of art, you should include a primary image and a detail shot or two. If you have a framed or installed view, that is good to include as well. Don't forget to list the artwork title, size, medium, and year of creation right next to or under the images. The more information the better, so you may even think about writing a sentence or two about the meaning or inspiration behind the work. This can help your audience engage with the piece and fall in love with it! Some artists decide to be transparent with all or some of their prices, but that is entirely up to you. If you choose not to show the price, you should at least include a link to where each piece can be purchased or a note that interested buyers may contact you for more information.

Updating Your Works

Mark your works as "sold" or "unavailable" if they cannot be purchased. It can be disappointing for potential clients when they reach out to you only to find that a work they really wanted isn't something they can actually buy. Some weeks and months may get incredibly busy, but try to keep your inventory updated and accurate to make the best experience for your potential clients.

BOOSTING SALES WITH A WEBSHOP

Creating a webshop can help you boost art sales. We'll go into this in more detail later in this chapter, but if your website supports e-commerce, look into setting up each piece on a product page so that clients can buy from you directly online, rather than having to contact you first. Not ready for that yet? Simply include a page with available works that you keep up-to-date for potential buyers, or establish a standard way of noting that pieces are available throughout your site.

Bio & Artist Statement

Your site should include a brief bio that contains relevant information about who you are and your background, in addition to a statement that explains what your work is about. Be sure to refer to the chapter on writing your artist statement (see page 30) if you need additional advice on how to craft one specific to the work you create. To add a personal touch, you may also want to post a professional headshot or photos of you in your studio.

Please note that your bio and statement are different, although some artists like to combine or list them together on their "About" page. You can take a look at Kat's website's "About" page for an example: https://www.katerinapopova.com.

Her artist biography shares all about her passions as both an artist and entrepreneur, including why she launched Create! Magazine, Art & Cocktails, and The Art Queens. In Kat's artist statement, she focuses solely on the meaning and inspiration behind her work. Some artists like to note where they currently live and work at the end, so you can include this if it is of interest. Kat prefers to keep her bio in the third person, but many artists we admire write theirs in the first person. Both options are fine—just keep it consistent.

CV

Create a separate page that lists all your notable exhibitions, press, and awards for a potential collector or gallery to see. You can format this to look the same as your artist resume, which we will discuss in the next chapter (see page 20). If you prefer to not copy your full CV online, you should include a link to a downloadable PDF version of it on your "About" page. We also think it is a good idea to provide direct links to any of your press features that can be accessed online.

Contact Page

Including a way to reach you is essential, for obvious reasons. As you grow your network, exciting new opportunities and interested buyers will come directly to you. Be ready by having a simple way to allow people to connect with you whether that is by email, phone, or both.

Most websites come with built-in contact forms that link to your email, and this is certainly an option that you can use if you do not wish to list your contact information directly. However, these forms can be a bit clunky and are not always the most user-friendly, so test it out before settling on this option. Alicia had an issue once where her contact box messages ended up in her junk mail, and she missed an opportunity to be interviewed for a blog. A writer had seen one of her pieces advertised as a headline image for a show in New York, but Alicia didn't find the note until months later, way past the closing of the exhibition. So disappointing!

While it may concern you to have your email available publicly, there is a low likelihood of being contacted for anything other than professional requests. It is worth mentioning here that you should already have a dedicated email for your art practice that is different from your personal email address. If you don't, now is a perfect time to make a separate address, and you can use the same guidelines as for choosing a domain name to select an appropriate and memorable email address. Gmail is a great free option, or website hosting platforms often offer email services so that you can have an address like info@yourwebsitedomain.com.

Do your best to respond to inquiries promptly, within approximately twenty-four to forty-eight hours on weekdays, which will invariably increase your success rate. If someone reaches out intending to buy one or more of your pieces, it's a good idea to have a price list and shipping details figured out beforehand, but we'll help you out with this later on in How to Price Your Art (page 54) and Smart Strategies to Sell & Market Your Art (page 64).

Upcoming Events or News
It's fun to find new fans and followers of your art online, but it still doesn't quite compare to how you can connect with your audience when you meet them in person. Include a section on your website that lets others know of upcoming events where they can see your work next. You never know if someone is local to you or traveling in the area where you have an exhibition. List the time, date, and location details of any significant shows. Feel free to also mention any upcoming workshops you will be teaching, open studios you will be hosting, artist talks you will be giving, or other exciting events that your audience may be interested in attending.

If you'd also like to include press mentions and awards, it might make more sense to call this page "News" instead and use it more generally for all of your exciting updates, not just events.

Mailing List Sign-Up
Your website should include a sign-up form for your mailing list. Any email marketing provider you use will likely provide a code that you can embed in one of your pages, or a link to the website. So don't forget to find that and plug it into your site! Squarespace, for example, connects the form to your mailing list provider so that the new addresses are input automatically. If you do not have a way to integrate new contacts in this way, make sure that you collect and import them into your mailing list provider on a regular basis. This list will be your access to patrons and collectors interested in purchasing your work, attending your exhibitions, and supporting you.

Blog

This is optional, but you can also maintain a blog on your website in which you share your process, travels, inspiration, tips, advice, or photos from exhibitions and events. Don't be scared to reveal a little behind-the-scenes look into your creative practice and introduce yourself to the world. Collectors who like your work will enjoy the opportunity to get to know more about you, so let loose, get creative, and give your website visitors an inside scoop on how and why you do what you do.

If you're going to include career experiences and advice or tutorials on your process, blogging can bring new traffic to your site and help your search rankings. Think about clever titles to grab people's attention, but don't get sucked into worrying too much about SEO (search engine optimization). You're an artist, not a blogger, so the focus should always be your work. This is a potentially useful tool for those who already have an interest in writing and marketing; otherwise, you shouldn't force yourself into doing it.

Shop

If you are not yet represented by a gallery, or if you have an agreement with your dealer regarding selling your own work, you can add a shop directly on your site. When Kat started marketing her art, she processed her transactions with simple PayPal invoices, but these days most website providers have an incredibly easy-to-use e-commerce system. Squarespace and Wix, for instance, both have a shop feature where you can set up and add your available work that can be linked back to your PayPal profile, bank account, or credit card. These online stores can offer features such as customized shipping rates and often automatically mark work as "sold" as each purchase is completed (a nice time-saver!).

Tip:

We suggest including a return policy on your webshop, even if it is to say that you do not accept them. For the best customer experience, however, we recommend trying to be flexible with your customers, without being taken advantage of. If you choose to have a website, you may also want to include an FAQ page that answers common questions, such as which types of payment you accept, how shipping works, and if your pieces come framed.

Your shop doesn't just have to feature original works. Including prints, as well as specialized services like commissions, will help you appeal to a variety of clients with a range of budgets. A sale is a sale no matter how small, right?

Many artists prefer not to include prices on their website because doing so used to be viewed negatively in the industry. Now, it is common to share the cost of smaller, more affordable works and to encourage buyers to contact you if they are considering any larger, more expensive pieces. This is a personal decision that you will have to make. There is no right or wrong way to include pricing, but be sure you are consistent and give everyone the same information, whether it's by listing it on your site or sending it privately in an email. The art industry is evolving, and transparent pricing is becoming a selling point for many collectors.

Once you have the basic structure down and have all the essential components of your website ready, you can add more features, customize the look and feel, add e-commerce capabilities, and more. Before you launch your website, have a friend look over all the pages to make sure there are no blurry images, typos, or broken links.

Having a clean, easy-to-use website will help you attract buyers, land gallery partnerships, and get press coverage. While social media is fantastic for contemporary artists working today, it never depicts the full picture of your creative practice the way a website does. You need to have space on the Internet that is owned by you and gives your patrons or dealers the information they are seeking all in one place. By creating a quality website, you will establish yourself as even more of a professional in the field and impress your visitors, especially if you are new to the market.

Include a link to your site on all your social media accounts, mailing lists, and printed marketing materials. Be proud of your work and the website you've put together to showcase your incredible portfolio online.

CHOOSING YOUR WEBSITE HOSTING PLATFORM

As mentioned previously, there are numerous platforms available to create beautiful artist websites. With user-friendly templates and easy-to-follow guides, you don't need to be a website designer or programmer to create a professional website.

Following are a few reputable website hosting platforms that will allow you to build a site from scratch, even if you're new to creating websites.

Squarespace
www.squarespace.com

This is the platform that we use for *Create! Magazine* and what Kat has been using to host her site for several years. We love that it is easily integrated with an e-commerce shop and is intuitive to use. Squarespace includes beautiful free templates and upgrade options, so you can sell work directly from your site and run your studio practice like a small business.

Weebly
www.weebly.com

Alicia used Weebly's free version for her first artist website right out of college and experienced no issues—save for the contact page/email box fiasco mentioned previously. As that happened many years ago, this glitch has likely been fixed since then. Otherwise, it was a simple and professional design that only took a few hours to put together.

WordPress
www.wordpress.com

WordPress is a very popular hosting platform with a variety of templates that many businesses, both large and small, use. Since this is the case, it's not a bad idea to familiarize yourself with using WordPress, even if you don't end up choosing it for your artist website. WordPress offers much more customization than any of the other listed platforms, but the downside is that you will need to spend more time tweaking it, potentially purchasing a separate design template, and adding plugins. Kat used WordPress to create her first business site and had success, but she eventually switched to Squarespace to save time.

OTHER POPULAR WEBSITE PLATFORMS TO EXPLORE

www.wix.com

www.format.com

www.otherpeoplespixels.com

www.bigcartel.com

www.behance.net

or find your own!

WEBSITE BUILDING ASSISTANCE

www.upwork.com

www.fiverr.com

Shopify
www.shopify.com
Shopify is designed to work as a storefront for small businesses and is perfect for anyone processing multiple orders each week. It's pretty straightforward and can be customized by purchasing premium templates. This platform makes it incredibly easy to create shipping labels, track your sales, and more. It's slightly more limited in terms of design, but developers are quickly improving its capabilities.

FINAL WEBSITE CHECKLIST

- Current artwork, thoroughly labeled and organized by medium and year
- Contact information
- Sign-up form for email newsletter
- Bio, Artist Statement, and CV
- Shop or list of available works
- Links to social media
- Blog (optional)

TAKE ACTION

- Browse your favorite contemporary artists' websites for ideas and inspiration on design and organization and different hosting platforms.
- Decide on your domain name.
- Plan the organization of your artist website so you know what features you will need.
- Choose a hosting platform and template/theme that allows you to create all the pages, sections, or galleries that you need.
- Build your website, being sure to include all the relevant website essentials we've mentioned!

THE smARTist GUIDE TO WRITING
A PROFESSIONAL RESUME

RESUME

Have you taken the time to update your resume recently? If you can't remember when you last sat down to look at it, perhaps now is a good time to do so! This task is always easy to put off, but it's important to do periodically—even when you are not actively searching for a new job or other opportunity. Whenever you review your resume, you'll likely find that you have at least one significant thing to add, update, or edit.

For a document that is so widely used and serves as the all-important summary of your career, it seems strange that there isn't really a standard format for resumes. Preferences vary from industry to industry, and asking for advice from five people would almost certainly yield five completely different answers. While the basic information that should be included tends to remain fairly constant, thoughts on what supplemental information should be listed, the order and spacing of sections, the ideal length, and even the font choice can vary.

We can't say there is just one right answer to crafting the perfect artist resume, but by following the key tips outlined here, you will ensure that yours isn't remembered for the wrong reasons.

RESUME TIPS

All about Formatting
Your name should be the largest piece of text on the page, and it should be at the top. We've seen creative resume templates with names in all lowercase letters, which is fine if that is the look that you prefer, but it is most common to capitalize the first letter of both your first and last name, unless you choose to have your full name in uppercase letters.

Although you can take some liberties with the design of your resume, be very careful about using too many colors, and absolutely make sure that the font is readable. We highly suggest asking for feedback on this from a friend or colleague. You can use either a serif or sans serif font, but opt for something simple. A few popular fonts are Arial, Times New Roman, Helvetica, Georgia, and Garamond.

If you are skilled in Photoshop, Illustrator, or InDesign, feel free to create your resume using these programs to add a bit of design flair. For inspiration, we recommend taking a look at templates from programs like Canva. That said, even artist resumes do not have to be particularly artsy. Just like with your website, less is often more. You never want the design of the document to distract the reader from your accomplishments. There is nothing wrong with sticking to Microsoft Word or Google Docs. Straightforward and readable, with a clear summary of your background and achievements, should be your primary objective. In addition, we advise that you use your composition skills to leave necessary blank space. Sometimes it is tempting to try to fit as much as possible on the page, but, as with a painting, the eye needs areas to rest. Implementing properly sized margins and spacing between sections will achieve this effect.

Be Consistent!

If you are going to use bullet points, periods at the end of a sentence, italicized titles versus titles in quotations, etc., do it throughout the whole document. The same goes for verb tense: use either past or present, not both. It is most common to present information in reverse chronological order within each section (education, exhibitions, publications, etc.). People reading your resume will be most interested in what you have been doing over the last two years, so make that information the easiest to find. Also, do your best to avoid abbreviations, even if you think they are obvious. Try not to leave it to the reader to guess what you mean by something.

If you do not have more than one item under a category, find a way to include that item under a different heading. For example, if you have only been invited to give one artist talk, include it under an awards section if you have won other awards, rather than in a section by itself. You can also include sections for curating or jurying experience or art-related teaching roles at the end of your resume, but it is not necessary to do so when applying to juried shows or calls for artists.

Proofread, Proofread, Proofread!

This shouldn't need further explanation, but if you only have seconds to make a first impression on the person reading your resume, you definitely don't want them coming across an accidental grammatical error or typo. Ask a friend, family member, colleague, or trusted advisor to do a quick read-through. You should always have at least one more set of eyes look over your resume before you apply to anything!

GENERAL TIPS

File Format & Name

Unless otherwise specified, send your resume as a PDF to avoid formatting and readability issues. Word files can become distorted from being opened in a newer or older version of the program, and then it becomes difficult for the person reviewing your resume to read it. You wouldn't want your application to be discounted before the person in charge of selecting candidates for the opportunity even has a chance to get to know you!

Name your file with a simple title such as: *yourname_resume*. Naming your file correctly seems like an obvious tip, but this is another mistake we've seen happen, and for the person in charge of reviewing hundreds, or even thousands, of submissions, it's absolutely crucial that you add your name so the reviewer can easily find your resume and not confuse it with someone else's.

Tip:

*File size is generally not a problem for a document file,
but it's always worth double-checking that you are not
sending an unnecessarily large file via email.*

Create Multiple Versions of Your Resume

Depending on where you are in your career and how varied your experience and achievements are, consider having more than one version of your resume. We especially suggest this as you grow in your career. The more specifically you can write your resume to fit the opportunity that you're applying for, the more likely you are to get it!

Alicia once applied to a position at a museum for which she wrote her experience exactly based on the bulleted list of qualifications given in the job description. She later learned that all of her coworkers hired in the same position had prior connections to the institution, whereas she did not. Her application was the only one out of hundreds that was selected based solely on how she presented her experience and interest in the position, rather than on who she knew. In this case, it was essential that she had written a tailored resume for the job.

> *"The more specifically you can write your resume to fit the opportunity that you're applying for, the more likely you are to get it!"*

It's easy to make this tip work for you as well. You might have one version of your resume that includes all the exhibitions you have participated in, as well as the auxiliary sections mentioned previously, and another that is more concise, with just the most relevant and recent exhibitions, awards, etc. This comes in handy when applying to multiple types of jobs, grants, exhibitions, and more, as they may be looking for different information. Creating tailored versions of your resume for various opportunities in advance will save you time later when you will probably be on a deadline to submit materials for an application!

Spend some time thinking about what you would be looking for if you were reviewing submissions for the specific opportunity you're interested in. For example, when applying for employment, focus on your related work experience, and for grants, highlight your exhibitions and awards. This is another mistake that we've seen often. It's great to be proud of your accomplishments, and we always want you to be excited to share them, but don't spend half of your resume on your teaching experience if you're applying to be represented by a gallery. The key is to include the most relevant information on your resume so that you'll be seen as an obvious fit for the position, exhibition, or award.

Resume Length

Keep in mind that all the most important information should be on the first page of your resume, as people may not read beyond that. Entry-level art positions could easily see hundreds of applications, so yours must stand out from the very beginning.

For this reason, when Alicia was early on in her career, a graduate school professor once recommended that her resume should never be longer than one page. Often, she still sticks to this advice, as it forces her to keep all the information relevant and concise. That being said, in her experience, she tended to receive more responses from potential employers when she sent a two-page resume, rather than one. However, this does not mean that you should pad your resume by using large spaces between sections to make it fit onto two or more pages instead of one. It's very obvious when people do this and does not impress anyone.

As long as your resume looks clean and includes the necessary information that the application or call for artists is looking for, whether it is one or two pages shouldn't make much of a difference. For an emerging or mid-career artist, we recommend a resume between one and three pages, at the most. Even if you've participated in many exhibitions and publications, you can cut down the list to the most recent ones in the past five or ten years.

Tip:

If your resume is longer than three pages, it might be more of a CV (curriculum vitae). A CV is a fuller, more detailed account of your career. You might see an application listing ask for this, so if it does, don't confuse the two. Remember that your resume is a shorter snapshot of your experience and accomplishments that you can tailor to each opportunity. Because your CV is a longer overview of your career, it doesn't have to be adjusted as frequently and is usually longer than two pages.

FINAL NOTES

We get a lot of questions from emerging artists about resumes, but this isn't something you should spend a ton of time stressing over. For any call for artists, the juror will focus the vast majority of their time on examining your work, not your resume. Your only concern should be making sure not to weaken your application with glaring mistakes or by failing to include your resume at all.

Gaps in your artist resume are fine. Life happens and people understand that! If you were embarking on a new series and needed time to build up your portfolio, there's no need to worry that it will detract from your submission. Even when you're applying for a job, if you took time away to raise a family or travel, be open about it. Perhaps consider addressing it in your cover letter and sharing how that experience shaped who you are now and gives you a unique perspective that you can bring to the position you're applying for.

Speaking more broadly about honesty, you also should never include something on your resume that isn't true. While we heartily encourage using strong action verbs to describe your experience (e.g. managed, improved, directed, etc.) and going after higher positions than what you've had previously, you can't say that you curated a show if your only role was to hang one piece. People will find out eventually, and you wouldn't want to fall into a situation where you're hired at a job that you're not actually qualified for. The art world is small enough that your reputation will follow you, so doing this can hurt your chances of being hired or taken seriously in the future.

Another question we are frequently asked is what to do if you are a self-taught artist. In this case, you can either choose to leave out the section on education altogether or include it at the end. However, if you don't have anything to list besides where you went to high school, it's probably best to skip it. Even if you did earn a bachelor's or master's degree in another discipline, unless it is relevant to the work you are creating right now (for example, if you studied law and now make politically inclined art), then it's simply not necessary to list where and what you studied. While someone looking

RESUME RESOURCES

Writing Tool

College Art Association
www.collegeart.org/
standards-and- guidelines/
guidelines/visual-art-cv

Free Design Tool

Canva
www.canva.com

over your resume will likely at least glance at your resume, if not do a quick read-through, they will be primarily concerned with your artwork and deciding if it is a fit.

Emerging artists may not yet have many exhibitions or awards to list on their resume. When Alicia graduated from her BFA program, in the Business of Art course (required for all senior students), some of her peers only had one item to include: the senior thesis exhibition. Yet, there had been numerous opportunities on campus and beyond to submit to local shows or be published in the student-run literary magazine.

Even if you don't have a lot of money, you can always find free open calls for artists or make up your own exhibition opportunities at a neighborhood cafe. There's not much you can do to make limited experience look like more than what it is on paper. You have to simply keep putting yourself out there and finding new ways to exhibit your art, earn awards, volunteer, intern, work, and more!

Unless your resume is poorly written or badly designed, it probably won't make a huge impact on your acceptance rate for exhibitions, but if you're applying to jobs and grants, it is essential that you put together the most professional resume to give yourself the best chance of being selected. Again, we urge you to consider thinking from the reviewer's perspective. If they asked for certain qualifications, did you remember to address all of them? When you make it easy for that person to see that you're not just a good fit, but the perfect fit for the job or opportunity, we know you'll start seeing the acceptances and responses you've been hoping for! Keep tweaking your resume based on your successful applications and adding new information whenever significant career changes happen.

Tip:

We also suggest comparing your resume to those of other artists around the same point in their career as you, as well as those of artists further along in their careers. They should be readily available on the artists' websites to either read or download. Don't forget to add yours to your website when it is finished!

ARTIST RESUME TEMPLATE

- Name
- Website
- Contact Information: Email, Phone, Address
- Education: Year, Degree Earned, School, Location
- Solo Exhibitions: Year, Title of Exhibition, Gallery or Institution Name, Location (You may substitute with "Two-Person" or "Three-Person" if you do not have any solo shows, or you can also include these if you only have a few solo shows.)
- Group Exhibitions: Same as above
- Honors and Awards: Year, Title of Award or Honor, Person or Institution Granting the Award or Honor
- Publications and Reviews: Year or Date, Author, Title, Publication, Website (optional)
- Collections: This should list the names of institutions, not your private collectors!
- Residencies: Year, Institution or Program Name
- Artist Talks and Presentations: Year or Date, Title, Institution, Location
- Gallery Affiliations: Name, Location, Contact Information (website can also be included)

With the world becoming increasingly more global, some say that you don't need to include a phone number or address. And if you're moving to a new city or country and are already job searching, including this information from where you lived previously could make your potential employer think that you're not in the area yet and, therefore, that you couldn't start immediately. You definitely wouldn't want that to be the only reason you weren't considered more seriously, so in this kind of instance, you don't have to be specific with your contact info. Ultimately, it is up to you, but you must at least include an email address where you can be reached.

The same holds true with including a photo, which is sometimes asked for in Europe. In the United States, it's rare to include a picture of yourself in your resume, so we recommend that you omit this. If you're applying outside of the country, check if including a photo is common practice when it does not specify in the job listing.

ART JOB RESUME TEMPLATE

Gallery, Museum, Art Fair, Auction House, etc.

- Name
- Contact Information: Email, Phone, Address
- Education: Year, Degree Earned, School, Location
- Relevant Work Experience: Title, Company, Location, Duration of Position, Duties
- Other Work Experience: Only include this if there are relevant skills to mention
- Skills: Software Programs, Languages, Soft Skills, etc.
- Honors and Awards: Only include this section if relevant
- References: Name, Title, Contact Info (or you can put "*References available upon request" at the bottom)

You'll notice that we do not include an "objective" at the top. This term is a bit outdated, as it is now more commonly called a "summary," but either way, we've both gone our entire careers without ever writing one. You may have noticed that LinkedIn will help you write a summary on your profile, so you can start there for an example. If you can write something concise and catchy that truly adds value to the profile of yourself that you've created in your resume, go for it! That being said, it can sometimes be more trouble than it's worth.

RESUME VOCABULARY

When you're writing a resume for a job opportunity, you want to use strong words that best communicate what you did in your role. Without twisting the truth, try to use words like the following terms to add a little oomph to your experience. Don't sell yourself short by being passive! Instead of saying, "I was in charge of," say, "I led" or "I directed" or "I oversaw."

Power Verbs!
- Managed
- Improved
- Directed
- Initiated
- Produced
- Launched
- Led
- Generated
- Founded
- Oversaw
- Increased (Doubled, Tripled, etc.)
- Sold
- Ran
- Supervised

Artist Career-Related Verbs
- Curated
- Wrote/Edited
- Designed
- Crafted
- Taught/Educated/Instructed

TAKE ACTION

- Look over the most recent draft of your resume and see if there are any major accomplishments missing. Is there anything that is no longer relevant that you could cut out?
- Check your formatting. Do you have a readable font, enough negative space throughout the document, and consistent verb tense and punctuation?
- Think about what you most want to highlight and make sure that is on the first page or at the top of the page. Also, pinpoint what is required for the opportunity you are applying for and make sure that is clearly addressed in your resume.
- If you're submitting your resume for a job, add a few power verbs whenever possible.

STRESS-FREE ARTIST STATEMENTS

Artist statements tend to be a dreaded topic in the art community, and we understand why. It can be difficult to translate all the thoughts and ideas behind your work into a concise, coherent summary, especially if writing is not your forte. While drafting a standout statement does not have to be a priority in your career, you do want to avoid a poorly written one. A statement that is too vague or informal or riddled with artspeak (i.e. trite art-world jargon) can leave a negative impression.

The vast majority of opportunities to which you will apply require you to submit a statement along with your images or website, so it is crucial to have one. For example, every time you have an exhibition, write a grant proposal, or want to submit your work to a leading art blog, you need to have this document ready. Rather than waiting until an opportunity arises, and risking having to scramble to piece something together last-minute, set aside time now to think about and then write your statement. It doesn't have to be long—a paragraph or two will usually suffice.

> *"Your statement is a chance for you to help your audience make a deeper connection with and gain a more thorough understanding of your work."*

The good news is, unless you are producing very different types of work in a short period of time, you won't have to write a statement often. Depending on how long you work within the same series, style, and/or medium, the same statement could last you from a few months to several years. If what is at the core of your work has remained the same, with only slight differences, it's likely you can revise your existing statement with a few small tweaks rather than doing an entire rewrite.

While artists do need to have professional statements, people know that you aren't spending the majority of your time working toward becoming a best-selling author. Nobody is expecting an award-winning essay. They just want to learn more about what you do to help them make a decision about whether to purchase your work, include it in an upcoming exhibition, or give you funding for your dream project.

We believe that much of the fear and dread surrounding writing an artist statement comes from artists overthinking what it is. Reframe your mindset, and remember that your statement is simply an easy-to-understand description of what your art is about. You don't need to be an amazing writer to get these ideas across to your audience. Be honest and use your voice. It may help to imagine writing as if you are describing your work to a good friend or better yet, an industry professional you admire. Your statement should give a clear, genuine snapshot of what you create, as well as how you do it and why.

There is something to be said about artists wanting to let their work speak for itself. Indeed, you can never guarantee how a viewer will interpret your work, even with an explanation or insight from you. Each person's perception of your art will be completely different based on their life experience, culture, and interests. But equally important to note is that they may fall in love with your art even more once they get additional information from you. Your statement is a chance for you to help your audience make a deeper connection with and gain a more thorough understanding of your work.

Ask yourself this before you begin: what do you want your viewer to know about you, your process, and your work that is not immediately evident just by looking at it? This answer is the most important aim for your statement and will help inform your writing.
If you can't answer this yet, perhaps you still have some work to do on building your portfolio. Writing an effective statement is impossible without a completed body of work to describe. Come back to this step once you've finished a strong series of art that you want to begin exhibiting and selling.

Now, take a deep breath, grab a cup of tea or a glass of wine, and follow these steps to draft your artist statement with ease.

EASY TIPS FOR WRITING YOUR ARTIST STATEMENT

Read, Read, Read

Reading is important beyond helping you craft your artist statement. You become a better writer when you consistently read quality writing. Invest in art publications to develop your vocabulary and learn about how others write about art. Take time each week, or hopefully at least once a month, to read the arts section of *The New York Times*, browse through a copy of a recognized industry magazine such as *Art News, Elephant, Art Forum,* and *Frieze,* or peruse another artsy publication or blog that inspires you.

Reading also allows you to see what everyone else is doing. If you're really lost, this practice can generate ideas for you to start with. Visit the websites of several working contemporary artists and see how they've approached writing their statements. Note the tone of voice, style of writing, and word choices. Think about their art and see how effectively (or not) they communicate what it is that they create. Do the two connect seamlessly? If not, what is missing? Note any gaps or missing information for yourself so that you can avoid those mistakes.

Comparing other artist statements can show you that there are certain traps you can fall into, including rambling or being too informal, but it will also help you get a sense of how diverse, vast, and unlimited your possibilities are! You don't have to sound like a robot, nor do you need to reinvent the wheel. Be clear and straightforward and your audience will respond. *Note: This goes without saying, but please never copy or try to replicate anyone's work in art or writing. Take cues, but don't steal!*

Brain Dump

Grab a journal or your sketchbook if you prefer writing by hand, or pull up a new blank document on your computer and make a list of things that you think about when painting, sculpting, taking photographs, etc. This list doesn't have to be full sentences yet, so don't filter yourself here. Write freely and note as much as you can think of in the moment. Ask yourself questions like: Am I looking for a specific mood when creating? Do I like telling stories? Who or what inspires me? If you are looking for additional questions and exercises to help you brainstorm, we suggest the book *Art-Write* by Vicki Krohn Amorose. In it, she offers a few important questions, such as:

- *Why did I make this?*
- *What do I believe in?*
- *How did I make this? (Materials, Process, Location, Etc.)*

Start with these, but feel free to get creative and come up with a few questions of your own!

Jot Down Thoughts throughout Your Day

If you are walking to grab a cup of coffee in your favorite neighborhood and suddenly get a random idea, write it down! Sometimes hearing inspiring song lyrics or listening to a podcast gives you the words and phrases you need to describe your work. For Kat, the descriptions and ideas about her work usually come during the painting process. You can easily write down words, phrases, and thoughts on your phone or in a notepad, even if you are in the middle of working. Inspiration is everywhere.

Put It All Together

Gather your notes and write a first draft of your artist statement. You can begin with an outline of the most important ideas you want to mention if that helps, or go sentence by sentence, rearranging things as needed. Focus on the themes that came up repeatedly in your notes and only use other relevant information about your art. It may feel rough at first, but that's fine for now. Don't fixate on over-editing yourself in your initial draft.

Review & Edit

Once you have a completed first draft, put it away for a bit (ideally, at least a day) and come back to it with fresh eyes. Do a quick read-through for typos and grammar mistakes, and then look at it more critically. How well does it connect to your work? Edit and adjust as needed if it still doesn't quite reflect who you are as an artist. Then read your writing out loud a few times. You can often catch mistakes and odd sentence structures more easily when you hear it spoken aloud. Repeat this process two to three times, and then have a trusted friend, colleague, or mentor check it for errors and give you feedback. Ask them if they think it was clear, relevant, insightful, or interesting.

Tip:

Install Grammarly on your computer to automatically suggest edits as you write and, at the very least, go through one round of spell-check before sending your draft to anyone to review.

If you still feel uncomfortable with your writing, there are many affordable options to have a professional edit your statement. If someone close to you isn't available or you'd rather invest in hiring an editor, you can find them online via freelancing platforms such as Fiverr or Upwork, among others.

When you are done, ask yourself the following questions:

- Does this make sense to me?
- Would someone with no knowledge of art understand this?
- Is it true?
- Does it reflect what I want the viewer to know about my work and process?

If the answer is yes to all of the above, congratulations! You now have a finished artist statement. Add it to your website and save both a .doc and .pdf version so that you will be prepared for any submission opportunity that comes your way!

RESOURCES

How to Write About Contemporary Art by Gilda Williams

Art-Write: The Writing Guide for Visual Artists by Vicki Krohn Amorose

www.fiverr.com

www.upwork.com

Here are a few examples of stellar statements from contemporary artists in our community! Notice how each artist explains their work in a way that is true to them and uses the statement as a way to add insight into their art and practice.

Eliana Marinari
www.elianamarinari.com

My paintings, created by superposition of glazing layers of aerosol paint on ink and pastel drawings, are a surreal representation of the subject, speaking of both the distorted quality of memory and the ephemeral nature of our experiences. The vestigial image, composed of transparent imperceptible paint particles, mimics the process of creating a visual representation of an image in our mind, which is matched in our memory to attribute meaning. The hazy quality of my portraits challenge the viewer, as the process of face recognition becomes more difficult, semantic associations become more important. The introduction of abstraction in my work brings time, memory, loss and an emotional narrative to the image so that the work becomes as much about the viewer as of the person who is in the painting.

Erika Stearly
www.erikastearly.com

Named using the street address of the residences depicted, I make paintings of the spaces where people live. Convinced that multiple approaches to painting are valid, the imagery in my work balances an impulse to faithfully render household objects against the emphasis on the hand of the artist. The combination of abstraction and representation romanticizes these spaces in a way that invites the viewer to construct their own narrative of the scene.

Over the years, I have developed a mixed media technique that allows me to combine the characteristics of watercolor and acrylic paint. Delicate shapes can quickly be sketched in or large blocks of color can be refined with watercolor pencils. The heavier bodied acrylic paint can fully cover existing passages and retains its brushstrokes. Using both types of paint together produces a more nuanced range of painterly effects.

Scott Hutchison
www.scotthutchison.com

My paintings and drawings are comprised of overlapping figures stitched together in one composition. They are multifaceted, abstracted, and meant to evoke the idea that our identity is in flux. Though we are singular beings, our psyche is not. We are molded in part by time and our life experiences.

The subjects in my paintings personify the strength and frailty of consciousness and the depths to which we experience the human condition. The figures are displaced, out of sync and stitched together from a multitude of people, like ghosts or layered memories, both timeless and self-aware.

All of my work can be seen as a journal entry, the manifestation of a deep concern for place and purpose in this world. I reassign faces and body parts through a mixture of trial and error, coupled with random chance and the need to create something from nothing. During this process, I am fully aware that I am seeking answers to a larger question: Are we in control of what defines us as individuals, or are we a product of our culture and our experiences? My art is meant to tug at the viewer and suggest that there is more to the material world. Each piece is intentionally shrouded in mystery, letting the viewer interpret its multitude of meanings.

Elisa Valenti
www.elisavalentistudio.com
I grew up in a time when eating in public was shameful, stomach rolls made you unworthy, and shopping for clothes was traumatic. I grew up before being plus size was normal.

My work reflects the images I wish I had seen—beautiful, luscious women doing ordinary things, just like everybody else. They are a reflection of my own battle with body image and my journey to mental health.

If you've ever been made to feel insignificant, I hope they inspire you to own your image of yourself and never give that power to someone else.

TAKE ACTION

- Read industry publications to build your art vocabulary and learn how others write about art.

- Look for examples of professional artist statements from a few contemporary artists.

- Do a few brainstorming sessions where you write down thoughts and ideas about your work.

- Write an initial draft, edit it yourself first, and then have a friend or peer do a final review.

CRAFTING YOUR PORTFOLIO

Although coming up with and producing a consistent body of work can feel complicated, it doesn't have to be. The best way to start putting together your initial portfolio, if you have never done so before, is to brainstorm ideas and create your own guidelines for how the final series will look. Of course, some things will change throughout the process, but have a general idea of the basics, like what sizes you'll be working in and the materials you will use. We'll provide you with additional questions for getting started later on in this chapter. This will help you create a beautiful collection of pieces that you will eventually be proud to present in the opportunities you've been dreaming of, whether that includes exhibiting in galleries and at art fairs or having your art featured by the press.

> *"Identifying and then emphasizing what defines your distinctive style elevates the quality and rarity of your art."*

You can also use this method when designing a new series or shifting gears in your practice. These moments can feel intimidating as well, but armed with the following tips, you can approach this process with the tools you need to successfully push yourself in a new creative direction—even if you're starting from scratch!

What is most important to remember throughout this process, in addition to creating work that you feel connected to and invested in, is that curators, galleries, and your clients will be looking for consistency within your body of work. Though this can take many forms, there should be a common thread that ties the pieces together in some way. It may be your subject, an exploration of a specific medium, the general size you're working in, a unique technique that you use, or something else that identifies your work as unique to you. Identifying and then emphasizing what defines your distinctive style elevates the quality and rarity of your art. These key characteristics are what will help you promote and sell your work.

STUDYING THE WORK OF OTHERS

Take a few moments to look at the websites of your favorite contemporary artists. Notice the elements that connect their pieces together. This will vary from artist to artist, but it will give you ideas on how you can create a series that doesn't feel restrictive or repetitive. On the other hand, some artists enjoy setting limitations as part of their creative practice, such as on their color palette or chosen subject matter, for example. The beauty is that it is up to you how you want to approach achieving consistency in your work. You can try several methods until you find what works best for you!

Getting Started

To start, you need to decide a few necessary details about your art collection. Think about the materials, the size, a timetable of how long it will take to complete (especially if you are preparing for an upcoming exhibition or other event), an approximate budget, and, of course, the subject or theme. Allow yourself to get lost in the infinite possibilities of what your work could be, and get wild! You will hash out more of the details as you start doing the work and can adjust accordingly.

Keep in mind that the actual art and specifics will fully reveal themselves after you begin working, so try not to stress over or worry about how the series will turn out before starting your first piece. Don't be a victim of "analysis paralysis." Be open to the pleasant surprises that may happen throughout the process, rather than letting any minor setbacks keep you from moving forward. Use your imagination to create an idea of what you want the complete collection to look and feel like, to the best of your ability, and work backward from there.

Planning a new series is not meant to be restrictive, so if your initial ideas start feeling that way, you can always pivot to something else and try again. Setting up a few guidelines beforehand should help you create a framework to dive deeper into your practice and ultimately get more out of it. Establishing a theme, style, or another cohesive element in your work also demonstrates to your viewers, galleries, and critics that you are a professional artist who has spent time developing your ideas.

FAILING FORWARD & EMBRACING YOUR IMPERFECT WORK

Note that you will have to create more work than necessary for the final collection, because not everything we make works out on the first attempt—and that is okay! Keep showing up, work on multiple pieces at a time if that suits you, and feel free to walk away from or paint over those that aren't turning out the way that you wanted.

On average, artists usually end up discarding around 50 to 80 percent of the art they create. Scrapping work isn't a failure; it's something that all artists deal with, so if you're worried you haven't made a piece you really love in a while, it's not just you! We all go through periods where we know we're not quite onto our best work yet. You can recycle the pieces that didn't work by painting over them or using them for collages or anything else that you come up with.

That being said, we can also be our own biggest critic, so don't get lost in the chase of perfection either. If there is a sliver of hope that you can turn something into a masterpiece, then keep it. Step away and come back to it later with fresh eyes, rather than giving up too quickly. Imagine how disappointing it would be to have thrown away a piece you later realized you could have made great!

We've put together the following list of questions to consider and answer before you get started on creating your best professional portfolio of work. Make notes of your thoughts and responses in a notebook or your sketchbook and then . . . get to work!

Pro Tips:

- *Be patient with yourself. Creating quality artwork takes time. Stay committed to your practice, show up consistently, and don't get discouraged by issues or obstacles that arise. We know you've got this!*

- *Embrace improvisation during this creative period, as it can push your new series further than what you initially imagined.*

- *We recommend having a minimum of ten, but ideally closer to twenty, pieces within a series before pursuing galleries or other opportunities. Having enough inventory is essential and will save you a lot of stress when the right exhibition comes up or a collector decides to invest in multiple pieces. Not to mention, if you have only finished two or five works, you might not have made your favorite or best works in the series yet.*

QUESTIONS TO ANSWER FOR DESIGNING YOUR NEW BODY OF WORK

1. What theme, topic, or subject do you want to include in your work? What have you been excited about recently, even if non-art related? Brainstorm and observe
    your current interests.
2. What media will you use to complete the series? What materials do you need to purchase or find? Does this project require grant applications or crowdfunding campaigns to help cover your expenses?
3. About how many pieces do you aim to create in this series? What are the sizes and how many of each do you wish to include in your ideal solo exhibition?
4. How long will it take to complete the entire portfolio? Create a tentative timeline for yourself with either weekly or monthly goals. Then stick to it!
5. Which other artists, both contemporary and historical, are inspiring you at the moment? List them and do research to discover common themes, materials, color choices, and anything else that unifies your interests with these creators.
6. How will this work feel to you? What emotions and moods do you hope to convey through this series?
7. What do you hope viewers and collectors will experience when looking at your new artwork? What do you think will help achieve this response?
8. How and where will you present the works when they are complete? The experience of viewing art changes in different environments. Would you prefer your works displayed in a traditional white box gallery, museum, commercial space, cozy cafe, or somewhere else? Start imagining an ideal solo exhibition as you work on the series and manifest it into reality.
9. We hope that these questions get your ideas flowing. Feel free to include any additional questions of your own that will help develop your plan for your new art series. Remember that the magic happens in the studio, so spend your time doing the work and not overthinking it! In his book *Do the Work,* Steven Pressfield states, "Don't prepare. Begin." While we might not agree with jumping into a new body of work without any preparation at all, we do like the reminder to just start and go for it.
10. When you have at least ten strong pieces that you are proud of, the following chapters in this book will be your guide on how to promote them to new collectors, curators, dealers, editors, and more!

- Determine the guidelines of your portfolio or new body of work.
- Review and respond to the Questions to Answer for Designing Your New Body of Work.
- Get started! Create a schedule for yourself and work toward creating at least ten pieces for your collection.

CREATING BUSINESS STATIONERY

Though printed documents are becoming less and less common in our industry, often replaced by Google Docs and PDFs viewed on iPads and laptop screens, there are several key pieces of business stationery

> *"Designing your business documents with the same aesthetic as your website or other branding builds and reinforces your brand awareness."*

that can help you with sales and marketing. Whether you use physical copies or share them online, start thinking about and putting these pieces together now so that you'll be prepared when you meet new potential clients or a prospective gallery, or are in touch with a writer who wants to feature your work.

DEFINE YOUR IMAGE

Designing your business documents with the same aesthetic as your website or other branding builds and reinforces your brand awareness. Help the people you come in contact with remember you! Consider making a simple logo for yourself with your name or business name. Then you can include this on your website, social media accounts, and more, so that it is cohesive throughout. Along these lines, you might also use a similar color palette, font family, or layout. If you've already built a website that you love, this can be the basis of your overall style. Otherwise, peruse magazines or other printed material to find inspiration for what you want your business stationery to look like. Kat has a very defined style that ties her businesses together. She primarily uses white, black, and a soft pink, sticks to between two and three fronts, and has a script logo of her name.

TYPES OF BUSINESS STATIONERY

Business Cards

Alicia always carries at least a few business cards in her wallet at any given time. You never know when you might meet a great, new professional contact. Whether you have your business card professionally designed, do it yourself, or use a template from a website or printing service, make sure to include at least one way to contact you, in addition to your name. For artists specifically, you should also list your website. You can choose whether to include a title, but it may be helpful so that it is easier for people to remember you when they see your card again days, or even months, later. Finally, don't forget that this is an opportunity to show off your work. Choose one or a few of your current favorite pieces to put on the opposite side of your information. It could be a conversation starter and even lead to a sale!

BUSINESS CARD TEMPLATE

- Name
- Title
- Email and/or Phone Number
- Website and/or Social Media Page

Postcards

We love postcards because they are incredibly versatile and inexpensive to print. They are most often used to make an announcement for an upcoming show, but we've also made some with special discount codes for *Create! Magazine* and others that say "Thank You" to send to clients who have made purchases or supported our work. In addition, Kat sometimes likes to print new or available works on quality postcards and send them to her collectors. This functions as both a marketing piece and a small gift to her collectors.

Price Lists

Of course, one of the most important documents you'll need to create for becoming a selling artist is a price list. If you're making a list for an exhibition, common practice is to include the works based on the order in which they are hung around the space. This can be clockwise or counterclockwise depending on how people are most likely to navigate through the space. When you want to create a price list for your available work, items can be arranged by size, year, medium, or alphabetically by title. You may also want to create a few price lists for potential clients, separated by series, medium, or size. It will be easier to send your price lists as PDF files, but also save the original Word files so that you can easily go back and adjust or update the documents as needed. Alicia has saved herself so much time when she needs to quickly send prices to clients by creating these templates.

PRICE LIST TEMPLATE

- Thumbnail Image
- Title
- Medium
- Year
- Price

Preview Sheets

When you have a potential client who is interested in your work, you may want to send them more than a price sheet. Designing a preview sheet with bigger images, multiple detail shots, and/or install views can help you close sales. If you are skilled in Photoshop or use one of the many apps available online that allow you to digitally place an artwork on a wall, you could add a rendering of how your art would look in their space. You might even consider writing a sentence or two about each piece. For example, you can talk about what the artwork means, what techniques you used, or something else that makes it unique. Again, we highly recommend creating an editable template for this type of document so that you don't have to start from scratch each time you make one.

Tip:

Here is an option for visualizing your art in a space if you don't know or aren't great at Photoshop: https://www. homestratosphere.com/wall-art-visualizer-software/.

Wall Labels

In recent years at art fairs, we've noticed a new trend of galleries hanging works without any labels, or simply writing the artist's name underneath in pencil. While some would argue that it is a smart sales tactic that forces anyone interested in the piece to ask the dealer about it, we don't suggest taking this approach. Some potential collectors or advisors working on behalf of their clients may not have time to stop and talk at every booth where they find an interesting piece. In this case, they would prefer to snap a quick photo of the label in order to be able to look it up again later, but if one isn't available, they could forget where they saw it or other important details.

It is also quite frustrating for us, as writers, to not be able to see the information right away. Since art fairs are often very busy for galleries, it has happened many times that the dealers and assistants who we'd like to ask about a work on display are already speaking with other people. We try to wait for one of them to finish their present conversation so as not to intrude, or circle back to the booth later on if we can. Unfortunately, as it's not always possible, the artist and gallery miss out on being featured.

You should trust that if someone is truly interested in buying a piece from you or learning more about it, they will ask about it—wall label or not. That being said, we're big proponents of transparency and think that you'll have more successful conversations with potential clients if they can easily find the basic information about your artwork from the beginning.

Tip:

Most artists and galleries hang wall labels near the bottom right corner of the work. Labels for sculptures are usually put on the pedestal where the piece is being displayed. For any larger works or installations, try to find a spot that doesn't distract from viewing the artwork, but is also close enough that your viewers won't have any difficulty finding it!

LABEL TEMPLATE

- Artist Name (in a group show)
- Title
- Medium (optional)
- Dimensions (optional)
- Year (optional)
- Price (optional)

Catalog

We're all for saving paper, but there is something special about seeing your artwork in print. You don't have to wait until you're working with a gallery to produce a catalog. Look for affordable rates from printing services online or see if you can work out a deal with a printer in your area. Do a small run of catalogs that you send to your mailing list to drum up interest in a new series or available works that you want to sell. Use templates available online to put it together, or invest in a graphic designer's services to help you with this project. Again, it's a nice touch to be able to give these to your collectors, and it shows an elevated level of professionalism. If you really prefer not to have physical copies made, to save on printing and shipping costs, that's fine too. You can simply create an online catalog and link it to your website or share it via your email list.

Resume, Artist Bio & Statement

For more specific information about your artist resume, please refer back to Your Artist Resume (page 20). We mentioned previously that just because you are a creative doesn't mean that your resume has to be. Unless you are applying for a designer position where your resume is another chance to show off your skills, you can keep it simple, so that whoever is reviewing it focuses on your accomplishments. On the other hand, adding your logo or keeping within the same color choices as your website and other business documents is a great way to stay consistent and cohesive throughout your branding.

The same holds true with your artist biography and statement, which we describe in more detail starting on page 14. You don't need to get artsy with your font choices. Remember that you want the reader to get a clear message about what your background is and what your work is about.

Other Marketing Collateral

Although not necessary in most situations, you could invest in a few types of informal marketing materials. Postcards are a great option, but making stickers, tote bags, t-shirts, or mugs can also be fun for your audience. We did an amazing collaboration with Art Girl Rising to make custom t-shirts with the names of five women artists we admire and the *Create! Magazine* logo on the inside label. What we loved about this partnership was that a portion of the proceeds of each shirt was donated to the National Museum of Women in the Arts in Washington, D.C.

Get creative with other printed materials or products that might be a fit for your work. They could even end up providing a small source of additional income if you list them on your website, but we more often use items like these as free giveaways for special event attendees, our magazine subscribers, or regular collectors.

TAKE ACTION

- Decide what you want your business image to look like. Is it something that you can design yourself with templates or do you need to hire someone else to assist you?

- Order business cards now, even if you don't have an immediate event coming up!

- Draft initial copies of your price list, preview sheet, and wall labels. Save a blank template document for each so that you can easily edit and create new versions in the future.

- If you haven't already done so, put together an artist resume, biography, and statement using your brand identity.

- Think about what other marketing collateral you might want to have, find quotes on pricing, and plan your designs.

CREATING SYSTEMS
TO STAY ORGANIZED

Let's start by debunking the myth that all artists are incapable of keeping their workspace, business, and lives in general organized. It's not true! You might not be good at it at first, but with a little bit of effort, you can establish processes and schedules to help you keep on track and boost productivity. There are ways to maintain order in all aspects of your creative practice, from how you set up your studio to how you break down the hours of each workday. We're going to focus on the main aspects that are the most important for us and what we do to stay organized within each.

YOUR ARTWORK

We highly recommend having some sort of inventory system for your work. You can input all of your information in a Word or Google document or Excel spreadsheet to allow for easy updating. If you have the means to do so, you could invest in a program like Artwork Archive for more detailed record keeping. Don't forget to consistently add your new works and note changes, such as availability or location.

Basic information that you want to track in your inventory includes:

- Title/year/medium/dimensions for each piece
- Where it is located (e.g. ABC Gallery, Studio Flat File Drawer 1, etc.)
- Whether it is available or has sold
- Price—you can consider noting all prices if it has increased over time

Additional information you could include:

- Framing details (helpful if a client asks to have another piece framed in the same way)
- Materials costs
- Shipping expenses to gallery shows or its collector
- Awards or exhibitions
- Potential clients who have expressed interest

YOUR WORKSPACE

There are definitely some artists who prefer to have all their brushes and paints out at once and can still be creative amongst a bit of chaos. If that is you, that's fine, and if it works, don't feel the need to change. However, you might consider setting up different areas in your studio for various tasks and for storing your supplies. For example, Kat's studio has a rack to hold her paintings along one wall, a table and open shelving for all of her paints and other materials against another wall, her easel in a corner, and a blank wall where she hangs works in progress so they are out of the way when they are still wet. After upgrading her studio to a larger space, she now has a second area that acts as an office, where she keeps books and extra copies of various issues of *Create! Magazine*, and has set up her desk for administrative work.

Not everyone has this much room to work with, but even a small area can be used in versatile ways. Think about investing a bit of money in a bookshelf, a set of drawers, and portfolios, or—if you have the space—maybe a small flat file or painting rack depending on the type of work you make. You definitely at least want a safe place to store your art supplies and artwork so neither will get damaged, used, stolen, or lost.

If you want to take it a step further, consider putting similar supplies together so that they are easier to find and labeling drawers or folders with their contents. Just make sure to stick to the system and only put items that belong there, or change the label if the contents are different. Artwork is usually stored by size, but it can also be organized by year or series. Decide which method would make it easiest for you to find a piece.

None of these organizational tips will make much of a difference if you also aren't consistent about cleaning your workspace! After you are done each day (or any time you have a session in your studio), aim to clean up everything that you have used. If you are busy and will be coming back to your work again shortly, you can get away with not putting everything away, but this can easily lead to a habit of leaving your studio messy. Doing tasks like washing your brushes, making sure that the lids of your paints are tightly screwed on, and checking that the caps of markers and pens are put on correctly ensures that your supplies will last longer, and that ultimately saves you money. Don't forget to sweep, mop, and dust every once in a while too, especially if you work in an older studio building. Finally, it's nice to do a thorough cleaning every six months to a year (Alicia's favorite!), so that you can keep your space fresh, get rid of anything you no longer need, and perhaps find some artwork for a mini studio sale. Who wouldn't want to make extra money with work that has just been sitting around?

YOUR DIGITAL FILES

Once you build up a body of work, you'll start to accumulate images of detail shots, framing photos, installation views, and more. Figure out the most convenient way for you to store all of these on your computer, and consider also storing them in a Dropbox account or on Google Drive. This allows you to access all of your important materials even if you need to work away from your home or studio and didn't bring your laptop. Again, how exactly you want to organize everything is ultimately up to you and should be decided by how you work best — we prefer categorizing art by year or series. However, if medium or size makes more sense to you, then do that!

The majority of your files will likely be artwork images, but you also want to keep track of all your gallery contracts, price lists, preview sheets, invoices, etc. Organize all these documents in separate folders so you can reference them again if needed. If you have numerous price lists, for example, you may also want to additionally separate them into different folders by year, medium, size, or series.

Another crucial thing to consider is how to consistently label your files. Even though application requirements may differ, for the most part, institutions or galleries ask that you include your name and title of the artwork for all of your image files. They may also request that you include the size, medium, and year, so you can choose to add that information if you like. You could also think about adding "sold" to the file name when your works sell, or simply move sold pieces to a new folder for works that are no longer available so you don't accidentally send a client an image of a piece that has already found a home with a collector! Other things you can add to the file name include whether the work is framed or unframed or if it is a low- or high-resolution image (also sometimes called "web" or "print"). Generally speaking, JPG or JPEG files should be fine for most submissions, but if the call for art requests a PDF instead of a Word Document or a PNG instead of a JPEG, send exactly what they ask for!

YOUR APPLICATIONS

Whether you want to pitch your work to media outlets, apply for awards, or submit to galleries and juried shows, you'll probably want a central place to keep track of everything. You can maintain a written list or text document, or Alicia recommends a spreadsheet so you can record where you want to apply, where you've submitted already, if you have sent a follow-up message, and what the result was (e.g. accepted, denied, or no response). You can also make a folder of supporting materials, such as essays you had to write for applications, various versions of your CV or resume, a list of references, annotated image lists, and anything else that is related.

It always seems like a lot of work to start on an application, but if you've done it once, you probably won't need to start from the very beginning. We'd never recommend recycling the exact same submission package you've sent previously, but you can always use certain documents as templates to save time when you put together a new application. Don't forget to proofread so you can avoid pitfalls like saying that you're so excited to apply for X gallery when you're actually sending it to Y!

YOUR CONTACTS

The great part about using an email service like Mailchimp is that in addition to keeping all of your clients' email addresses in one place, you can also add notes and input physical addresses, as well as what they purchased from you. If you don't use an email platform, we recommend saving the addresses in a spreadsheet or in the address book of your email provider, like Gmail. Definitely find a way to separate your clients' and VIP clients' information so that you can quickly locate them when necessary.

YOUR EMAIL

Are you always chasing inbox zero, or have you given up at this point? Just as some people can handle more clutter in their workspace than others, some creatives prefer to handle emails as quickly as possible, while others are fine leaving hundreds unread. At a certain point, when your career begins to grow, you may find that keeping up with your primary inbox becomes more difficult, so set up an automatic message and try to identify names or businesses that you should address right away. Look through your inbox right now and see what types of messages are unread. You may find that they are promotions, news, or other emails that aren't important for your art practice. Make it a point to regularly go through and unsubscribe from lists that are not relevant so that your artist inbox is strictly for discussions with clients, galleries, curators, etc. Your professional email shouldn't be bogged down by extra, unnecessary distractions.

For Alicia, she works best by leaving the most important messages directly in her inbox. If they are read, but in the inbox, that is a signal that she is still working on them. Once she has finished with the email, she moves it to a folder called "completed." If a message is unimportant, it can either be deleted right away or moved to completed. She also keeps folders for artist and writer submissions, various projects like books or exhibitions, and sales.

There are two folders that Alicia believes are key to have. One she calls the "keep" folder, which is short for "keep for future reference." This can include anything from directions about how to do something to conversations with certain clients, curators, galleries, and more. The second is a "pick-me-up" folder, in which you keep all the nice notes from clients, family, friends, colleagues, or anyone who wrote you something special. Whether it was an especially thoughtful thank-you message or someone simply reaching out to say how much they enjoy and relate to your work, we both love to have these readily available on those tough days when you're not feeling your best and need that reminder for why you keep doing what you do.

Tip:

Clean out your spam and junk folders periodically. Every once in a while, something valuable may accidentally end up there, and you wouldn't want to find it months or a year later.

YOUR SALES

You can get very involved with tracking all of your sales by using apps, but if you've set yourself up with Shopify, PayPal, or another selling platform, it's likely that you won't need to do much, since you can easily look up any order by logging into your account. For more meticulous record keeping, you may want to save a copy of all invoices in a separate folder, but again, most of this is already stored digitally with whatever program you use.

One thing you definitely want to track is payments! Set up a system that will help you track if a client or gallery still owes you money so that you can follow up with the appropriate people when needed. Things may come up on both sides and people get busy, but never back off of getting paid for your time, effort, and work.

YOUR TIME

If you're like us, you can't properly manage your work life without a calendar! You may like to use a wall calendar or planner, and sometimes it's nice to keep a written documentation of appointments and meetings, but syncing iCal or Google Calendar with your phone is probably the simplest option. Alicia prefers to color-code work, home, and other commitments so that she doesn't confuse them. Keeping all your activities in one place also helps you avoid double-booking yourself, which can easily happen if you try to keep multiple calendars. Also, if you can, don't just write the activity and time in the correct time zone, but think about adding the expected duration, location, and any other relevant details (e.g. Interview with gallery at 2pm, *bring portfolio and printed copy of resume).

Write down or schedule appointments as soon as they are set. If you don't have your phone or planner with you at the moment, try to find a way to remind yourself to input the meeting in your calendar as soon as you can so that you don't forget it!

When it comes to time management, you can be fluid and assign yourself tasks based on the projects you have going on at the moment, or you can allot certain days and times for different kinds of work. The latter is also known as time blocking and requires that you set up periods of time throughout the day where you focus on specific tasks. For example, you might set a timer and paint for two hours or take photos of your work for forty-five minutes. The point of this, and what makes it most effective, is ensuring that no distractions, like social media or checking email, come up during your blocks. If you are interested in this technique, look into artist and illustrator Lisa Congdon's online course called "Workflow, Time Management and Productivity for Creatives." [1]

Neither of us tends to use this method because we have a variety of deadlines to keep up with at once, as well as many projects that come up last-minute. However, using some of the ideas of breaking down your day into chunks or focusing time on tasks without looking at your phone are certainly useful for improving your overall productivity.

YOUR TASKS

Decide on one way to track all the projects you are working on. You can use a journal where you write to-do lists, create a spreadsheet, or, if you are digital savvy, perhaps you'd prefer Asana, Basecamp, or another task management program. Whatever you choose, remember to note key information, like what the project is, what you need to do, if there is a deadline and when the deadline is, and any important contacts or other relevant details.

You very well may find yourself prepping for an upcoming solo show at a gallery, submitting five grant applications, and launching your first online course in the same week. In order to do all these tasks successfully and on time, you need to have a place where you can write down not just the big-picture tasks that need to get done, but also each of the smaller tasks that you must complete to get there. For example, instead of simply writing that you need to prep for your gallery exhibition, put down that you need to order business cards, pick up work from your framer, hire an assistant for the install day, etc.

---

1 **Lisa Congdon,** *"Workflow, Time Management and Productivity for Creatives." Online course at creativelive.com.*

YOUR PRIORITIES

Once you know all the big and small tasks that you need to complete, organize them by urgency. Think about which of your deadlines are approaching soon and always aim to finish those projects before the rest. You can color-code your task lists to help you identify which projects are more important, and underline or put an asterisk next to the most pressing items. Just pick something that will stand out to you when you glance over your to-do list.

Alicia writes out her to-do list on a weekly basis. Unless she has to complete a project for an upcoming deadline, she assigns herself about two list items per day. Getting too granular about your list will overwhelm you, and it will be hard to stick to your plan if you feel like you accomplish very little overall. By only focusing on two to three big tasks per day, Alicia almost always ensures that she will finish everything and be able to cross them off her list (the most satisfying part!). Of course, little surprises can occur throughout the day, so be willing to be flexible, but this system has consistently worked for her. You can also choose to include non-work related items so that you can more accurately plan out your days, which we both do.

Tip:

If you don't work a traditional 9-to-5, Monday-through-Friday schedule, don't feel obligated to plan your time that way unless you want to. Feel free to start your weekly lists on Wednesday, or arrange your days on a 7-to-3 or noon-to-4 schedule.

Even if you don't have urgent projects at the moment, it may also help to create priorities. For example, if you notice that you've been putting off something difficult, try writing it at the top of your list. It takes getting used to, but usually it is better to abide by the famous words of Mark Twain: "If it's your job to eat a frog, it's best to do it first thing in the morning. And if it's your job to eat two frogs, it's best to eat the biggest one first." Unless there is a small task that will only take you a short amount of time to finish, get the biggest and hardest projects out of your way first so you don't end up scrambling at the end of each day or week.

Once you have your to-do list set up, you have to commit to it and review it throughout the day and week. Feel free to add and move tasks around as needed. If you don't get to a task today, try not to worry and simply push it to the next day or workweek. Your list should be fluid and adjustable, but also something that you stick to for best results.

Ultimately, you don't have to be incredibly organized to be successful. That being said, improving your organizational skills can have a dramatic impact on how effectively you work. Sometimes cleaning and clearing out your physical space helps your mind feel less cluttered too. For those of you who believe that organization isn't your strength, you may still recognize that there are aspects of organizing that you are good at or enjoy. Focus on those as you develop your career, and try incorporating other techniques when you are ready.

TAKE ACTION

- Create an artwork inventory and make sure to update it regularly.
- Arrange your studio or work area to have separate spaces for storage and making art, if possible, and aim to clean it daily or at least weekly.
- Label all files consistently with relevant information and set up a system for organizing your files into specific folders based on projects, by year, etc.
- Put together one document for tracking applications that you still need to do, those that are in progress, and those that have been completed. Add deadlines and whether you need to follow up.
- Consider making folders to categorize your emails so that messages don't get lost in your inbox. Definitely at least make one folder to save thank-yous and other positive notes from your clients, peers, collectors, and more!
- Set up a calendar and input all your appointments, important dates to remember, and meetings. We suggest including details like the location, and always try to add items as soon as the dates and times are settled!
- Plan your daily routine by thinking about your long-term projects and immediate tasks. Research more about time blocking if you think this method would work for you.
- Prioritize anything that is due the soonest; otherwise, push yourself to do the biggest or hardest tasks first.

HOW TO PRICE YOUR ART

One of the questions we get most frequently from emerging artists is: "How do I price my work?" The confusion surrounding this topic is entirely understandable, because there is no exact science behind placing monetary value on art. For better or for worse, the art market changes very rapidly and is often difficult to predict, thereby making the process of finding where your art fits within the market even more challenging. However, over the past decade we have collected a few tips that will help you figure out what to charge your collectors and how to get started with selling your work.

Tip:

Making art is often such an emotional experience that it feels difficult to put a value on your own work, let alone part with it. If you absolutely love a piece, make sure that your emotional value is accounted for in the price to some extent, but don't let this hold you back from selling successfully. Remember that clients are buying because they enjoy your art as much as you do! You have to be willing to let go in order to be part of their happiness and joy in collecting and owning your work.

While it may not happen on the first try, it is imperative to find a price point that not only results in sales, but also makes you feel comfortable and proud to offer your work for. Charging too little undervalues your talent and efforts. Plain and simple. You probably won't end up enjoying the process of selling to clients because it will always feel like you're giving your work away. This can become incredibly discouraging over time, and you may be tempted to give up, which is exactly what we want to avoid!

In addition, if you're selling too quickly you could run out of inventory, making it hard to send work to shows, fairs, or other commitments. You should be able to sell your art without missing out on opportunities to develop your resume and build your creative career. Even if you love the work you're currently making, nobody is a machine. You need to allow time for breaks, business or administrative tasks, and finding new inspiration. If you're constantly selling or taking new commissions to make ends meet you could very easily experience burnout in your artistic practice.

However, setting or raising your prices too high or too quickly will automatically cause some potential buyers to not even consider your work. Most emerging collectors have a budget in mind, and if you're too far beyond that number they'll think your work is out of reach. While we definitely want you to make a fair profit, some artists expect to earn thousands on the very first piece they create, or that as soon as they jump into a career as an artist they will suddenly earn the equivalent of a full-time income. That could certainly happen, of course, but it is incredibly rare. Most artists take several years, if not more, to increase their prices incrementally.

Always remember that you're asking your potential collectors to not just invest in your work, but in you as an artist! If you're still relatively new and "unknown" to the art world (i.e. you haven't exhibited widely, been published, or won awards), they are taking a bit of a risk in buying your work. We all hope that a viewer will fall in love with a piece and want to buy it solely because of that romantic feeling. But most are cautious with their monetary investments, and you should be aware that your potential collectors want to make sure that what they are paying for is actually worth the price. If you can't provide solid reasoning behind your prices you will likely lose sales.

If you set a price and don't get any inquiries, that can be as frustrating as selling to clients who are underpaying you. This isn't always a sign that you've priced your work above what your collectors are willing to spend, but it could be a strong indicator of it. For many artists, the initial price conversation with a potential buyer can feel awkward. If you provide a big number you're not actually confident you should be selling at, in the hopes of a payday, you'll likely give yourself away. Finding the right prices will help you present your work with ease and allow you to be firm if you have to negotiate with a client.

With all this in mind, we're sure that you're thinking is: what is the happy medium and how do I find it? Let's explore the following tips to find out!

FINDING YOUR PRICE POINT

Research Your Market

Visit a few galleries that show work by emerging artists who have a similar amount of experience or are at the same point in their career as you. Take notes on various sizes, mediums, and the subject matter to gain an understanding of the average prices in the market. Even if it seems intimidating, you're more than welcome to ask to see the price list at any gallery. The assistants at the front desk should be willing to help. Asking about the price list may also give you the opportunity to speak with a manager or director depending on where you visit. We certainly do not recommend taking up too much of their time, considering that they want to focus on clients actually interested in purchasing work, so be upfront with them on why you've inquired about pricing. This could even be an entry point into a quick elevator pitch about your art!

If you don't have access to galleries that you can visit in person, spend some time online looking at websites like Saatchi Art, Artspace, and other similar platforms to see the prices for work that relates to your own. Of course, not all 24 x 24-inch paintings are created equal, so we still recommend doing a little additional digging into the artist's background once you have found a style, size, and medium that you would consider comparable with yours. There is also a plethora of newer galleries that exist solely online and therefore almost always list their artists' prices on their website.

When you find an artist who you think is a good reference in terms of pricing, you could also try reaching out to them to ask about how they decided on their numbers. We believe in collaboration over competition. Hopefully, they do too and would be willing to give you some advice or perspective.

You may even consider looking at art auction houses in your area or online. Be careful here, though, as these businesses primarily deal in the secondary market, meaning that the artwork is being resold from the client rather than from the artist directly. However, since most houses list the results of their auctions online you'll know the exact amount that a piece sold for—or if it didn't sell at all. This might give you more realistic, big-picture ideas of what paintings sell for in comparison to sculptures or prints, as well as the various price points certain styles of artwork can sell for.

The great thing about the Internet is that you can type in any topic you need help with and get millions of results. Keeping in mind that some art you come across will be too cheap or too expensive, average out the prices until you are comfortable with a price point that you can use for your own work.

Ask a Friend

Artists are so close to their own artwork that sometimes it is great to get an outsider's perspective. Do you know a curator, art agent, art advisor, or even a fellow artist who is further along in their career than you? Any of these people might be a good resource for you to get a bit of guidance on what your prices should be. Make sure that this is a person you trust and who knows your work well; otherwise, it could turn into an uncomfortable conversation very quickly. Try to be open to their thoughts and suggestions, always remembering that you alone will make the final decision on whether you use any prices they recommend.

Include the Cost of Your Materials

It would be almost impossible to calculate exactly how much paint, clay, charcoal, etc. you use to produce one piece of work, but keep in mind roughly how much you spend on supplies to ensure that your prices take these expenses into account. The cost of materials is especially important to consider when you are just starting out and your rates may be fairly low already. Don't forget to include the costs of shipping supplies, such as bubble wrap and tape, which can add up quickly. Framing, mounting, or any special matting should be taken into consideration as well.

Again, even though you probably won't know exactly how much of each medium you've used in one work, we advise that you include an amount in your prices that is a general estimation of your overall materials cost, plus a little extra in order to ensure that you will recover that expense. After all, you don't want to either make a profit or have enough money to buy new supplies—you want both!

Keep Track of Your Time

While we think it's important to know how much time you are spending in the studio, you don't necessarily need to use this as the only point of consideration for pricing your work. Some artists spend long, tedious hours on each piece while others make a lot of work more quickly, and only select a few final pieces to include in their portfolio. Neither process is wrong or right, and this is another reason why pricing can often seem so complicated. This is why we suggest finding a number that you feel confident presenting to potential clients after doing your research, calculating your materials, and keeping your working hours in mind.

Some artists like to imagine creating their art as an hourly job and set their prices based on that. For example, if you were to pay yourself a wage of $15 per hour and your painting took you twenty hours, you would charge $300. While this is a much simpler way of coming to a price, we don't recommend solely using this method, as it doesn't factor in the cost of your materials. Wouldn't it also be disappointing to see that while you are selling your work for $300, a similar artist is selling each painting for $500 or $700? This is why we highly recommend doing some research before settling on your prices.

Tip:

Occupational employment statistics from the United States Department of Labor listed $25.08 as the average hourly wage for independent artists, writers, and performers as of May 2018.[2]

2 "*Occupational Employment and Wages, May 2018: 27-1013 Fine Artists, Including Painters, Sculptors, and Illustrators,*" *Occupational Employment Statistics, U.S. Bureau of Labor Statistics, last modified March 29, 2019, https://www.bls.gov/oes/current/oes271013.htm.*

Using these steps still involves a bit of guesswork. You can always try out your prices with a small studio sale or send an offer to your email list and adjust your pricing based on the response. That being said, we understand that some people might want a method for pricing based on more concrete math. Let's look at two different formulas that might work for you as an alternative to the process we've just discussed.

Art-Pricing Formulas

The first pricing formula is from the Artists Network website, where it was mentioned in a blog post by painter Lori Woodward. Start with the size of your artwork and calculate what it is in square inches.

15 inch x 15 inch = 225 square inches

Then multiply that number by a dollar amount that represents where you are in your career. For example, $.50 to $2.00 for artists starting out, or $3.00 to $7.00 if you are a bit more established.

225 x $2 = $450

Next factor in the cost of your materials. If you have to take into account a commission from a gallery, you may want to double that cost.

$50 spent in materials + $450 = $500

Or, if you work with a gallery:

($50 materials x 2) + $450 = $550

The vast majority of artwork is priced in increments of $10 or $25 (until you start selling in the $1,000+ range), so if the math comes out to a number like $324 consider rounding down or up to $300, $325, or $330.

Try this formula out with a few of your pieces and see what you think. It might take a few tweaks on the initial dollar amount to get it right, but eventually you should be able to land on what you believe is a fair price for your art.

A NOTE ON PRICING WHEN YOU ARE REPRESENTED OR CONSIGNED BY A GALLERY

Just because a gallery will take a 50 percent commission on any sale of your work (or whatever percentage has been agreed upon between both parties), it does not mean that you should increase your retail prices by 50 percent when you start working with one. You can double your materials cost to make sure you recover that expense, but not your whole price. While it might be tempting to do so, there are several reasons why this should be avoided:

Continue ›

• First and foremost, you should always maintain an honest relationship with any galleries you work with. If you tell them a higher price and they find out that amount is not what you usually sell for, you could potentially ruin the partnership you have with them. It's better to have an open discussion upfront about potentially raising your prices a little to account for their commission and you taking the next step in your career, which does merit a bump in prices!

• When a new gallery first takes you on, they will be introducing your work to their audience, but will likely also want to connect with the network you have already built. If you are suddenly selling work for much higher prices than your audience is used to they may no longer be willing to buy, and the gallery will notice.

• Working with a gallery isn't for everyone, and there are many pros and cons to consider. If you want access to their resources and client base, among other things, we always advise artists to choose wisely who they get into business with. See The Dos and Don'ts of Applying to Art Galleries (page 153) for more on this topic or Alternatives to the Gallery System (page 166) if you are considering other options.

A second formula option comes from an article by the massive online art marketplace Saatchi Art.[3] Saatchi works with thousands of artists, and this is the formula that they widely recommend based on their experience.

This method starts with doubling the cost of your materials no matter what. So, let's say your materials cost is $100.

$100 x 2 = $200

Then you will decide on an hourly rate for yourself, like we discussed earlier, and multiply that dollar amount by the number of hours it took to make the work. Let's use the same numbers from the previous section: $15 per hour and 20 hours to complete the painting.

$15 x 20 = $300

Next, add the two totals together for the final retail price.

$300 + $200 = $500

This result of $500 probably seems more reasonable for a painting that took twenty hours to complete, right? Now try this formula out with various sizes of your art and see if it generally works for you.

Even if you don't end up using either of these formulas, they could certainly be part of your research and experimentation process when you first start pricing your work. The biggest test of how successfully you've priced your artwork will be when you start presenting to clients, so try not to get stuck on this part for too long. Once you've gone through an initial sale (or a few, if you're newer), you can reevaluate and make any changes if needed.

Continue ›

3 *"How Do I Price My Artwork," Saatchi Art, https://support.saatchiart.com/hc/en-us/articles/206523267-How-do-I-price-my-artwork.*

‹ Continued

If the price of your work is too high, you might resist promoting your work or alienate fans of your art who would love to become collectors. If it's too low, you may feel depleted or even resentful toward your buyer. Test out your happy medium, and then commit to it for a year to get yourself established. Remember that to be professional and respectful in both your buyer and gallery relationships, you should remain very consistent with your pricing so that no one feels cheated. Even if you're showing in different cities (or even countries), the art world can be very small, and if one person finds out that you are selling for lower with another gallery or on your own, it could damage your reputation.

Don't get frustrated if you don't make any sales on your first try. Not all artists do! Be patient and don't blindly assume that you have to slash your prices. You simply might not be reaching your target audience yet, and in that case, you want to focus more effort on marketing before trying again.

PRICING DIFFERENT TYPES OF WORK

Research Your Market

All these pricing tips are great when you're pricing one similar body of work, but what if you make paintings and watercolors or small and large drawings? You'll certainly want to have prices for all the types of work that you do ready to go, in case a client discovers you and is interested. We highly suggest establishing a consistent price point for every size and type of work you create. Put all this information in a document that you can easily reference when discussing with customers or a gallery.

For example:
10" x 10" drawing = $100
15" x 15" drawing = $175
20" x 20" drawing = $250

and

18" x 24" painting = $500
24" x 36" painting = $750
36" x 48" painting = $1,000

Generally, you should vary your prices based on size (i.e. larger = more $) and consider selling different mediums at different price points. At the time of writing this book, Kat's 9" x 12"watercolors are $300, while her large oil paintings start at $1,300. Works that don't take as long to create or necessitate the use of expensive materials usually cost less. Drawings, sketches, prints, collages, watercolors, and photographs are likely going to be less than oil or acrylic paintings and sculptures. This, of course, is not a hard rule and there are many exceptions, depending on your specialty and focus as an artist, as well as where you are in your career.

HANDLING REQUESTS FOR DISCOUNTS

One last thing to keep in mind is that clients and galleries may ask for discounts. Ten percent is fairly standard in the industry and is often noted in artist contracts with galleries. Again, we don't recommend trying to covertly add an additional amount to your prices to avoid losing any profit. Be fair with your customers and work with them as much as you can if you can see that they really love your work. Your prices should already be set in a way that a small discount is doable and won't hurt your profit margin. If they ask for a lot more than 10 or 20 percent off, absolutely feel free to stand firm on your prices and suggest less expensive works or a payment plan instead. Unless it is an older work that you'd rather have find a home, don't let anyone make you feel pressured to sell for less than what the work is worth. Ultimately, you have to be HAPPY with the prices you choose, so that you will be excited and motivated to sell your art for years to come.

RAISING YOUR PRICES

Finding the ideal price range, where you're selling enough and consistently but not too much, is the first challenge. The second is deciding when to raise your prices and how much to raise them by. Now, there is certainly no obligation to increase your prices at all if you're selling well. We know numerous artists that have a set pricing structure, and this works great for them because it means consistent sales and income. It also encourages repeat buyers who are accustomed to paying a specific amount and might otherwise be turned off if they come back a few years later to find the costs significantly higher.

That being said, when you're continually working to develop your craft, investing in higher-quality materials, exhibiting more frequently and even showing with galleries, and/or being recognized by the media, you certainly deserve more monetary compensation for your work. A general rule that we agree with is that if you're selling over half of the work that you create in about six months or less, or if you have a sell-out or nearly sell-out exhibition, you should consider increasing your prices. [4]

Here are some other instances that may indicate it is time to raise your prices:
- If you only have a few works left in a limited edition series you may increase the prices due to their rarity. Alicia worked at a gallery where each subsequent piece in one cartist's limited edition series was more expensive than the last. This is not necessarily typical, and it only works when there is enough demand for the work, but it's something to keep in mind.
- If you're creating a new body of work that is bigger in size or uses more expensive materials you should raise your prices to recover your costs and support you in upgrading your studio practice.
- If your work has been purchased for an important public or private collection (by a recognized institution or collector—not just any sale) this is a major achievement, and it signifies taking a next step in your career.
- If your art has been featured in several prominent media outlets you can use this exposure as justification for increased prices. As with being purchased for a collection, this demonstrates strong interest in your work.
- If you have recently been awarded a prize, grant, or special residency opportunity this is usually another marker of leveling up.
- If you are working with a brand, business, or private collector on a commissioned piece, charging more for your work is appropriate and often standard practice. Instead of buyingsomething outright, they are asking you to create a custom work of art, which requires more effort and sometimes several rounds of changes depending on the project.[5]
- If you sign a contract to be represented with a gallery, as we mentioned previously, this could potentially be an opportune moment to discuss raising prices with them.

A 10-percent increase is a common percentage to use if you're incrementally increasing your price points. This is enough to make a difference in your sales and profit, but it shouldn't scare away previous clients who might want to make a second or third purchase from you. Keep repeating this process as often as needed, and if the 10-percent jump isn't enough, feel free to increase up to 20 or 25 percent if the demand is there. Keep working toward the ideal prices you'd like to be selling your art for. If you're not there yet, continue to push yourself and take small steps toward your goals until you make it.

Happy selling!

TAKE ACTION

- Visit a few galleries in person or explore online to research the work and price points of artists similar to you.
- Experiment with pricing formulas and your own work.
- Create a document of established price points for the various types of work you create.

ADDITIONAL RESOURCES FOR PRICING ARTWORK

How Do I Price My Artwork:
https://support.saatchiart.com/
hc/en-us/articles/206523267-
How-do-I-price-my-artwork

Simple Formulas for Pricing Artwork:
https://www.artworkarchive.com/
blog/how-to-price-consistently-
for-art-sales-success

How to Set and Raise Selling Prices for my Art:
https://www.artbusiness.com/
moreprice.html

Art Pricing, When To Raise Your Prices, How Art Prices Go Up:
https://thecuratorssalon.com/
artist-blog/2018/art-pricing

Artspace:
https://www.artspace.com

Artsy:
https://www.artsy.net/

---

4 Alan Bamberger, *"How to Set and Raise Selling Prices for your Art."* ArtBusiness.com, *https://www.artbusiness.com/moreprice.html.*

5 Gita Joshi, *"Art Pricing, When To Raise Your Prices, How Art Prices Go Up,"* The Curator's Salon, *January 18, 2019, https://thecuratorssalon.com/artist-blog/2018/art-pricing.*

SMART STRATEGIES TO SELL & MARKET YOUR ART

ARE YOU READY TO SELL?

We know that so many artists would love to be making more money from their work, but that alone isn't a reason to jump into selling your art. While we are huge advocates of starting before you are "ready," this is more a mental game than anything. There are some key basics that you do need to have prepared before you start offering your work to galleries and elsewhere. If you are a younger artist or just getting started, ask yourself the following questions first to make sure you are setting yourself up for successful selling!

Which works are you most excited about and proud to share?
This will help you when it comes to marketing and being authentic about why people should be interested in collecting your art.

Is it a complete body of work?
Aim for at least ten cohesive pieces to start with, ideally more.

Are all of the works finished? Have you thought about framing, matting, or adding a hanging wire on the back?
You can start teasing works in progress, but clients are more likely to focus on pieces that are complete and ready to hang.

Have you set consistent prices?
Be ready to respond when someone shows interest, rather than having to think of something on the spot and risk over- or undercharging them.

Do you have quality photos of your work?
This should go without saying! You need great images of your art to sell online. Period.

Which pieces are you able to package properly and ship in a timely manner?
Bigger works cost more to pack and ship, so save yourself a headache by buying the proper materials or even hiring an art handler or similar service to help. Customers usually expect artwork to ship within a few weeks, so make sure that is possible on your end.

Did you check that none of the pieces are promised to upcoming shows?
Don't get caught in a situation where you sell a piece that was meant to be exhibited (unless you really needed to make the sale, for whatever reason). You could lose the opportunity to be in the exhibition and cause the venue to question your professionalism.

Has your audience already expressed interest in certain work?
Take note of works that your audience has liked! Don't strive to make work simply because you think it will sell, but use your community to your advantage.

Checked these questions off your list? Great! Now you're ready to begin.

SIMPLE STEPS TO SALES & MARKETING

Early in your creative career, it may be tempting to think that you need to wait for someone to validate you before selling your work. It's common for artists to feel that they need a gallery or agent to sell and promote their work. The good news is, these days you can do it on your own and sell your art directly. With the rise of social media, online marketplaces for art, and unlimited resources to help you learn the basics of business and sales, now is the best time to be an independent artist.

Simply look at someone like self-taught artist Ashley Longshore, who opted out of the gallery system altogether and is experiencing tremendous success by marketing herself in nontraditional ways. Even if you decide to work with a professional gallery, you can still use the principles outlined in this chapter to help you make the most of every opportunity.

When Kat chose to be a fine art painter, she didn't get picked up by an agent and start magically making a living as an artist. On the contrary, it took several years of trial and error and tons of rejection letters before it clicked that she needed to take charge of her own career, and no one was coming to save her. Through a series of life lessons, investing in additional education, and personal development, she discovered that artists do not have to wait for anyone to make them qualified to sell and promote their work. We are living in an incredible time where a simple Google search, a book on Amazon, or an affordable online workshop can fill in the blanks and provide the tools we are missing to help us get to that next level. Embrace the entrepreneurial spirit for your art career and take it further than you even thought possible.

We hope to save you some time and offer a few shortcuts so you don't fall into the same limited art-world thinking that we did at first. Have the confidence to take charge as soon as you can. The best thing you can do for yourself is start treating yourself like a small business and learn how to put yourself out there. Regardless of whether you have a gallery or not, art lovers will be interested in collecting work, so let's make it easy for them to find you.

Continue ›

As scary as it can initially feel to promote your own work, we've learned a few simple things about what it takes to make direct sales to collectors online and through exhibitions. Even though Kat is represented by a gallery at the time of writing this book, she still invests her time and energy into learning marketing basics to ensure the relationship is beneficial to both parties. Alicia uses a similar approach when marketing our online gallery, PxP Contemporary, to maximize sales for the represented and invited artists.

When we were starting out in the art world, it was a common notion that an art gallery would eliminate many of our struggles and somehow outsource all the sales and marketing for us. Admittedly, Kat had a secret fantasy that securing gallery representation would allow her to paint in a faraway cabin in the woods and never have to worry about any other part of her art career. As you might have guessed, quite the opposite ended up happening, but that's definitely not a bad thing. In fact, it's been a blessing in disguise for us both. Over the years of learning and working together to launch multiple online projects, we took back a lot of power and independence when it comes to selling art. This has brought us outside of our comfort zones at times, but it has also relieved a lot of financial pressure. We had to show up for ourselves when no one else did, and it's now our passion to help other artists do the same.

Working with a gallery can elevate the artist's image, but you are not off the hook for doing the work on your end. We like to approach gallery representation as a partnership, instead of expecting them to "do something for us," and we continue to market and push out work ourselves to help sales. It is, of course, the gallery's responsibility to manage marketing and help connect their artists to a wider audience than they might have access to, but it's always extra helpful when the artist also does their part. This symbiotic relationship usually results in the most sales, which is a win-win for everyone.

If it is your ultimate dream to be represented by a great gallery, you can still work toward that goal and market your work until that happens. Chances are, you are much more likely to get noticed if you put yourself out there. Send a message to the world that you are ready to be recognized by treating both your studio practice and marketing like a professional.

Here are a few ideas we've used that can help transform your mindset around selling and marketing. Stop waiting for permission. If you want to make money with your art, start working on your business to invite and inspire new collectors to purchase art from you.

People Want to Buy Art. Help Them Do It!

A simple trick is to actually announce that work is for sale. This may sound silly, and we write and talk about this all the time, but often, when it comes to online marketing, you need to nudge your potential collector in the right direction. You want to make sure your audience is aware that they can be the happy new owner of the piece they noticed in your newsletter, on Facebook, or via an Instagram post.

A few ideas on how to announce and promote sales include:

- Create an album on Facebook titled "available work."
- Send an email newsletter announcing any new collections.
- List the phrase "inquire to purchase" on your website.
- Post art you recently got back from a show on Instagram with a caption urging clients to get in touch if they are interested. A caption such as "work available for sale, direct message or email me for details" or something along those lines makes a huge difference. Don't forget to always give your audience a way to contact you.

This should go without saying, but if you are represented by a gallery and only sell work through them, direct any potential clients to the gallery and share the contact with your dealer if that is part of your contract. Kat often hears positive feedback from the galleries that show her work because she not only does this, but also uses her audience to promote her art and the gallery. Her galleries have expressed how much they appreciate a simple shoutout via an Instagram Story or a post mentioning that a specific piece is available through them.

Remember that people want and like to buy art, and you are not being annoying by allowing them that joy. You know that people shop for expensive shoes, purses, and cars. So why not art as well? In fact, buying art can be a much more meaningful experience to a buyer than many of those other items might be, not to mention it is usually a better investment and lasts longer. Give your collectors the chance to own your work and support your career! Sometimes the fact that they are helping an emerging or living artist is significant for them as well.

Be sure to only post art for sale that you are TRULY proud of. If something in your gut tells you that you are not quite there yet, and you need to polish up your skills, don't rush. Take the time you need to develop a strong body of work, and then start selling with confidence. Reference Crafting Your Portfolio (page 36) before diving into marketing.

Use the Power of Storytelling

When interacting online or in person, harness the power of storytelling. Share a moment which inspired your current work or a situation that changed your perspective and made you passionate about a specific topic. We all have numerous stories to tell. By sharing them with others, you will find a common thread connecting you with your ideal clients.

When Kat started exhibiting her work, the theme in her paintings was nostalgia and homesickness for Russia, the place where she grew up. When she publicly opened up about her experiences and described the imagery and memories that inspired her paintings, it made the viewer feel like they were purchasing a special piece of her story. Several collectors invested in her early pieces because of their own memories, travels to Russia, or experiences with separation from home. We all strive to feel connected, and art has the power to visually express those sentiments that we share. It's your job to communicate how the viewer can connect to your work specifically and convince them why it's important for them to own it.

It doesn't always have to be profound, but be honest about why you create what you do and deliver the message in your own way. For example, Kat loves to share thoughts and inspiration in her Instagram Stories. The quotes and anecdotes she posts help her audience connect with what guides her when she makes her work. It's a way to show creativity, process, and personality, which helps attract and engage new fans of her art.

When collectors often see art or are looking to purchase art online, hearing the maker share something personal about a piece gives context and adds meaning. Storytelling doesn't have to be direct. Some creatives simply share a part of their process by making time-lapse videos. Others answer questions from their community via short clips posted on social media. If you're camera-shy, you can simply write in-depth Instagram captions to explain your art and studio practice. Experiment with how you want to present your story and step out of your comfort zone a little bit more each time you share.

Investing in Your Business Will Help It Grow!

You've probably heard of the saying "you have to spend money to make money," right? It's not always easy to hear when you're starting out, having a slow period with art sales, or trying to find work, but if you are able to allocate some funds to professional development it can, and often does, end up rewarding you with more than what you put in.

Creating a small budget to pay for affordable advertisements on Facebook and Instagram is a fabulous way to promote your art among new collectors that are not in your immediate network. Start by investing a few dollars each month to grow your audience through ads or reputable Instagram shoutouts, and then increase to $10, $25, or $50. We've both used these methods of advertising and seen great results, even if we spend as little as $5 to boost a post.

We will cover more in-depth tips for using social media in other chapters, but to get you started, begin thinking about your target audience. Consider the following: Who are they? Where do they live? What are their interests besides art? Instagram does set up an "automatic" audience based on your followers, but that may not be who would most likely end up buying your work, so don't necessarily run your ads with their default settings.

Here are a few other paid ways to invest in your art career at every price point:

Under $50

Buy an art book.
Whether it is business advice geared toward artists, the empowering story of a creative person you admire, or a glossy publication with images by an artist whose work inspires you, picking up a new book to read will both help you learn and give you a break from studio time, while still being productive. Or, you can also buy books in audio format and listen while you work.

Take a course or workshop.
Check local museums and art centers for classes on a subject of interest. You can also find online courses to take from home on sites like CreativeLive, Skillshare, and more.

Order business cards or postcards.
It's nice to have these ready to go when you're preparing for an upcoming exhibition and attending events such as gallery openings or art fairs. Nowadays most companies even offer easy-to-use, customizable templates that make designing professional-quality cards a breeze.

Submit to a juried exhibition or recognized art publication.
Not only does this add to your resume if you are accepted, but it can also help you grow your network and get your work noticed by new curators and collectors.

Under $100

Buy frames for your artwork.
You don't always have to wait until a show to make your work "ready to hang." Sometimes helping a buyer visualize how your piece will look like on their wall helps close the sale.

Consider purchasing art and shipping supplies in bulk.
Depending on where you shop for your creative and packing materials, you may find that they offer discounts on buying, for example, five canvases rather than one or two at a time. As long as you have room to store them, why not plan in advance? It's more than likely you will use them over time. Even if nothing is overtly advertised, you can always ask!

Hire a studio assistant to help with a project or exhibition.
While you may not have the funds to keep a studio assistant on a permanent basis, there are certain occasions when your time really is more valuable than your money. Use it to hire a local art student for a few hours to help with tasks that are time-consuming, but don't require you doing them personally.

Under $500

Book a session with a business mentor or artist coach.

If you want to improve your sales, marketing, and money-management strategies, a business coach might be the right fit for you to get one-on-one training and accountability. There are also mentors who specialize in working with artists and can assist with outlining the steps you should take to jump ahead in your career.

Have your work professionally photographed or buy a nicer camera.

It's great if you've been making do with your iPhone or a simple digital camera to shoot your work, but you will certainly see a difference in the quality of images that a photographer can provide you with or that you take with a more professional digital camera.

Make a mini catalog of your work.

There's just something special about seeing your artwork in print. Design a booklet to send to your collectors or have available at an upcoming show.

Upgrade your studio.

Consider investing in new or better tools and equipment, such as additional design software or other technology, a drafting table, storage racks, flat files, or anything similar that will add to your workspace.

Under $1,000

Take a course at a local university.

When you're looking for a little more in-depth coverage than a book or short-term workshop will give you, browse the course offerings at a local community college or university. Some may be able to offer a lower price point for auditing the class rather than taking it for credit.

Go on an artist residency.

Always wanted to travel? Combine your passions and seek out a residency in a place you'd want to visit. They often provide affordable housing and some will help with meals, so all you need to do is budget for additional food and transportation.

Over $1,000

Pay for a booth at an artist-focused art fair.

Selling online can be hard at first, as the majority of collectors still prefer to purchase work that they've seen in person. If you are not yet represented by a gallery, this is an opportunity to get your art in front of potentially thousands of art lovers and buyers. Find a fair that specifically focuses on artists showing their own work, like The Other Art Fair or Superfine.

Get a certification.

A great way to supplement your income from art sales is by broadening the scope of your freelance skills. Perhaps you can teach, do design work, or book photography gigs on the side.

It can seem scary to put precious funds toward your future when you can't see tangible results from them right now, but as Alicia's mother always told her growing up, "Your education is something that nobody can ever take away from you." Keep on learning and be willing to trust in your dream. This also sends a message to the universe that you are serious about being a professional artist. It doesn't have to cost a lot, but don't skimp on setting up the strong foundation on which you will build the rest of your career.

Keep in mind that investing in your art career doesn't always require you to spend money. Setting aside some time to work specifically on business and administrative tasks can be incredibly helpful and yield great results.

Here are cost-free ideas to get you started!

- Update your resume and website.
- Invite a few artists to your studio for a group critique or studio visit.
- Go to an art event and make a new professional contact.
- Clean and organize your studio space.
- Practice consistent self-care.
- Listen to art or business podcasts and read blogs for artists.
- Look for a free course, workshop, or tutorial to take.
- Send an email blast with recent accomplishments or news.
- Take photos of recent work and share them online.
- Have a show at a local venue.
- Get a former client to write a testimonial for you.
- Ask a friend or collector for a referral.

We hope that these ideas have given you new inspiration on how to invest in your creative practice so that you can take the next steps in your art career.

Prepare a Commerce Platform Before Announcing Your Art Is for Sale

Whether it's selling on Etsy, getting paid directly via PayPal, using an e-commerce platform such as Shopify, or creating a page on Squarespace, make sure you set up your shop and test it out first to ensure that your clients will have a satisfactory customer experience. If the process is too slow or complicated, it will be difficult for collectors to buy from you and you will lose sales. Simplicity is key!

Calculate your shipping costs, both domestic and international, and if the platform you use charges a fee automatically, just double-check that it does indeed cover the full expense. Do this by purchasing a scale (you can find one for under $30 on Amazon) and setting up accounts with UPS, USPS, FedEx, or your local mail carrier. Having direct accounts in place can save time and money, especially if you print labels from home and drop them off, rather than go to a post office and wait in line.

Remember that the client is normally responsible for covering the shipping cost, especially if it's a larger work. To encourage people to buy smaller pieces or works on paper, you might consider shipping small pieces or works on paper for free or for a flat fee. Or, if you want to close a deal with a prospective buyer, part of your negotiation might be to split the shipping expense.

We advise you to always be as prepared as possible. Get everything ready on your end in advance and act as if the sales will happen (because they will!). You can't anticipate every detail, but having a basic system in place will show your new collector that you are a professional artist worth investing in.

Your Reputation Will Follow You, So Make It Great

Whether you are represented by a gallery or not, be a great person to work with, not just a great artist to work with. Offer payment plans to potential clients who may not be able to pay your full prices right away, respond to messages or questions from your audience in a timely manner, and support others in your community when you can.

Building your network isn't just about making connections with clients, curators, and galleries. Friendly, courteous interactions with your fellow artists can also end up being rewarding. We have both not only made new friends in our art community, but also benefited from being connected to new opportunities by these peers that we would never have had otherwise.

We have said it before, but being a true partner to your gallery by pulling your own weight can multiply your success. And if you are selling on your own, starting your client relationships off on the right foot will help them remember you and they'll be more likely to add to their collection of your art in the future. Furthermore, if they loved buying from you they could very well recommend you to a friend and do the marketing for you!

During one of Kat's first few art sales, she received a compliment from an older gentleman collector who happened to be a lawyer. He told her how impressed he was with her professionalism, quick replies, and seamless sales process. Mind you, this was back in 2012 when she was using a simple email invoice and he was sending her a paper check! Do the best you can with the resources you have, and make upgrades periodically as you grow your business.

Heal Your Mindset around Marketing & Selling

Many of us have learned to associate selling with sleazy, pushy businessmen. But forget about this Hollywood trope when it comes to your approach to marketing and promoting yourself, because you can make it your own. That way it doesn't have to feel like you're acting and you won't be uncomfortable. People will only respond to you if you are true to your artwork and yourself, so don't use marketing techniques you think are inauthentic. You know you're a talented artist, so be proud to promote your work. Use your excitement to develop a way of sharing what you create that works for you and feels good. Trust your gut instinct. If it is telling you something doesn't seem right, change up your sales pitch or method and try again.

Collecting art is a personal process and varies from client to client. Be confident and follow up, but don't be offended if a sale falls through or doesn't go the way you hoped. Like any relationship, you are looking for a good fit, and you want both you and the buyer to be happy with the outcome. If you didn't end up selling a piece, that's okay. Sometimes a work of art gets scooped up right away, but more often than not it takes at least a few years to build your reputation and trust with collectors. You'll start to see steadier sales once you reach this point in your career, so work hard to get there.

If the right buyers haven't found you yet, or if you have already connected with potential clients who are not quite ready to purchase for whatever reason, be patient and understanding. Alicia bought directly from an artist at an art fair almost a year after initially inquiring about her work. She didn't forget; it just wasn't in her budget at the time. But upon seeing the artist's impressive showing at the fair, she knew she had to finally pull the trigger — and she's so glad that she did! Continue confidently sharing your work to help convince the clients who may be on the fence or who were interested previously but haven't followed up in a while.

Don't Just Sell Art — Make It an Experience

Come up with innovative ways that your audience can engage with your work. Create a unique event or experience for your collectors that they wouldn't get anywhere else, like hosting a studio visit with refreshments or a special online sale via email and social media. One thing that Kat used to do was periodically mail out postcards and small catalogs with new pieces directly to her client mailing list. This was a smart approach in two ways. First, these quality-printed materials served as small token gifts, showing her appreciation for having supported her over the years. But second, they also put her available work in front of their eyes for them to start getting excited about and to consider adding to their existing collections.

Getting out from behind the computer screen is also really important, so when you start participating in local exhibitions and events, be sure to introduce yourself to any interested patrons and get them to sign up for your newsletter to stay in touch. Seeing art in person can be a memorable experience for many collectors and creates a wonderful way for you to grow your mailing list.

TAKE ACTION

- Answer the questions on page 64 to determine if you're ready to sell.
- Set up your commerce platform and shipping accounts before you announce your art is for sale.
- Remember to be patient and keep confidently stepping out to share your art with potential clients!

TAKING THE LEAP
& LEAVING YOUR DAY JOB

ADVICE FROM KAT

Are you an artist or creative who dreams about leaving your day job and making it on your own? If so, this chapter is for you! After more than three years of being self-employed, I want to share my experiences and advice to help you take the leap when you are ready.

My intention is to encourage you and help you understand that being your own boss in the arts is possible, but I also believe in sharing the behind-the-scenes reality of what it's like, especially in the beginning. I welcome anyone who feels that they are meant to follow this path, which is both challenging and exciting, to join me, but I also want to be completely transparent and helpful in preparing you for what may be ahead.

Should you simply hope for the best, be positive, and put in your two weeks' notice to pursue your dreams? Not at all—at least not yet. I've been there, and I know what it takes. You have to be strong mentally, financially, and emotionally to take this leap, and while I love to encourage everyone I meet to chase after their dreams, I want to empower you to make an informed decision by sharing my journey first.

EMBRACING YOUR DAY JOB

If you already have a job or career that you enjoy, aside from making art, that allows you the time and freedom to create while giving you security and an income, that is incredible and you should embrace it! That was my original plan, but I wasn't satisfied with any of my employment experiences, which is why I decided to carve my own path. I think finding a job that supports your lifestyle and allows you time for making art is honorable. You should be proud of it—even if it's not related to your creative passion. I know many artists who enjoy what they do at their day job, and the arrangement works for them. This chapter is for those who dream of being their own boss or are deeply dissatisfied with their current employment.

I promised myself that once I started making headway in my own career as an artist, I would "send the elevator back down to someone who needs a lift." I do not have all the answers or solutions to your unique situation, but hopefully my experiences can give you some ideas and perspective on what life is like once you make the jump, as well as show you how I got to where I am now. These are the things I wish I had known when I was preparing to leave my job and trying to learn about who I wanted to become.

When I started out on my career path, I was worried about all the wrong things. I had many insecurities that held me back and a negative mindset that was probably the reason behind many great missed opportunities. I was resistant to change. But my experience and level of education, which I thought would affect how others viewed me, played much smaller roles in my career than I expected. I now look back and find comfort in these mistakes and try not to slip back into negative patterns of thinking when hard times arise.

Now that you read through that disclosure, following are some helpful tips that will prepare you, empower you, and build you up to be the person you want to be when you are crazy enough to take your art venture out into the world. You are capable, strong, and talented, and I am rooting for your success!

Be Your Own Investor

When you start working for yourself as an artist or creative, you have to think of yourself as a business. I was hesitant to embrace this idea for a long time, but once it all clicked, my life changed. You are the CEO of your art career. You have to take full responsibility for your successes and failures. This means making wise choices about your money, your time, and how you present yourself to the world.

If you are still working your day job, use it as your "angel investor." I know many day jobs don't pay nearly enough to even cover the bills or your student loan payments, but do your absolute best to save as much as you possibly can—you will thank yourself later. Nickname your bank account "dream art career" or "studio fund" and put away any extra dollars after your necessary living expenses are covered. Save up for the time when you will leave, and use any additional money for building a website, photographing your work with a quality camera or hiring a photographer, covering application fees, and buying the materials you need to create your next body of work.

During my waitressing days, I used the extra $100 to $200 I had for purchasing canvases, visiting exhibitions in bigger cities, and applying to dream opportunities. I also always had a budget for art books and magazines so that on my work breaks, my mind would be filled with things that I aspired to be around, not the noise and negativity of my workplace environment.

Emergencies and unexpected expenses always come up, so instead of hoping for the best, plan ahead to make sure you have a cushion. Before I quit my day job, I had only six months' of living expenses set aside, which I frankly regret, because it wasn't enough. After a handful of massive setbacks in the first few months, I ended up having to use most of that saved money unexpectedly, including my retirement fund. Always save a little more than you think you need. Trust me, it's worth staying at your job for an extra few months if it means you can be comfortably focused on your work instead of having a meltdown like I did. Remember that it's tough to be inspired (if not impossible!) when you are having a panic attack over not being able to pay your bills.

Use Your Free Time to Build Your Career

Right after I graduated with my BFA, I was so discouraged that I couldn't find art-related employment that I would sulk, binge on Netflix, and cry about how miserable I was and how unfair it was that I had a college education and still had to work minimum-wage jobs. I dreamed of being hired by a gallery or museum and basically waited around someone to come and save me. But no one ever came. Eventually, I realized that I had to rescue myself and build the life of my dreams on my own terms.

One day, after a year of rejections from every single art job I applied to, I said, "I will figure this out on my own." I got a job at Macy's in the makeup department (my most creative gig yet) and decided to just make the best of my situation. I aggressively painted in the mornings before my shift and on weekends. I used my phone on work breaks to research calls for art and get ideas for future paintings. During my lunches, I sprinted to Barnes & Noble and hungrily consumed every new art magazine while sipping on a cappuccino. I started to enjoy my life, even though my employment wasn't ideal. I began to be happier and even more motivated in my painting practice.

Not surprisingly, the good energy radiating from the new determined me eventually landed me more opportunities than I'd ever had before. I got an exhibition in Philadelphia and sold my first large painting to a brand new collector I'd never previously met. These accomplishments gave me the encouragement I needed and fueled my positivity.

Around this time, I also got the idea to start my first independent publication, *FreshPaintMagazine*. I remember having a "lightbulb" moment, and I excitedly began researching how to make it happen. The first publication was scrappy, to say the least, but I'm so glad I was inspired and bold enough to do it. I was building an online community and getting deeper into my own work, while balancing the world of retail and the catty cosmetic department (a bunch of bored women standing around all day). I don't remember exactly how it happened, but I started meditating and practicing affirmations to protect my passion and positive attitude, which was especially crucial in an often-depressing work environment that could easily bring me down. I knew that I was getting somewhere, and this inspired me to keep pushing myself.

Invest in Lifelong Learning

I spent a lot of time at the bookstore poring over magazines in those early days, but I also started getting into business literature and self-development books. I was so motivated to make my dream a reality, even though I really didn't know what it would look like. I started consuming as much knowledge as possible, first dabbling in art career books, but later stumbling across empowering titles like *#GIRLBOSS* by Sophia Amoruso.

A new world began to open itself up to me. I realized I could speed up my progress by learning how others did it and applying any relevant aspects to my own life. I started to see patterns in how others from similar backgrounds made it happen. It gave me hope, and it made me feel closer to my dream. I slowly began diving into the world of social media, using it to market my art and new magazine. It was a steep learning curve and I had no idea how to write captions or what to post, but I improved over time by educating myself and experimenting.

I remember the first time I sold something through Facebook and Instagram and how amazing it felt. At first, I thought it wasn't legitimate and that I was a fraudulent artist because I didn't have a fancy gallery representing me, but I'm so glad I kept going because that is how I make much of my living now. As my social platforms began to grow, my community started to develop, and eventually I was picked up by the gallery that currently represents me.

Practice Daily Commitment

I recommend that you take time each week, or even each day, to learn something new that you know you need help with. It might be business tactics, art techniques, social media tips, or anything else. Head to your local library, search the millions of free articles online, download podcasts, or watch instructional YouTube videos. We live in an incredible time where almost anything we need for success is right at our fingertips. I never thought of myself as a businessperson, but I am thankful that I kept an open mind and took the time to educate myself so that I could later support myself as an artist.

In her chapter on starting over (page 226), Alicia mentions how important it is to research to prepare for any aspect of your life and career, and I wholeheartedly agree. It's never going to be perfect, but having a general understanding of what you are getting into, coming up with a plan for making money, marketing yourself, and managing your schedule can alleviate a lot of anxiety. I invested in several workshops and courses before I left my last employer to strike out on my own. I took Marie Forleo's B-School program, classes by Lisa Congdon (available on CreativeLive, a favorite website that offers tons of other incredible courses), and attended a few in-person workshops. You can't prepare for every situation, but investing in affordable education directly related to your field can make a huge difference in your progress.

Get Involved

After graduating from college, I volunteered at art openings and wrote articles for an online art magazine in exchange for free admission to museums. These responsibilities forced me into a professional upgrade as I started working harder to reflect these new environments. I began meeting many more artists and creatives, building new friendships, and even improving my own art. I got new ideas from being around quality exhibitions at major institutions and impressive work that challenged and excited me. Though I am naturally an introvert and sitting at home was my favorite activity besides making art, I knew that wasn't the person I dreamed of becoming. I hated the socializing at first and even got massive social anxiety before any art opening, but I kept pushing through until it became second nature.

I like to remind myself that even though I did not take a "traditional" career path (if there is such a thing!), all my experiences—even those that scared me or that I thought were negative at the time—shaped who I am today. For example, many of the exhibitions and opportunities I had in my early career came from meeting people at events that I attended or volunteered at.

Figure out Your Finances

So, how do you know when you're ready to go out on your own? As you begin consistently selling your artwork and diversifying your income streams, put together an estimated budget of how much you need to generate for a sustainable income that will support your lifestyle. You want to make sure that your art, freelancing, and side gigs bring in enough money to provide for your living and business expenses. Personally, I earn money through a combination of art purchases, magazine sales, commissions, speaking engagements, and curating. Once I knew that I could maintain a consistent mix of all these revenue streams to pay for my bills, it helped me decide that I was ready to quit my day job. Become familiar with your sales and other sources of revenue from your creative business, and double-check them for overall consistency so you

SURROUNDING YOURSELF WITH INSPIRATIONAL PEOPLE

A former mentor once quoted Jim Rohn's inspiring words to me: "You are the average of the five people you spend the most time with." This relates to finances, fitness, relationships, business, and many other parts of life. Many find that if they work this equation based on income across their five people, it tends to be incredibly accurate. This doesn't mean you have to let go of friends you truly care for, but it is a reminder to make a conscious effort to be around those who have achieved more than you, in some way, to let your brain know that it's possible for you too.

Continue ›

can confidently leave your current employment. Each time I had a breakthrough or figured out something new that worked financially, I took notes and got excited because I felt one step closer to my ultimate goal.

I recommend that you test your side income for at least a year before taking the leap. I experienced an unfortunate business partnership breakup with my first magazine, which slowed down my growth. While this is unlikely to happen to you, life gets in the way sometimes, so be as prepared as possible. Don't think of it as a rainy day fund, but instead as an investment you can use to grow your career if everything goes smoothly (which it will!).

Remember That You Are Your Personal Brand

The last job I had, at a Capital One call center, taught me the importance of being your own brand. This means that you represent yourself everywhere you go, and it's your job to show up, work hard, and have the best attitude possible (even if you eventually want to move on to another job). I am happy I had the sense to take this advice to heart. By being my best, even at a job I wasn't excited about, I was able to build amazing relationships with my team members and managers. I pushed myself as a salesperson and customer service representative, no matter how frustrating it was, and my managers rewarded my efforts with extra days off to paint. This eventually let me transition to working part time, and then finally allowed me to leave on good terms with the option to come back "in case things don't work out."

I know life can get aggravating when you aren't in an ideal situation with your art career, but putting forth your best effort, no matter where you are, creates a support system that may end up helping you land your dream position or smoothly transition to self-employment. There is something empowering about having a group of people rooting for your success — and knowing that you always have the option of going back to a day job, giving you peace of mind and more certainty when you're ready to take the plunge.

I hope this summary of my experience helps you craft your own plan to make it on your own one day, if that's your dream. Remember, if you're still at a day job you love or earning money through other freelance work, even if it's not creative, more power to you! I have so much respect for educators, art therapists, designers, consultants, and the many other professions that are both creative and demanding. I also love hearing about how artists support themselves while working in fields like finance or engineering — and who love their second career outside of the arts.

Don't feel pressured to make your entire income from art sales alone. This is something I struggled with in the beginning. It's rare for self-employed artists to support themselves solely by selling their work. Usually we all have to hustle to make ends meet in between those big painting sales.

I wish you all the best on your journey, and if self-employment is your ultimate goal, I can't wait to toast to your success!

TAKE ACTION

- Start saving money now, putting it into a separate account and adding to it as often as possible.
- Calculate your monthly expenses so that you can save at least six months' worth of income before leaving your job.
- Work on your art and marketing in any free time you have.
- Test out how viable it would be to rely on your art long-term.
- Add additional revenue streams to your financial portfolio (see Diversifying Income Streams, page 85, for ideas).
- Figure out how much of each type of work you need to sell to comfortably support yourself—don't forget to include taxes, emergencies, and recreation in your budget.
- Develop your studio practice by investing in education and art materials.
- Build a supportive network of new contacts to help you launch your new independent career, while still maintaining your other professional relationships.

NOW WHAT? THINGS TO CONSIDER AS YOU BEGIN SELF-EMPLOYMENT

ADVICE FROM ALICIA

Leaving your day job to start working for yourself is an exciting and empowering moment. But despite feeling thrilled, you may also find that you miss the sense of security or structure in your daily routine. Not having a clear plan of what you will do once you start self-employment may lead you to question or regret your decision. Rather than falling into this frustrating position, I'm sharing a few things we've both learned about how to maximize your time and productivity once you are your own boss!

"Go" to Work

Even if you work from home, shower and get dressed every day (unless you aren't feeling well), and don't spend all your time with your laptop in bed. Set up your desk, easel, or other working space in a different area of your house or apartment so that you can separate work tasks from the rest of your home life.

Take Breaks

I used to be guilty of eating "al desko" every day and working straight through lunch. As much as I thought I was multitasking, not taking a proper break only made me rush through my meal without enjoying it, and not taking my eyes off the screen all day left me exhausted. I finally realized that eating lunch away from my workspace not only allows me to slow down and appreciate my food, but also helps me come back to my work later feeling refreshed and ready to tackle whatever task I want to focus on.

Create Routine

Establish a new daily routine for yourself. This doesn't have to be strict, unless you want it to be, and it may vary on different days of the week. Make a general plan for when you will work on making art versus administrative tasks, for example, and stick to it. Be sure to add in time for exercise, as well as taking breaks for food and rest.

Kat has set up a weekly calendar for herself. She spends Mondays, Wednesdays, and Fridays in the studio. The other two weekdays are dedicated to business tasks and her work with the magazine. After some trial and error, this is how she decided to best organize her schedule. As you create your own routine, think about when you're typically most productive and work around that. If you're not a morning person, don't force yourself to start painting at 7 a.m. every day. It probably won't be sustainable, and you may actually start to dread getting up in the morning.

In 2019, I started reading first thing in the morning. It makes me feel productive, helps me learn new things (I switch between personal development nonfiction and fiction novels), and it discourages me from checking social media and email first thing upon waking up. I always notice a positive difference when I begin my day by picking up a book rather than my phone. You could also try doing this at night if mornings don't work for you.

Be Intentional with Socializing

One of the things that you might not consider about self-employment is the emotional effect of working by yourself. Even if you didn't enjoy your former employment, it at least likely included daily socializing, which you lose upon leaving. If you're spending a lot of time at home or alone in your studio, force yourself to make new connections. This is the best time to practice and utilize your networking skills. Meet the other artists in your studio building, set up weekly meetings or calls with people in the industry who you've wanted to get to know or collaborate with, or start a critique group with several of your peers. Get in at least some regular face-to-face interaction with people aside from those you live with. Kat and I keep in touch via daily messages on social media or through emails, but we also try to have weekly video calls on Skype. We often have business meetings or ask to record podcasts with artists and other arts professionals whom we admire. This doesn't have to be complicated. Something as simple as asking someone out for coffee to catch up is a great way to stay social!

Respect Your Work

When you have a flexible schedule, it can be tempting to want to accommodate other people's availability. Unless it is someone very important or a task that needs to be completed on a deadline, stand firm in your own availability. You and your work are not less important than anyone else's. If you have dedicated studio time between 2:00 and 4:00 p.m. and you get a meeting request for 3:30, don't be afraid to say that you'd prefer earlier in the day. Provide alternate options, rather than feeling like you should sacrifice your schedule for theirs. Letting others dictate your schedule can leave you feeling disappointed or resentful, so stick to your routine as often as possible. Eventually, people will start adjusting to it.

Manage Money Wisely

When you've just begun working on your own, be as frugal as you can with money. Some months may be great, but you'll inevitably have a slow period and if you've been spending too freely, you'll suddenly feel stuck and stressed about how you'll afford your bills. Set up a budget, track your expenses, and learn about taxes — there are special rules for those who are self-employed. Kat uses TurboTax, and I hire an affordable accountant to handle my yearly filings. Both options are great, so you can choose either, but do not forget to submit your taxes annually!

Making the transition to self-employment is a huge step, and we hope that you use these tips to make the most of the experience. While it seems strange at the beginning, especially if you're used to a corporate job, it will become more comfortable and familiar as you establish yourself in your new role. You may need to make adjustments as you go, but soon enough you'll go from surviving to thriving.

TAKE ACTION

- If you're starting your self-employment transition (or perhaps are already self-employed), take some time to sit down and work out a routine and schedule to help you make the most of your time and resources. Don't forget to allow time for breaks and meals to refresh both your body and mind.

DIVERSIFYING INCOME STREAMS

During our college days, we often wondered about how artists make money. We spent hours researching the lives of creatives, asking around in our community, and desperately trying to figure out if there was some secret about making a living in the arts. How was everyone else making it work? We knew a handful of ways our peers pursued creative careers, such as teaching or in museum and gallery employment, but these options seemed limited, especially considering how few open positions were available at the time.

One of the suggested career paths by our college professors was to pursue our MFA degrees and teach—but this isn't for everyone, and we both knew that it wasn't for us. If you don't feel passionate about this field, it won't be a pleasant experience, despite the steady income, and it can be just as competitive to find steady employment. Though we respect and honor the educators in our life (we wouldn't be where we are without them!), we both wanted to try something different. At the same time, we also realized that selling enough work to support ourselves at an early stage in our careers was not sustainable.

There is no reason why selling original work alone should be your focus. While it's an incredible feeling to find a new home for your art, making this your only source of income can put immense pressure on your studio practice. Many professional artists juggle multiple side gigs to support themselves. Artists who create work that isn't easily salable or doesn't fit the aesthetic of an average home still need to develop financial cushions. If you are an installation or performance artist, selling to collectors may be challenging, particularly at the beginning of your career, but don't feel pressured to give up the integrity of your artwork and make art you think collectors will buy just to make money. It's never worth it.

There are other reasons for adding multiple sources of income beyond accounting for the salability of your art. Say, for example, you are selling consistently, but decide to take time to develop new work. That likely means you'll be holding off on promoting anything new. Or, imagine if you were invited to have an exhibition at a major museum, and it will take you months or years to build up the work required for this opportunity. How will you support yourself if your only income stream is selling the work you create?

When Kat quit her day job, she relied heavily on sales of original art and prints. She experienced a lot of success, but also knew she was limited in taking risks, at the cost of not making any income that month. While it's possible to make a living from just selling original work, it's not for everyone. It's also a good idea to create a financial cushion in your life in case you want to switch gears, take a break, explore something new, decide to have a family, or experience a life circumstance that temporarily prevents you from making art. In terms of practicality, it is a known fact that there are slow seasons embedded in each year—which we quickly learned during our transitions from day jobs to being our own bosses—and it's advisable to prepare for these times.

Continue ›

‹ *Continued*

Like clockwork, every summer sales die down and we end up scrambling to figure out a way to make ends meet. Slow times are common in every industry, but for someone who makes a living as a creative, it's so important to prepare and plan to prevent financial damage. Cash flow for artists, freelancers, and creative entrepreneurs is one of the most challenging aspects of building a creative business, because it can be so sporadic. One day you may feel like you are swimming in cash, selling everything inside the studio, while the next month you have to borrow money from your family to pay your bills. We are here to help prevent this from happening to you, and to ensure that you have a steady and diversified financial portfolio going forward.

Following are some of the most common ways for artists to earn money, both in their studio and beyond. We will start with a few obvious options and dive deeper into more niche opportunities. Think like an artist and explore these options for your career. Try to be open-minded and think beyond these existing income streams. In what ways can you use your interests and passions to generate some extra cash? Consider your interests and skills that aren't necessarily art-related and think about how you can capitalize on them to earn more. Are you good at accounting? Maybe you can help other creatives figure out their taxes. Do you enjoy painting with kids? Run a summer program in your studio. Growing your Instagram at lightning speed? Help someone who is struggling with social media by offering freelance services. The possibilities are endless! Before we explore existing income ideas, take a pen and paper and brainstorm specific ways in which you can potentially earn money outside of selling your art.

DAY JOBS

While we talk more about day jobs in other chapters, we want to reiterate that there should be no shame around any employment that supports your livelihood and studio practice. Of course, we all want to be comfortable and fulfilled, but sometimes in the early stages of our careers we have to hustle and humble ourselves to make ends meet. We have both worked in various uncreative environments, including restaurants, banking, fitness, retail, and more. Even if you aren't where you want to be just yet, you can still work toward your goals and strive for a different life, while remaining proud of where you are right now. Don't judge yourself too harshly if it helps you pay the bills and make art in your spare time. (We share more on transitioning from your day job to an "artrepreneur" on page 75.)

We both learned to be more open to various income streams, such as side gigs, workshops, commissions, and public projects. Eventually, Kat even started *Create! Magazine,* and two years later we launched the online gallery PxP Contemporary together. Having multiple income streams took the pressure off Kat's artwork and resulted in some of her best paintings. A combination of all of these income streams has helped us both work for ourselves.

INCOME OPTIONS

Direct Artwork Sales

This is an obvious category and is probably what first comes to mind when you think of making a living as an artist. Direct art sales can be highly profitable but require you to use your inventory. Please review the chapter on pricing your art (page 56) to make sure you get paid appropriately for all the hard work you do!

When selling directly from your studio or through a gallery to a collector, you want to make sure your collection includes works at different price points. Include a few large, premium works for high-end collectors, a few medium-sized pieces, and small affordable works that are an easy sell online or in person. Kat has sold many watercolor studies by making them available online and mailing them directly from her studio. You can promote your art on social media and announce the release of new collections. If a gallery represents you, help them out by notifying your followers and teaming up with the gallery to maximize your marketing efforts.

Often, selling smaller pieces can be an entry point for a new collector to commit to a more expensive work later on. Over the years, Kat has had several collectors who started with a small watercolor and decided to upgrade to investing in a large oil painting later on. Alicia has seen this happen consistently with her gallery clients as well.

Selling your expensive work can provide income for a month or more, but you can achieve the same financial results by selling several smaller pieces throughout the month. The most important thing is to maintain your collector and gallery relationships and let them know that you appreciate their business by sending them notes, postcards, or a friendly thank-you email every once in a while.

Commissions

Your artistic style and aesthetic may attract collectors who want a custom piece. It's important to establish your rates early on so that you are prepared for the time when you are contacted by a client requesting information. We recommend referencing the chapter on pricing (page 56) to ensure you're compensated fairly and tacking on an additional fee for custom labor. Only you can decide how much would make it financially worthwhile for you to complete the given job. For example, if you sell an 8" x 10" piece for $200, a commissioned piece at that size may cost $250, $300, or $400. Keep in mind that commission work means you may have to go through one or more rounds of revisions (unless you negotiate otherwise), spend more time on research and preparatory sketches, and do other tasks that aren't a part of your regular practice.

We also recommend creating a simple contract with your buyer and asking them to make a deposit on the artwork before you even get started. Find a simple contract template online and tailor it to your needs and timelines. Set up an easy payment method, such as PayPal, Venmo, or an online checkout form for your client and get started on your work! If you love doing commissions, make sure you include a section on your website that includes information on your rates and expected completion times, how to contact you, and examples

Continue ›

of previous work. Notify your audience that you are accepting commissions on social media and through your email marketing. Kat, for example, started commissions early on and relied on them through college to supplement her income. At the time, she was painting florals, but as her style and skill evolved, she began getting inquiries about painting a client's bedroom or home as well. When someone is interested in your work, but has their own vision, you can offer them a unique piece to suit their desired taste.

Selling Prints or Reproductions

Prints have become widely popular over the past decade. They are a fantastic way to nurture new collectors and introduce them to your work in a budget-friendly way. There are incredible web retailers offering reproductions that mimic the quality and texture of your original art. Luckily for us creatives, technology has come a long way, and using it to make more affordable versions of our work has helped many artists supplement their income.

You can either choose to sell unlimited reproductions of your work through print-on-demand sites like Saatchi Art and Fine Art America, or you can work with a local high-end printer to create limited-edition reproductions of your work. Some artists even add hand-painted details and sign their prints to create a more unique piece for their collectors. Many clients prefer to buy this type of print, which still has a bit of the artist's personal touch, so this is something to consider if mark-making or detail work is an important feature of your art.

If you are someone who works in a digital medium, finding a good printer is essential to your practice. Make sure to test out printing services in order to maintain the quality of your work for your collectors.

Tip:

When signing a contract with a gallery double-check that they approve of print sales beforehand if this is something you want to pursue. Some galleries only prefer to promote original works and so it won't be an issue, but others do limited-edition print releases together with the artist.

Workshops & Teaching

Teaching is a fairly standard income stream for artists, and has been for centuries. Art and teaching go hand in hand, and this avenue can be incredibly fulfilling. Even if you prefer not to work in the education system, holding a workshop in your studio or at a local museum can help you connect with your community and share something you are passionate about on your own terms. With the marketing power of social media, you can promote a course or workshop you want to host directly to your audience. For example, you can create a Facebook event to attract attendants and charge cash at the door or use PayPal and credit card processors, such as Square, to get compensated for your time and expertise.

Common Ways Artists Make a Living from Teaching

- Teaching in a traditional K–12 school setting
- Becoming a university or college faculty member
- Organizing classes for adults or children at a local art center
- Leading a summer camp for kids
- Hosting a workshop or masterclass at their art studio
- Traveling to hold seminars or demonstrations of how they make their work
- Instructing paint-and-wine nights at restaurants, boutiques, and more

Online Education

One of our favorite aspects of the internet age is the incredible opportunity to share both our art and unique skill set with anyone in the world. Websites such as Skillshare, Udemy, CreativeLive, Creativebug, and others offer classes and instruction on any topic, from painting flowers to the business side of art. Have you ever thought of a skill that you are particularly proud of that could potentially generate additional revenue for you? Don't overthink this one. You don't have to be a total expert to be able to teach others, but do try to learn as much as possible on whichever topic or skill you choose to teach as you go along.

We have both invested money to learn from other artists or entrepreneurs and have also shared our experiences and knowledge via online resources. You can use a website such as Teachable or Kajabi to create your course or workshop or host a live webinar in exchange for a fee. Don't keep your expertise to yourself. Empower your audience with knowledge in what you are good at!

Freelance & Contract Work

We have both worked jobs in other fields, such as retail and the fitness industry, to earn more income, but there are many other opportunities to find regular, paid work that doesn't necessitate working full time or outside of the arts. While you likely won't receive benefits and may have to keep nontraditional hours, the flexibility of making money on your own time and terms is appealing for many artists. Take a look back at the list of strengths that we suggested you write earlier in this chapter. Do any of those sound like something that can be turned into freelance work?

Alicia turned her experience handling social media and email marketing for her previous gallery and auction house employers into a small side business. After she had moved on from these roles, she continued to manage various clients' social media channels remotely and write email newsletters periodically. Through referrals, she was able to add more paying clients to her roster who were looking for these specialized services. She also made sure to continue learning about social media by taking extra workshops and online courses so that her expertise would be the most up-to-date and she could provide ample justification for her rates. Now, she focuses more on freelance writing opportunities and dedicates time either weekly or monthly to pitch new publications.

If writing or social media is not your forte, there are many other options to consider:

- If you are skilled in carpentry, you could freelance in framing, set building, or exhibition design.

- We know many artists who earn a substantial part of their living wages from art handling. If you can safely and securely package, install, and ship artwork, this may be a viable choice for you.

- Photographers can, of course, do commercial work in addition to their fine art pieces, or they can ask their local contacts to see if anyone needs professionally shot images of their artwork or installation views of gallery and museum exhibitions.

- Our biggest tip is to remember to not sell yourself short. You don't have to be an expert to start making money from a skill you have. If you are simply better at something than most people, you can likely find someone who will pay for the convenience of having you do it better and more efficiently than they can!

Other Skills That Can Be Monetized in the Arts

- Painting (residential and commercial spaces)
- Exhibition design & installation
- Artwork packaging & shipping
- Inventory & archive management
- Artwork conservation
- Framing
- Photography
- Graphic & web design
- Social media management
- Email marketing
- Blogging
- Accounting
- & more!

Tip:

If you are working with a contract, see if you can have a clause inserted that specifies when you will get paid and consequences for your compensation not being delivered on time. This will likely only apply with bigger companies, but it gives you security in the event that the employer fails to follow through. This unfortunately happened to Alicia at a previous job, so we want you to be proactive in order to avoid this situation.

FINANCIAL TIPS

There are a few things to keep in mind, whether you choose to pursue steady freelance work with a contract and set hours or choose less structured, occasional opportunities.

1. Set a fair hourly rate for yourself or, if you'll be paid per completed job or project, make sure to include the cost of your time, as well as any materials or transportation expenses.

2. Always establish what you will be paid in advance and set a deadline for when you will be paid. We know that conversations about money can be awkward, but it's even more uncomfortable to have to chase someone down for an unpaid invoice months after the work is done!

3. As with any other income that you earn, save a percentage for taxes. If it helps, transfer it into a separate account so that you won't be tempted to spend it. You should also ask if you will be provided with a 1099 form, which you should be if you earn over $600 from a single client.

Internships & Apprenticeships

This option is definitely not for everyone, but for Alicia, when she was in school and shortly afterward, completing several internships were essential steps in her career that led to full-time jobs and other important opportunities. Do research to find paid positions, but keep in mind that Alicia actually did two that started as unpaid, but quickly turned into financially lucrative roles due to the quality of her work. Paid internships and apprenticeships will generally be more competitive and may have a rigorous application process, so be diligent about putting together your best possible submission package and not missing the deadline.

Most of these positions won't bring in the equivalent of a livable wage, but the right ones can allow you to earn some extra cash while providing an excellent networking opportunity. Always weigh your options and don't be afraid to negotiate. You should not agree to work close to a full-time schedule if they can't pay you for it just for the "experience" (in some states this is illegal!). Ask to cut down to one or two days a week if the budget only allows them to pay you adequately for those hours.

Grants

As Kat mentions in Navigating Artist Residencies (page 246), she has relied on grants to help her travel abroad and create new work. Though grants can be highly competitive, they are tremendously helpful to someone who is trying to get their foot in the door of the art world. We strongly suggest that you start sending out your work to as many relevant grants as possible. Some opportunities are based on merit, while others require a proposal or call to action. Our recommendation is to start with local organizations, because they tend to be smaller and less competitive. Then, once you've been successful at acquiring funding there, move on to the bigger, more prestigious grants.

Licensing

Have you ever noticed the artwork sold by home goods chain stores? There are artists behind those pieces of art, and they make money from it. Licensing work means that you sign a contract with a major company, such as Michael's, Target, or Anthropologie, to sell reproductions of your work and earn royalties based on the sales. This usually means that you give away your right to the image, so this is something to seriously consider before you proceed. (To learn more about how licensing works, refer to our highlight interviews with artists Lisa Krannichfeld and Jenny Brown starting on page 303.)

Public Works, Murals & Brand Collaborations

As you build up your career and establish your reputation, you can start applying for opportunities to create murals, public sculptures, and installations, depending on what fits your work. Kat has had several paintings purchased for public collections at a university and a corporation. Some artists get commissioned to create work for hotels and other public spaces. If you work with a gallery, sometimes they will arrange for this to happen for you, so let them know if these projects are of interest to you.

Murals add personality to a space and can attract a younger clientele. If you don't have a gallery or agent to seek out public art commissions like this for you, browse online for open calls or reach out to businesses with big blank walls that might be open to the idea of you creating something for them. Make sure to think about pricing beforehand so that you're ready if a potential client is interested. You may have to cover the cost of your own materials, and don't underestimate the time and effort required to complete the piece. We learned more tips by speaking with muralist Tyler Kay. Read her interview on page 96 for her specific advice on finding and completing mural commissions.

Once you become more established, you may get contacted by major corporations, such as home decor, makeup, and fashion brands that are interested in hiring you for partnerships. Though this is a huge honor and potentially exciting opportunity, we want to make sure you are prepared to ask difficult questions to ensure you get clear on what you will gain from this opportunity, know how much money you will earn from each product sale, and more. We asked artist Ashley Longshore to share her approach to working with influential brands in order to help you make the most of it when the time comes. See her interview on page 94.

These are just a few common examples of how you can start earning additional income as an artist. The possibilities only continue to grow, as more and more brands want to partner with artists and designers to stand out in the marketplace. When Kat first became self-employed, she partnered with a real estate agent who helped her get painting commissions of her clients' homes. Pay attention to the people in your community, and see if there are any ways you can partner and benefit from each other's skills. Think beyond your artistic knowledge and utilize any interests and passions alongside your art to make sure you can support yourself and your family as you grow your art career.

TAKE ACTION

- Make a list of skills and passions that could help you earn additional income outside of your art practice.

- Brainstorm what excites you and what you can spend hours doing even without compensation.

- Do some research online to learn how other creatives are making a living using your set of skills.

- Take action each week to build out your income streams by working on a sales website, finding a printer to make reproductions of your art, recording an online course, teaching a workshop in your studio, or anything else that comes to mind!

MAXIMIZING BRAND COLLABORATIONS

Ashley Longshore

Louisiana-based painter, gallery owner, and entrepreneur

www.ashleylongshore.com

At what point in your art career did you decide to start reaching out to larger brands and corporations for partnerships?

I did not start reaching out to them; they came to me. I think that's something important for artists to realize. It can be frustrating to go out cold-calling these huge corporations. They have agendas; they watch what's happening. This is why it's so important to cast a wide net. Are you using your social media? Are you doing pop-ups? Are you getting out there?

I think sometimes artists think it's just about social media, but there are so many other things you have to do to be out there and be seen.

The other thing to remember is that I have been doing this for twenty-six years. You can't think that right out of the gate, you will get started, and all this stuff is going to happen. For some artists, it might happen that way. For others, keep going, keep putting yourself out there, and the right people will see you, and the right partnerships will come along. When they do, it's important to think about who your audience is, who your collectors are, and making sure that you are maintaining the value for them as well. I always think about my collectors before I accept a partnership.

Share a few creative ways you used to approach brands at the beginning.

Again, I wasn't approaching brands; they were approaching me. That being said, when I did have a phone call expressing interest, I would go all in and spare no expense. For example, when Anthropologie came to New Orleans and I knew they were scouting for talent—and this was so many years ago, about fourteen years ago—I told my friend, "Oh my god, well they have to eat lunch. Can I have lunch for them at my studio?" I spent every dime I had, emptied my bank account, getting flowers for my studio, ordering sushi, sake, and sparkling water. I put on a presentation in front of the president, Wendy Wurtzburger, and fifteen of the buying executives. Fortunately, they chose me to do a chair project, and we ended up making lots of fun housewares.

It was the beginning of a great relationship in which I learned a lot about merchandising, manufacturing, design fees, and how this type of collaboration works.

What advice would you give emerging artists for partnering with fashion designers and high-level companies?

First of all, there are two phrases that I despise for big companies to throw at me, and they are "this is standard" and "this is how we always do business."

Every business deal has an opportunity to be more creative or less creative than the next. There is no such thing as a "standard" contract or business deal. So if somebody tells you they're only going to pay you a $1,500 design fee and you don't get any royalties, that is BS. It doesn't have to be that way.

You need to figure out how much exposure you are getting. Where are they running ads? How many stores are they putting your work in? How many of the actual products are they making? What price point are they selling them at? What does it cost them to manufacture these?

When you ask all these questions, you can't be aggressive about it. You should be tactful, gracious, and enthusiastic.

If you do a little research on what they want you to do and the products they are creating, you will find that there is plenty of money for everyone. Unfortunately, with so many of these corporations, they're cheap, they don't want to pay, and they want you to work for exposure. If you are going to work for exposure, ask lots of questions.

I had a huge billion-dollar company that wanted me to do a partnership with them and then told me that they weren't going to pay me and that it was all about exposure. And I said, "I've done my research on your company and you don't spend any money on advertising." Needless to say, this partnership did not work out. You have to ask those questions.

Once you started working with exciting collaborations, how did you leverage the experiences to get future opportunities?
Using social media, using Constant Contact and email marketing platforms, and making sure that the partnerships and opportunities you are taking on are bringing value to what your current collector base has invested in you.

It's impossible to not create a very wide net. It's sort of like when the sharks start attacking; they all smell blood. I think all these corporations are looking for exciting, innovative, fun, in-the-moment expressions of humanity. You just have to make sure that you take on the right opportunities. Work with people who also teach you something. Those are the best experiences, more so than just the money. But also, don't undervalue yourself. As an artist, there are only so many days to be creative in your life, and there is plenty of pie for everyone.

Doing business with these companies is like making a big birthday sheet cake. You deserve your own corner of that cake, and there is plenty of cake left for everyone to go around. Just make sure that they don't stick you in the corner with the bowl. No artist should be licking their fingers while a big corporation is making a lot of money off their talent.

GETTING STARTED WITH MURALS & STREET ART

Tyler Kay

Painter and mural artist
www.tyler-kay.com

How did you get started with being a mural artist? What was your first experience like, and how did you leverage it to get more gigs?
My first experience—or experiment, I'd like to call it—painting a mural took place when I was eleven. My mom let me paint a small Care Bear mural on my little sister's bedroom wall. After completing that mural, I painted a handful more here and there for family members and friends.

Fast-forward ten years and I made the decision to pursue a career as an artist. I had taken a position as gallery director at Bisong Art Gallery in downtown Houston. In this position I had the opportunity to sell my canvas pieces, instruct painting classes, and essentially surround myself with art enthusiasts.

My first commission for a "professional mural" was received from an individual who participated in one of my painting classes. This mural measured approximately 20 x 40 feet and was for J-Dance Company in South Houston. I recall feeling overwhelmed with excitement and determination when working on this project. My main takeaway from this mural commission was the lesson to create a fully detailed and colored design prior to beginning. All of the compositional changes that occurred while working on the piece could have been avoided with better preparation beforehand.

My success in continuously receiving future mural projects, I believe, is dependent on several factors, which include my professionalism, my attentiveness to detail and dedication to deliver my best work every single project, and my enthusiasm. Your network is truly your net worth, and I can accredit my former clients, colleagues, family, and friends all equally responsible for marketing my service and contributing to my success in this profession.

Share a few tips on pricing murals when getting started. What hidden fees or costs should artists consider when offering this service?
When pricing a mural you should always consider five factors:

1. Dimensions (square footage)

2. Intricacy of design (The complexity and detail within a mural directly affects project length.)

3. Location (Will you need accommodation? What will your daily transportation expenses be? How will you get to and from the site?)

4. Material cost (What painting medium will be used to complete the mural? Will any additional equipment be required, such as scaffolding or a lift? Will any surface preparation be required?)

5. Working conditions (What will your access to the mural location be?)

6. I personally provide free consultations where I will briefly discuss dimensions, composition ideas, and provide an estimate to the client. To proceed into the design phase, I always require a nonrefundable deposit. Securing a deposit provides you, the artist, compensation for your time developing the design, enables you to schedule a tentative start date for the project, and ultimately weeds out the inquiries that are not serious.

What is the most challenging part of doing public art and balancing your work as a traditional fine artist?

Due to the large scale of my public art works, it has been quite the balancing act to simultaneously maintain production of canvas paintings. My large-scale mural projects are incredibly consuming, of both my energy and my creativity. The various unpredictable factors of mural artistry that vary from project to project make it challenging to schedule canvas painting production. I can never predict what my next mural will entail, regarding dimensions, complexity, location, etc. With this being said, a studio would not be beneficial to me, simply because I am typically not in the same location for an extended period of time.

I have found it is very important to set myself goals, but at the same time avoid creative burnout and not force myself to produce pieces when I don't feel inspired or I'm feeling exhausted. For example, at the beginning of every year I set a goal to exhibit in one art fair and to produce (x) amount of paintings per month. I then go on my phone calendar, month by month, and set friendly reminders to myself.

Examples:
• *Four months before art show* "Have you started your painting for the art fair?"

• *Random day, midweek, during my mural busy season* "Take a break today and paint for yourself."

• This is an effective way I've found to hold myself accountable while also avoiding artwork production that can begin to feel robotic or overwhelming.

What has been the most rewarding part of being a mural artist?

I have found the most rewarding aspect of being a mural artist is having the ability to utilize art in public spaces to engage individuals with their surroundings. Whether or not community members are included in the physical production process of the mural, I still feel as if the accessibility alone provides an interconnectedness between the individual and the space. My murals have been utilized as backdrops and settings for proposals, wedding ceremonies, family pictures, and various community events. Each of these instances I've witnessed are examples of how individuals formed their own unique connection with the artwork and the setting. I find nothing more fulfilling than utilizing my artistic passion and abilities to contribute to meaningful interactions and connections.

The Fine Artist's Guide to Social Media & Marketing

USING INSTAGRAM FOR YOUR ART CAREER

Over the past few years, it has been hard to miss the rapid growth of social media and its impact on the art world. Instagram, in particular, is a popular platform for creatives, given its visual nature and easy-to-use format. While this app isn't absolutely necessary for your art career, it can help you make connections, gain recognition, reach collectors, and even boost your art sales. For example, many of our virtual relationships have led to in-person studio visits or coffee dates and have allowed us to build an incredibly supportive creative network over time.

When we first started using this platform, we had no idea how big an impact it would make on our art careers. Over the years, this powerful tool helped Kat promote her paintings, make sales, launch a magazine, and leave her soul-crushing day job. Alicia has shared her writing, found new collectors for the artists she represents with PxP Contemporary, and earned substantial extra income as a social media specialist. Of course, none of this happened overnight.

As we slowly discovered that we could use platforms like Instagram and Facebook as marketing and sales tools, our perspectives began to shift and we dove into educating ourselves on how to best utilize these platforms. There are a few basic tips we learned, and still use today, that helped us grow our personal and business accounts. For example, *Create! Magazine* grew from a small community of hundreds to thousands to now more than one hundred thousand engaged followers.

FOUR TIPS FOR GROWTH ON INSTAGRAM

Tip 1: Be Yourself

When Kat created her first account, she was instantly drawn to Instagram's simple visual format. She didn't start out using it as a business tool for her creative career, and it took a few years to find a way to connect to her audience in a way that worked for her.

At first, she was overly strict with the content she posted and shared only her paintings, but after realizing that it felt unnatural, she experimented with how she presented herself to her virtual audience. Posting too many details from her personal life felt like oversharing, which can distract viewers from the art and turn off potential followers. Eventually, she found her flow and stopped putting so much pressure on what content to post.

This platform can be fun, spontaneous, and inspiring, and there is no reason to set too many strict limitations. Focus most of your posts on including something related to your work and vision. Sometimes it's easy to forget, but most accounts (excluding bots) have a real person behind them—and they're often looking to make connections, just like you are.

Tip 2: Find Your Voice

When Kat found her voice and her own approach to sharing online, that is when she truly began finding her tribe. She started having real conversations through posts and messages. Others reached out to share their stories or send images that they thought she would enjoy. The "followers" revealed themselves to be normal people who understood her work and what she was trying to do. She still has meaningful conversations with collectors and peers today via Instagram and finds that it is one aspect of the platform that she most enjoys.

When it comes to writing messages and captions, Kat tries to be as transparent and real as possible. She shares moments from her day, what she's currently inspired by or excited about, or something she's struggling with, talking to her audience as if they were a friend she hasn't seen in a few weeks. Kat makes it a point to be personable, candid, and fun via her social channels. Rather than posting every day, she often utilizes Instagram Stories, which are a great outlet for sharing daily moments and personal details that wouldn't necessarily contribute to her feed.

We cannot stress enough that social media works most effectively when you find and use your own voice. This is true for both your art practice and developing your online persona. Don't try to be like another artist or influencer. You can be inspired by other people, but what the world really needs is your unique voice and perspective. So, if you'd like to be as open as Kat is, that's great and you should do it. But it isn't for everyone, and if you prefer to focus more exclusively on sharing your artwork with less posts about your life, selfies, or inspirational quotes, don't feel obligated to post more than you're comfortable with.

"Be yourself and your audience will find you."

The way Kat has amassed her following on her personal painting account is only one way of doing it. We've seen tons of great artist accounts with thousands of followers that strictly post artwork photos or focus on a certain tone, like humor. What matters is that you are consistent! You can be thoughtful or poetic, hilarious or goofy, or maybe you're more philosophical or academic. Just be yourself and your audience will find you. The more you're able to hone in on your voice, the more likely you'll be able to attract and connect with those who will be most interested in your content.

The general rule is to have the majority of your feed represent your art and aesthetic, so that when a potential collector or media contact comes across your account, they will have a clear understanding of your work and style.

STORIES, IGTV, & REELS AS SALES TOOLS

Stories, IGTV, and reels are useful Instagram features for when you want to share behind-the-scenes videos of your creative process, your travels, inspirational content, and more. These tools can add character and depth to an otherwise two-dimensional feed. A few ideas for using stories include sharing the following:

• Process videos and time-lapses

• Studio views and materials you use

• You introducing or speaking about your art

• You answering questions from your audience

• Works you currently have listed for sale

• Announcements or reminders for important events

• Sales and successes that you want to celebrate

Once you grow your account above 10,000 followers you get extra perks, such as the "swipe up" feature in stories, which links the user to a website of your choice. You can have your audience visit your shop, promote an article you were featured in, or share details of an upcoming show. If you're just starting out, it may take a while to make it to 10K, so in the meantime, add your website to your profile so that users can easily access it. Truly interested patrons will find a way to reach out to you, even if it's just through a direct message, but having your link right in your bio helps simplify the process for them. Once you receive a comment or message with an inquiry, try to get the potential client over to your email so you can send them your pricing, images of the available work, and any other details (framing, shipping, special offers, etc.). Perhaps even mention that you want to keep track of the interaction as a reason to have them provide you with their email, Instagram does not currently let users organize their DMs.

Respond to emails and messages promptly. Expressing gratitude for their interest and for connecting with you is an important part of starting a conversation with a potential client. Always share your work and prices with confidence. Even though not every interaction will result in a sale, acting as if any message could yield a successful result is excellent practice for when the right collector does come along.

Tip 3: Be Consistent

Remember that Instagram is just a snapshot of your life and career as an artist. What are the most important things that you want others to see, considering that you're only sharing a small part? We use and suggest the simple rule that the majority of your posts be about your art, studies, exhibitions, and works in progress. We've also found that highlighting media features gives confidence to a prospective client and encourages them to invest in your art.

Be mindful of how each post relates to one another, both visually and in terms of content. You can also post images that relate to your work, such as travel, references, inspiration, other artists that inspire you, etc. Give your new followers a good idea of who you are, and then introduce the fun details periodically.

Think of your feed more like an exhibition versus individual paintings. Look at the bigger picture! Though this is completely up to you, some people commit to using a select color palette, filter, and white balance in their posts to create a powerful first impression. We tend to only follow this rule loosely, but a feed with a consistent aesthetic does help capture and engage viewers when they first encounter your page.

Nowadays, you can use social media management programs, such as Hootsuite, to plan your posts in advance and see what your feed will look like. When Alicia worked as a freelance social media consultant, she often planned out posts by week or by month so that she could not only visualize how the content would look together, but also save time! It helps when you don't have to worry about what to post each day and can instead focus on responding to comments or messages and connecting with other accounts. In addition, it allows you to ensure that you're still posting regularly, even if you're busy or traveling.

Aim to post your art with minimum interruptions, but don't be afraid to post a selfie or your favorite pets once in a while. People want to see the real you, the person behind the scenes. It's likely your followers will also love seeing works in progress, studio images, and messy palettes. There is something human and relatable about these little details of your life and practice.

Tip 4: Be Engaged

Like and follow artists and galleries you admire. Support them in a genuine way by leaving positive comments if something they post excites you. Feel free to send a message with content he or she may enjoy, but don't tag them randomly unless you have permission to do so. We love when fellow artists send us a new painter or book they think would inspire us. Being an active part of your community, both online and in person, does eventually come full circle and will boost the chances of new, amazing opportunities coming to you.

You never know if a curator or editor will stumble upon your page or click on your profile. Be gracious regarding any constructive feedback you receive, and remember that there is a human behind every username. If you have a negative interaction online, do your best to ignore the comment, block the user if you feel uncomfortable or threatened, and get back to sharing with those who care about you and your work. More followers always equals more people who think that they know you and have the right to share any opinion about you or your work. We talk more about how to deal with these "negative Nancies" in Good Vibes Only: Negativity in the Art World & How to Fight It (page 235), but in general, it is best practice to not respond at all. They're not worth your time!

ADVANCED WAYS TO CONNECT WITH YOUR ONLINE AUDIENCE

Partner with an Influencer

While you should focus on growing your Instagram in organic ways, getting featured by a big account that has more than 50K engaged followers will give you a boost. However, just because an account has a lot of followers doesn't mean it's legitimate. Pay attention to the interactions on the posts, because unfortunately there are many who buy fake followers or use bots.

When Kat was featured by The Jealous Curator, she quickly ended up with more than 1K new followers on her page. The same thing happened when she was featured by other art influencer accounts, such as The TAX Collection. Any trusted brand or influencer with more than 100K followers who are loyal, active, and interested will help you connect with a new audience.

There are also paid art shout-out services that charge anywhere from $20 to $100 per post. Do your research to make sure the brand offers quality content that aligns with your aesthetics and vision. We have used several of these services in recent years, and it has helped us attract new followers and collectors, as well as boost sales, over time. Continue to submit your portfolio to bloggers, writers, and magazines and it will help you grow both your collector base and your online presence.

In order to get featured by an influencer, it's important to respect their submission guidelines. Don't just blindly send an unlabeled image via a private message. We also often receive messages like "you should feature my work" or "post my work if you like" on the *Create! Magazine* account, and that doesn't grab our attention either. Take the time to read the influencer's requirements, review previously featured work to ensure that your art is a fit, and follow the instructions. It may take a few tries, but showing up like the thoughtful and professional artist you are will get you much further than mindless tagging and messaging.

Tip:

Never buy followers or bots. You will end up with a bunch of spam, it will lower your overall engagement, and they will almost always be removed by Instagram later on. It can be tempting to create the illusion of numbers, but doing so will prevent real potential customers from seeing your posts. It's better to have 100 loyal and active followers than 100,000 fake ones.

Invest in Instagram Ads

Kat started using Instagram ads to promote her studio sales several years ago. At first, she experimented with the feature and paid as little as $5 to promote individual posts, which yielded some results. As she learned more about the platform and found a match for her target audience, this investment started to result in sales. Today, Kat rarely invests more than $50 per week on each ad, but this tool has helped her find new clients and promote her work beyond her existing contacts. Using ads can be a powerful way to break out of your community and get noticed by others outside of your immediate following. In order to take advantage of this feature, you must have a business profile on both Facebook and Instagram.

This feature is easy to set up in your profile settings on Instagram, and then you simply click on the "promote" button on the bottom right corner of any of your posts to boost a specific painting you're trying to sell, raise awareness for a new body of work, announce an exhibition, or advertise a big studio sale. These are just a few ideas of how you can push your work forward online with a small budget.

Working with Instagram and Facebook ads requires you to create a clear vision of your ideal collector. Think about the type of person they are, where they shop, and what other activities they enjoy— this will help you accurately target them. You can tag specific interests, organizations, other artists, and brands when setting up your ad, so we recommend that you brainstorm these traits of your ideal collectors before you decide to run a campaign.

Instagram also allows you to set the duration and budget for each promotion, so start with a minimal budget first to see what works. After looking at the results in the Insights tab, you can change your audience, shorten the amount of days the ad will run, or add more money. Do always check your campaign as it is in progress. If you don't see a lot of clicks, comments, or new follows, consider pausing it so that you don't waste money on an ad that isn't performing optimally. Try new methods, audiences, and formats to see which ones yield the best results. Instagram offers many resources for how to use its ads. Learn more by visiting: https://business.instagram.com/advertising/.

Link Your Shop to Your Account

Instagram and Facebook both allow you to link your shop or e-commerce platform directly to your feed. If you choose to list your prices online or sell prints of your work from your webshop, this is a perfect tool to incorporate into your marketing strategy. Learn which platforms can be linked and how to do so by visiting this helpful guide for additional information and details: https://www.facebook.com/business/instagram/shopping/guide. Remember that you need to have a business account on both Instagram and Facebook in order to have access to this feature.

INSTAGRAM POSTING GUIDE

Many of our posting tips apply to both Instagram and Facebook, but there are a few key differences between the two platforms, so don't simply repeat the exact same post on each. It is always easy to tell when someone has let Instagram share a post automatically to their Facebook page, and your posts will look much nicer when formatted correctly to the appropriate channel.

General Tips
- Use high-quality photos.
- Proofread captions so that there are no grammar or spelling errors.
- Write captions in a friendly tone and (almost always) include a call to action.
- Consider using vertically oriented images, which users are more likely to engage with, rather than square or horizontal.

Content Ideas

- Post Individual images of your artwork.
- Post "throwbacks" to older pieces you haven't shared in a while.
- Include detail shots.
- Post works in progress.
- Share installation views and gallery exhibitions featuring your work.
- Share private or public collections that include your art.
- Post quotes that inspire you, designed in a style that matches your aesthetic.
- Share other people's art that informs your practice (with appropriate citation, of course!).
- Post studio shots.
- Post process videos and time-lapses.
- Post sketches and studies.
- Answer questions from your audience or poll your community about a topic related to your art.
- Share photos or videos of wrapping, unwrapping, or shipping artwork out to clients and shows.
- Share books or podcasts you like.
- Comment on relevant art news.
- Share how you first became interested in art or started your art career.
- Talk about recent challenges, milestones, or accomplishments.
- Teach your audience about your process and your favorite art materials.

General Tips

- Preferably post at least two to three times per week, up to once a day if you are very new and initially trying to grow your account.
- If that is not possible, aim for as many posts per week as you can commit to.
- The best times of day to post are: early morning (before work), lunch break, evening commute (during the week), and Sunday evenings—but this, of course, depends on your location or where in the world you'd like the majority of people to see your posts at the ideal time.

HOW TO USE INSTAGRAM HASHTAGS

Besides ads, hashtags are some of the best tools to reach new users on social media. People love to explore hashtags to find exciting content that they haven't seen before. Utilize them strategically to help artists, art lovers, and collectors land on your page and then follow you. Currently, you can use up to thirty hashtags per post. If you're starting out, we definitely recommend using the maximum. Once you have grown your following, you can cut down to fewer. For example, for *Create! Magazine* we tend to use around ten to fifteen hashtags per post.

Look for hashtags that have between 10,000 and 1 million posts to maximize the reach while also making sure your posts are not lost in the mass of uploaded images. For example, try something like #chicagoartist instead of #artist, depending on your location. Using a few popular hashtags is fine, but we don't recommend doing so for all thirty.

Create Hashtag Lists for Easy Posting

Save yourself time and effort by creating several hashtag lists that are relevant to your practice. Enter these lists into your phone's Notes app, a Google document, or an Evernote file so that you can easily copy and paste them after you post something new on Instagram. Following are a couple of ways to incorporate hashtags with your posts.

Hashtag Option 1

Put a few hashtags in the initial caption (three, for example) that are most relevant to the image being posted. For example: #yournameart (or #yournameartist) #artpainting #contemporaryartist. Then copy and paste the rest of the allotted hashtags in the first comment. Depending on your aesthetic preference, you can post the block of hashtags with several ellipsis dots above it so that they are hidden. For example:

.

.

.

#hashtag4 #hashtag5 . . .#hashtag27

Hashtag Option 2

Use all thirty hashtags in the first comment. We prefer this option so that the caption only includes the relevant information about your post and your audience won't be distracted. Sometimes a huge block of hashtags doesn't look clean, so it is a nice alternative to move these to a comment instead. You can also choose whether you want to include spaces between your hashtags or not. They work the same either way but are visually cleaner with spaces.

Sample Hashtag Lists

We've compiled the following lists of hashtags that we use depending on what the post is about. You can also do your own research if these do not apply to you, and experiment to see which yield the most engagement. You can also utilize free hashtag services online or tweak what you use on your own posts and check your audience response with the Insights tool on your Instagram profile. When used correctly, hashtags are an efficient and free way to connect with a like-minded audience. Instagram also allows you to "follow" specific hashtags so you can discover other creatives in your community or field of interest.

(Remember you can use up to thirty hashtags at a time!)

Studio & Process

#creativeminds #process #canvas #worksinprogress #onthetable #paintbrushes #onthewall #artstudio #sundayvibes #artiststudio #carveouttimeforart #painting #artiststudio #studioscenes #myworkwall #doitfortheprocess

General Art

#contemporaryart #modernart #art #artist #artsy #gallery #photooftheday #creative #instaart #artoftheday #dailyart #artstagram #artlover #artoninstagram #artgram #artporn #artdaily #artistofinstagram #instaarthub #painting #drawing #artgallery

Tip:

Pay attention to the hashtags others in your niche are using to tag their work. See if there are any hashtags that they use regularly and borrow them for your hashtag lists.

ADDITIONAL HASHTAGS TIPS

Use Medium-Specific Tags
For example: #gouacheonpaper #sculptures #artpainting #dailydrawing #textileart #installationartist

Use Specific Geographic Locations
For example: #philadelphiaartist #phillyart #germanart #artinparis

Tag Specific Events (Like Important Art Fairs) When Relevant
For example: #artbaselmiami #artmiami #scopeartshow #friezefair #artexpochicago

Mention a Demographic
For example, women artists might post: #womenwhopaint #womenartists #womeninart #femaleartist #womanmade

Use Interests to Attract Your Dream Collector
For example: #potterybarn #apartmenttherapy #elledecor #vogueliving #anthropologiehome #mywestelm

Researching hashtags doesn't take long, so sit down for a bit when you have half an hour or so to determine which might work best for you. For quick inspiration, take a look at this article from Displate, which lists over 500 art-related hashtags: https://displate.com/blog/500-art-hashtags-for-instagram. Alicia has also put together a free downloadable PDF of 700+ hashtags for artists split into blocks of thirty that can be accessed at the following link: https://mailchi.mp/3fa326f2a849/700-hashtags-for-artists.

FOCUS ON YOUR GOALS

It can be tempting to spend a lot of time and energy on growing your social media or comparing yourself to others online. We encourage you to focus on your final desired outcome. Do you want a big social media following, or do you want a blossoming art career? Remember, thousands of followers doesn't automatically translate into thousands of sales. Focus on quality, encouraging sales when you can, and building a trusted network of peers and collectors. This will ensure your time spent online benefits your art career.

TAKE ACTION

- Think about what you can write in your future captions to share your story and personality with your audience.
- Make a list of potential influencers and accounts that you wish will share your art in the future. Research their submission process and prepare your best work.
- Brainstorm future ad campaigns based on your budget. Do you have inventory you want to sell? Do you have an upcoming exhibition you want to promote? Consider where your advertising budget would be best spent.
- Create a few hashtag lists to keep on file where you can easily access them for quick and easy posting.
- If you are trying to sell your art online, include contact information, clearly mark work as "available for sale," and note any other important details in your posts.
- Reply to and follow up on emails and messages with inquiries from any potential collectors.
- Go through your recent posts and reply to any new comments about your art to engage with your peers and future clients.
- Share any media features, exhibitions, or other exciting moments to show your collectors that you are an artist on the rise.

GETTING NOTICED ON INSTAGRAM

You may have heard that many galleries, curators, and writers now discover new artists they end up representing, exhibiting, or interviewing via Instagram. It's pretty incredible that social media has created platforms that allow any artist to share their work worldwide. That being said, there are so many talented creatives showing their art on Instagram that it can seem like it is a competition for followers and it's impossible to get noticed. But neither of these negative notions are true. We are here to help you make sure your feed stands out for all the right reasons!

USE QUALITY IMAGES

We know . . . we say this all the time! Because Instagram is a visual platform, it makes sense that all your images should be high quality, never blurry. But this doesn't mean that you have to spend hours to get a perfectly lit shot of your studio or an artfully messy image of your palette and brushes. Focus on clean, cropped images of your work that can easily be reposted. Make it easy for your followers or bigger accounts to share your art.

To that end, while it is fun to mix up the type of photos you share—detail shots, an installation view, and works in progress (or even your cat!)—make sure you regularly show finished pieces. We recommend uploading a completed work for every three to five posts, depending on how much work you have, how often you post, and how quickly you create new pieces.

There have been many instances when we have come across a really incredible artwork that we want to share on *Create! Magazine's* Instagram, but when we go to look up the artist's profile and start scrolling along their feed, not only can we not find the piece we're looking for, we can't even find one single image of a nicely photographed work cropped to the edges! We don't want this scenario to happen to you. If you're not posting at least a few images that others could easily share, you're missing out on an easy marketing opportunity.

DON'T POST WITHOUT A CAPTION!

As we discussed in the chapter on writing your artist statement, nobody is expecting Pulitzer Prize–quality writing, and this is true with your social media captions. In fact, we love that social media allows us to be slightly more informal and personal than we are with our statement or artist biography. That being said, there are still ways that you can be strategic about what you include in your captions.

Get Clever with Captions

You have to give your audience context for your images, so you should at least include a title and consider adding the medium, size, availability, and potentially the price for every artwork you post. If you're sharing exhibitions or media features, link to the other accounts so that they see your post, maximizing the chance that they will repost or comment, improving the engagement on your own photo. In addition, include relevant details about the dates and locations for exhibitions, where people can read the full articles you're highlighted in, listen to podcasts you've been interviewed for, etc. Include action words that invite and encourage your followers to engage with your post, like "**Comment below** if you love this color palette," "**Email me** to inquire," or "**Visit my exhibition** at (insert name here) gallery to get a first look at my new series." It's incredible how this one small tweak to your captions can make a huge impact on how your audience responds to your content.

Go More In-Depth

Feel free to write longer captions that explain the inspiration or meaning behind a piece or share something about yourself. Your followers will likely enjoy hearing things that may help them feel more connected to you, and this reminds potential collectors that when they buy your art they're supporting a real person, instead of just a face behind a screen. Our only advice here is to space out the text so that it looks visually pleasing. Fewer people will read your full caption if they come across a big block of text. It's also fun to intersperse a few emojis for emphasis and to visually break up the caption. It might be easier to draft longer captions in an email or in the Notes app on your phone first, as typing captions directly within Instagram sometimes automatically lumps it together in one long paragraph. You can also use this handy website to force spaces in your Instagram captions: https://apps4lifehost.com/Instagram/CaptionMaker.html.

Tip:

If Instagram keeps pushing separate paragraphs together, you can separate them with a dash or dot.

For example:

Paragraph

.

Paragraph

Or

Paragraph

-

Paragraph

Use Smart Sales Strategies in Your Captions

Using sales strategies in your captions is one way to entice potential clients. While you might be thinking that you're selling abstract paintings or pop art sculptures, what you may actually be selling to your client is "chic, modern decor" or "fun and whimsical conversation pieces." Steff Metal, in a guest blog post for *The Abundant Artist*, notes that these are called "features" and "benefits."[6] Take a moment now to think about what those might be for your own work. You might be accustomed to saying that a watercolor painting you made has rich tones of raw sienna, ochre, and crimson, but for your potential clients you could instead mention that by purchasing this work people would "surround themselves with their favorite fall colors all year long" or that the piece has "hues that will add warmth and light to any space." This tactic can help convince your audience that they don't just like your art, but that they need it!

Your Feed is Your Business Card

Kat has a personal rule that the majority of her feed is her art, and if you look at many of the artists who have been successful on this platform, this is something they abide by as well. This strategy means that when a potential buyer or curator visits Kat's profile, they have an immediate understanding of her work. While it's fun to share selfies, travel photos, and studio shots, alternating the images with your work, even if it's an older image, will help your profile be a virtual business card.

In fact, Kat often uses her feed during networking events to quickly show new acquaintances her artwork. If you have an urge to share personal moments, like we often do, you can fully utilize Instagram Stories, which disappear after twenty-four hours and are not a huge commitment. Instagram Stories are also a great way to introduce yourself to your online community and can be a strong supplement to your feed. You can post time-lapse videos, more candid studio shots, and share daily inspiration. Kat likes to engage with her followers by using the "question" feature, in which followers ask her something about her work and she answers in the form of text, video, or images.

Something to consider is that a perfectly polished feed with the same filter on all your photos may work for some artists, but it can also end up looking artificial. Kat noticed that being herself and sharing some images of her personal life helped her foster meaningful connections online that go beyond art sales and features. Posting an occasional selfie helps others recognize her during art fairs, exhibitions, and workshops! It's always powerful to solidify a contact made online through a real-life interaction. Experiment and research successful accounts to see how they approach their online marketing. Strive to create a strong aesthetic on your feed that genuinely represents both you and your work.

---

6 **Steff Metal,** "Artists Who Sell: How To Write A Killer Sales Page (And Why)," The Abundant Artist, https://theabundantartist.com/how-to-write-art-sales-page/.

Use the Right Hashtags

You can find specific examples of hashtags we've used successfully in Using Instagram for Your Art Career (page 99), but the general rule is to be relevant to your work while not being too broad, or your posts will get lost in the mass of images.

Recent statistics claim that up to 95 million images are uploaded to Instagram daily! Find niche hashtags to connect your art with a more focused audience that is more likely to respond to your posts. For example, if you make sculptures you could use the hashtags #sculpture or #sculptures, but if you search either of general terms on Instagram it will bring up millions of posts. When this many images fall under a hashtag, your post will be buried within minutes (maybe even seconds) of uploading, leaving very little opportunity for anyone searching this hashtags to see it. Instead, try something more specific like #sculptureart or #sculpture_art.

Share Your Work with Influencers

It might be your goal to get reposted by a larger "influencer" account, like an art blog, magazine, or curator. However, avoid direct messaging them to ask for a feature or randomly tagging them unless they explicitly request this as a way to submit your art for review. These strategies, while easy to do, simply aren't professional and rarely result in a repost. So why waste your time? Instead, take a few extra minutes to look for how each account accepts submissions. They usually mention simple directions in their bio, such as using a specific hashtag on your posts to share your artwork with them or e-mailing them for collaborations and sponsored content.

We look through our own hashtags with *Create! Magazine* regularly and love seeing the great images that the artists in our community share with us! Keep in mind that Instagram doesn't allow influencers to sort through all their received messages. With the volume of direct messages we receive at *Create! Magazine*, after a day or two it is hard to go back and find a specific one, even if it was an artist that we liked. If you do end up sending a private message to someone, make sure you include basic information, treating this interaction like you would a professional email. Begin with a greeting, introduce yourself, send a link to your work, include any important details, and thank them for their time. Make it easy for others to quickly learn more about your work in a friendly and respectful way.

Many influential accounts, including Avant Arte, Contemporary Art Collectors, Aureta, The Jealous Curator, The TAX Collection, Unit London, and more, have posted Kat's work. One thing she has noticed is that once a large account shared her work, many others followed suit. While banking on these features shouldn't be your goal, they can undoubtedly impact your career in positive ways and promote your art among a wider audience than you'd normally reach. Even though you can't guarantee that your account will go "viral," one way to increase your chances is by sharing strong images of your art that are easy for others to share. Remember that your follower count and online presence doesn't always correlate with your sales, so don't let this be your primary focus.

Stop Obsessing Over Your Followers

While we can't speak on behalf of other publications or curators, at Create! Magazine we personally don't care what an artist's follower count is. If we like the work, we will reach out for an interview or repost the art whether they have 50, 500, or 50,000 followers. There's no need to play games by following a bunch of accounts, hoping that some will follow you back and then unfollowing them a few days later. People definitely notice and will remember you in a negative light.

Instead, make connections with other artists, curators, galleries, and arts publications that you genuinely like. This way you can meaningfully engage with their posts. For example, if you leave a particularly nice or interesting comment on a post, it is probable that they'll click through to your page. It pays off to be a friendly follower. Additionally, don't feel pressured to post new content all the time! It's likely that only a fraction of your followers will see any given post, so if one has performed particularly well feel free to share it again later. It is a great idea to keep putting your best work out there, especially as you grow your audience — you never know when a new writer or curator will end up on your feed!

When your work is inevitably shared, repost it on your profile and be proud of your accomplishment. It's also good practice to leave a comment thanking the account or publication for the feature. Hopefully one shared work will cause a chain reaction leading to more! That happened to Kat with a piece she didn't expect and to Alicia early in her career as well, with a completely different type of work than what she usually made. Be patient and consistent with your posts and it will happen to you too!

You Don't Have to Start Over

If you are reading these tips and have the sudden urge to delete all your images and start over, you don't have to. You can start building your ideal Instagram feed right now. Unless you have embarrassing images that would harm you professionally in some way, you don't need to remove any old posts. As you start posting quality content, your feed will automatically upgrade and gradually draw attention away from your older posts.

Kat likes to occasionally scroll down to her first posts for fun to see the evolution of her work and social media savvy. With technology, her images improved over the years, but she also worked hard to find her voice online and that helped her connect with more art lovers across the globe. You'll likely notice a shift in the type and quality of content posted on other accounts over two years old. Scroll through a few of your favorite artists to check! You can even make notes of what improvements they made and borrow those ideas for your own feed.

You're Not Way Behind

Aside from feeling overwhelmed because your old posts might not be of the quality that you'd like going forward, you may be worried that starting now won't get you to the same level as artists who have been using Instagram for years and seem like seasoned pros. Sometimes we joke that the secret to Instagram is to have started your account five years ago, before people were as cautious as they are now about how many other profiles they are willing to follow and having a curated feed. There is a small bit of truth to this, but if you're launching a brand new account and uploading your first post, know that you can still grow the following you need to reach your goals.

We opened our online gallery, PxP Contemporary, in May of 2019 and within six months, Alicia had grown its Instagram audience to thousands of followers. We've shared all the tips we have used to grow this account, as well as our other accounts, and you can tailor these to suit your needs—even if you're starting from the very beginning! And if you're just getting into social media, you'll be able to implement best practices from the get-go, so your feed will be sharp and impressive to potential collectors from its debut.

Above all, none of this is important if you aren't yet happy with your work or don't have finished pieces to show. Put in the time in your studio to get to the point where you have a really strong body of work to post about first and then, trust us, the rest will follow.

Tip:

During the process of writing this book, Instagram made yet another major change to its platform by testing out a new feature that hides the amount of likes on each of your posts from other users. Take this as yet another reminder that you shouldn't solely rely on this one social media channel or worry about mastering it because it can be altered and updated at any moment. You never know if one change could affect how people decide to use this platform in the future.

TAKE ACTION

Take a few moments to review your feed, and then ask yourself the following questions:

- Would someone visiting my profile be able to identify what I do in thirty seconds or less?
- Are most of my images clean and cropped or professionally photographed and representative of my art?
- Do I have an overall aesthetic that would help viewers identify my unique style? If not, what can I do to tie my posts together?
- Can my images, the type of content I'm posting, or my captions be improved in any way?

YOUR FACEBOOK GUIDE

Social media has become an invaluable tool for many artists in recent years, giving them a comprehensive and mostly free platform on which to market themselves and share their work. It takes time to build a following; therefore, we recommend that you focus on no more than two channels to make the best use of your time and gain momentum in your marketing efforts. The best advice we have is to find a platform that works for you in terms of presenting your work, connecting with your audience, and navigating with ease. If you prefer a certain platform, you're more likely to commit to using it and developing your presence, which is how you'll experience the best results when it comes to building your audience and even making sales. The key to growth is consistency, so choose platforms that you know you are good at or enjoy using.

Video artists might gravitate towards sites like YouTube or Vimeo, or you might find Twitter to be the most relevant for your work, but it is likely that most artists will benefit from focusing on Facebook and Instagram. Unless you have concerns over privacy or politics, we suggest setting up a Facebook business page promoting your artwork, if you haven't already.

Facebook is one of the original social media networks, and should not be discounted, even though new and exciting platforms may emerge and surpass it in popularity. The company continues to buy out other social media apps and tends to appeal to the widest audience, which becomes useful if those who tend to buy your work fall into an older demographic. Having a Facebook business page is also the only way that you'll be able to purchase Instagram advertising, so this alone is a smart incentive to set one up. As we've discussed, ads on Instagram can be a powerful way to grow your art career and get your work in front of the eyes of new potential collectors.

To utilize all the tools we share in this chapter, go ahead and create a Facebook business page now, if you don't yet have one. It's free and a quick step, which you can learn more about at www.facebook.com/business/pages. Your business page will allow you to take advantage of ads, engage specifically with your art followers, encourage inquiries about your work, and more.

TAKE ADVANTAGE OF UNIQUE FEATURES

Albums

Even while Kat was still in college, she started utilizing Facebook's unique features, such as the ability to share photo albums, provide links, and create events. This platform has a wealth of tools that are especially useful for artists and small business owners. When Kat finished her first body of work, she carefully documented her images and uploaded them in an album. Doing this helped her promote her senior exhibition and even resulted in her first few sales. She still regularly shares albums anytime she completes a new series or has a special offer for her audience.

If you are new to Facebook marketing, your following most likely consists of friends and family, but don't underestimate the power of your network. Even if, for example, your aunt buys your first piece, you never know who will see it in her home or even on her own Facebook feed. Often, our early collectors are people who are already in our general community, and we should embrace the opportunities that already exist within our small circle.

Create a new Facebook album each time you release a body of work that you are ready to share, launch a studio sale, or want to promote your exhibition. Make sure you include the medium, size, and any other important information for each image. Provide a link or a way to contact you to purchase the work you feature in each album in the body of the main post. As a bonus, when a work sells, mark it as "sold" to create excitement and a sense of urgency for any potential collectors who are following or happen to land on your Facebook page!

Once you create an album, we encourage you to share each work individually in separate posts. You want to offer a place where your entire body of work is shared, but then break it up into bite-sized pieces until it catches the eye of a potential buyer. You can also cross-promote each piece on Instagram and other platforms of your choice for maximum results.

Events

Facebook events are a great way to support your upcoming exhibitions, open studios, artist talks, workshops, or art fair appearances. Even if the organization that you are working with has an event page, create your own or become a co-host to better engage with your community.

When you create an event, include a memorable image that quickly introduces the audience to what the event is and lets them know what to expect. Provide the time, location, dates, and any supporting links in the description. You can choose to invite only certain individuals, if you want to target specific collectors, or your entire following if there's no limit on how many people can attend. Be sure to share the event by posting it on both your business page and personal feed.

Facebook Live

Facebook Live allows you to introduce collectors to your work, answer their questions, share exciting news, and genuinely engage with your audience. If you feel too camera-shy to show your face, share a live documentation of your process by setting up your phone, digital camera, or video equipment to film you as you work. Our days can get busy, and it may seem easier to just jump on when you have a free moment, but scheduling a time to go live and letting your followers know in advance will allow more people to join you! You can and should save your live videos on your feed so that others can watch them later.

Facebook Groups

If you need support or encouragement, or are seeking resources for exhibition and grant opportunities, Facebook Groups is your place to be. You can search for topics, such as "art opportunities," "artist networking," "artist support," "call for art," or something similar to explore your options. Most private groups require you to answer questions in order to be approved, so don't skip over that part or the moderator may not accept your request to join. We create groups for our workshops and encourage the members to share issues and successes and help each other by offering guidance and support. There are so many other groups that provide a similar sense of community, so we strongly urge you to find ones that will support you in your career! We even started a group called "Strong For The Studio" to encourage artists as they focus on health and wellness, in addition to making art. Accountability is a powerful tool in any aspect of your life, and your art business is no different.

Advertising

If you have a business page, start educating yourself on how to use advertising to expand your community and reach more collectors. The process is similar to Instagram ads, which we discuss in Using Instagram for Your Art Career (page 99). You always want to start with a budget in mind, and we recommend starting with a small amount, such as $10 to $50, so you can test it out without making too much of a financial commitment. At the same time, it's also worth noting that even these small amounts can make a significant impact.

You can promote a post with

YOUR AD AUDIENCE

Before you run an ad, you have to create an "Audience" for it. Facebook allows you to target your ads by certain demographics, including location, age, and gender. You can also plug in specific "interests" for your potential clients. This is important, and you want to be as specific as possible. When you include keywords such as "painting," "Saatchi Art," and "landscape painting," the app will find users with a mix of these interests. Take time to really think about what interests your potential collectors would have. Are there blog titles, magazines, hobbies, or stores that you can mention to hone in on those who'd be most likely to purchase your work? You can even use specific institutions, such as "MoMA," as an ad "interest" category. Don't worry about gauging whether you've added too many or too few parameters; Facebook will indicate if your audience is too broad or specific.

a single image (an artwork you hope to sell, for example), an exhibition or event, or you can create an ad campaign to grow your general Facebook page audience. One particularly useful aspect of advertising on Facebook is how specific the platform allows you to be. You're given the option to tailor your ad based on whether you want more page likes, interactions with your posts, website visits, sales, or email signups. Knowing this, make sure that you know exactly how you want your ads to work for you before launching any new campaigns.

Before you "boost" a post (this is the term Facebook uses for advertising an individual post) or promote your page, it's also essential to understand who you are trying to reach. We recommend jotting down notes on what kind of person is interested in your art. Brainstorm a list of potential galleries, art companies, websites, and blogs that feature works similar in style as you. These are parameters that you can add to the audience section of any ads you create in order to most effectively reach your ideal buyers.

Check how the ad is doing during its run. If it is not working well, you have the option to pause or delete it, which you should do in order to save your money and put it toward a new edited ad. Based on the insights of how each boost or campaign performs, you can experiment, track what works best over time, and adjust your ads to make sure that they give you the best possible returns on your investment. Give each new audience that you create a name and save it so you can easily reuse the campaigns that were successful in terms of reach and engagement.

To learn more technical details about advertising and Facebook's policy, visit www.facebook.com/business/ads.

Tip:

The optimal size for each type of ad varies on Facebook, which can be frustrating and confusing. You don't want to use something incorrectly or else the photo may be distorted, and you risk lowering the effectiveness of the ad. Luckily, there is an amazing resource from Sprout Social that gives a breakdown of what sizes of images you should use where: https://sproutsocial.com/ insights/facebook-ad-sizes/.

Remember to experiment with your audience, pay attention to what works, and include a call to action on each post. If you are running an ad to promote a studio sale, don't forget to include your website, shop link, or email!

BEST PRACTICES

Now that we've highlighted some basic features that can help you in your art business, here are some best practices for using Facebook. Use the following tips to help you come up with great content, grow your online community, and maintain a consistent voice.

General Rules for Posting

- Include images with every post. All images should be quality photos: not blurry, well-lit, and cropped to the frame or the artwork edges.
- Proofread all captions to avoid grammar or spelling errors. Use proper English, without text-speak (c u there = see you there). Facebook does a better job of handling longer captions in a more visually pleasing way than Instagram, so take advantage of this!
- Captions should be written in a friendly tone and should almost always include a call to action: visit my website for more information, email me to learn about commissioning an artwork, etc.
- Facebook prefers posts with images that have minimal or no overlay text (this is important if the image is being used for an ad) and also prioritizes posts with video content.

Tip:

Instagram gives you the option to automatically share a post to a connected Facebook account when you upload a new photo. However, while this can save time, the formatting does not translate seamlessly. One of the biggest giveaways is that tags of other accounts will not show up properly on Facebook, and you lose that opportunity to connect. It's better to use a social media management tool to schedule your posts instead.

Engaging with Your Facebook Audience

- Tag art fairs, other galleries, and museums to help increase how many people see your posts. For example: "See my new solo show at @Gallery." Only tag those relevant to you and your work! Avoid trying to get noticed by tagging galleries that you are not associated with (unless it's part of their submission protocol).
- You do not need to use hashtags on Facebook. Some people do, but it's not as common for people to search through hashtags as it is on Instagram or Twitter.
- Consider changing the profile picture and your cover photo periodically—this is a good opportunity to showcase new works.
- Make sure that your "About" section is always up-to-date, add information to the "Our Story" section (if you've set your artist page as a business), and set up automatic responses for when people send messages to you. Facebook reviews business pages and rates them on response time, which is made public on your profile. You don't want to be identified for not replying to messages in a timely manner as it isn't a good sign to potential collectors.

Ideas for Content

- Photos of artworks, especially new works and commissions.
- Post when works have sold and, as long as you have permission, post client homes with your artwork installed.
- Gallery photos or a gallery booth at art fairs with your work.
- Studio and process: photos of your studio, works in progress, you at work, etc.
- Holidays, including your birthday and/or your favorite artists' birthdays.
- Exhibitions: themed works on display in a gallery or in your studio, or your art in other public collections.
- Relevant art world or art market news and occasional posts about where you live or are traveling to and major exhibitions around the world you're interested in.
- Videos of any of the above!
- Motivational or funny quotes, memes, or gifs.

Posting Frequency

- Preferably a few times a week and up to once per day—posts can be scheduled in advance within Facebook or by using a social media management tool like Buffer or Hootsuite.
- If you're posting less often than daily, ideally post between Wednesday and Sunday for higher impact.
- The best times of day are early morning before work, lunch break, evening commute (during the week), and Sunday evenings.
- Utilize paid boosts and ads for your business profile, if you have the money to do so.
- Boost the most important posts for which you want a higher guarantee that people will see and engage with them—for example, works you want to sell, an invite to a gallery show, etc.
- Consider a monthly ad that promotes your page on Facebook to get more website views or page followers.
- Create a targeted audience and ensure that it aligns with the post content! For example, you can target people with an interest in art or art collecting, select an age range and location, etc.

TIPS FOR ENGAGING WITH YOUR FOLLOWERS

Respond to all messages and comments in a timely fashion to improve your ratings with Facebook, ideally within a few hours, but at minimum, aim for a twenty-four to forty-eight-hour response time. Remember, it's a good idea to simply set up away messages to respond automatically to other users so that your ratings are not affected. Also be sure to regularly revisit each post and make sure that everyone who has liked it has been invited to like and follow the page. To do this, click the likes under a post to view the names as a list, then click the invite button by each person's name who hasn't already liked your page.

TAKE ACTION

• Set up a business page for your art on Facebook, including descriptions on the "About" page and "Our Story" section, away messages, a variety of images, and other ways to contact you.

• Establish a content schedule and a realistic number of posts you can commit to per week.

• Experiment with ads and set up a few target audiences for artwork sales and other announcements.

MORE WAYS TO CONNECT WITH YOUR AUDIENCE

Building meaningful relationships with your community and collectors sometimes necessitates getting out of your comfort zone and trying new things. Don't settle for only creating a support system on social media when there are so many different ways to take your professional relationships to the next level. When interacting online, you may miss great opportunities to connect with others if you're just going through the motions!

In this chapter we'll share a few different methods you can use to improve your image, engage with your audience, and deepen your connection with your community.

TOKENS OF APPRECIATION

Over the past few years, we have made and maintained relationships with many different artists, several of whom have sent us beautiful prints of their work after being published in the magazine. These prints are excellent examples of what we mean by tokens of appreciation—and you don't have to send something big or costly. Whether it's a small print, stickers, or a handwritten card, a physical thank-you is always more memorable than a direct message or email. So, next time you are given an opportunity or close a sale, ask the person if it would be okay for you to mail them a thank-you gift. Make sure your package is neatly presented and that it reflects your personal brand.

Kat often uses high-quality postcards featuring her latest artwork to thank her collectors and supporters. These cards can be framed and therefore double as a mini print. She also occasionally sends copies of magazines she was published in, as well as catalogs with new works. In return, she always receives excited and grateful messages from her community. This is a great way that she strengthens the bond between herself and her clients or artist friends.

We have also used this strategy for Create! Magazine by giving away stickers, tote bags, and free issues, or by writing special thank-you letters. Everyone loves to be remembered and appreciated, so why not make someone else's day?

PRIZES & GIVEAWAYS

A great way to create excitement online is to do a giveaway of a print, a small original work, or something else that represents your art practice. Not only will this attract new followers and potential collectors if done correctly, but it will also help you notice who is consistently excited about your work. Those who share the most enthusiasm can end up being potential collectors of your work.

When you launch a contest or giveaway, be sure to have a call to action included in the directions of how to participate. For example, you may request that entrants use a particular hashtag, follow you, comment on a post, tag a friend, join your email list, or something else that suits your intention. In exchange for your gift, you should get your audience to provide you with their contact information or help draw attention to your account so that you continue to grow your network.

Best Practices for Giveaways

- Choose something to gift that is easy to ship.
- Make sure you have great photos to entice your audience.
- Create a timeframe for the contest.
- Draft a caption with the rules on how to enter or participate.
- Ask the participants to tag a friend or multiple friends.
- Offer additional entries for sharing the post or subscribing to your newsletter.
- Promote the contest via social media and your email list.
- Use an app to select a random winner!

To take it a step further, you can ask a few podcasters, bloggers, or other art influencers if they would be interested in sharing the giveaway on their platform. Some might be willing to feature it for free, but others may only allow you to promote it if you pay for advertising. We recommend starting small and experimenting first. Only invest in paid ads when you have the money and really wish to build momentum on a larger, established platform.

ARTIST-RUN FAIRS

Another way to step out from behind the screen and make more connections in person is to participate in an artist-run fair. These events, which are typically hosted in larger cities, are designed to allow artists to curate their own booth, engage with their audience, and, of course, make sales. For Kat, participating in a fair was important because she wanted to meet collectors from outside of her immediate network in Philadelphia. She was instantly drawn by the idea of exhibiting in New York and ended up signing up to participate in the Brooklyn edition of The Other Art Fair.

If you are not yet represented by a gallery or don't have a relationship with one, we suggest that you look into this opportunity. While a fair is a significant financial investment, and there is no guarantee you'll make a profit or break even, it can have benefits that go beyond making sales, such as networking with other artists, being exposed to influential media outlets, tracking which of your work(s) your audience best responds to, and more.

If you're curious about art fairs, we cover them in more detail in Tips for Surviving an Art Fair as an Artist (page 253), but we encourage you to consider this option at least once in your career. When you're ready to commit financially, you may find that it is a good fit for you and your art.

POP-UP SHOWS

If you live in an area with vacant storefronts or creative boutiques, restaurants, or cafes that host art shows, organizing a pop-up exhibition can generate a lot of excitement for your art, as well as lead to valuable new connections. Several artists in our community have created their own opportunities for shows by partnering with large retailers, such as Macy's and Lord & Taylor. You can pitch your own unique idea to a business if your work matches the company's mission, aesthetic, or values. Search for a person you can contact in the organization who is in charge of events, business partnerships, or marketing. If it is a small company, don't be afraid to reach out to the owner or CEO directly. Present a clear message of what you want to do, your plans for coordinating the show, and most importantly, how both of you will benefit from working together.

If you don't feel ready for a solo exhibition, see if you can curate a group show or host an event featuring several artists at a yoga studio, art supply store, hotel lobby, or another venue of your choice! Invite your artist friends or creatives you admire to join you. A group event can also help split up the work of putting the show together, and it can drum up additional interest in the event when more people are involved who can help promote it.

BLOGS, VIDEO CHANNELS, OR PODCASTS

Many artists now solely use Instagram as their website and don't have any other place online where people can access their writing, opinions, or inspiration. This is not ideal for a number of reasons, one of which is that you do not own your Instagram account like you would own a website. For example, we know of an artist whose profile was deleted, and she lost images of her entire portfolio. This experience was traumatizing for her, and we'd never want it to happen to you, which is why we encourage you to invest extra time and resources into housing your work and ideas in more than just one location on the Internet. We share the importance of having a website in Your Artist Website (page 9), but if you want to take it a step further, there are several other outlets available.

While podcasting and blogging can both involve a significant time investment, they also provide incredible opportunities to share your story, document your journey, and give others access to your ideas and thoughts. Since starting her show Art & Cocktails, Kat has been surprised and delighted by the shift in conversation she has had with fellow creatives. Every week her inbox is now flooded with messages from listeners. The artists openly share their struggles and successes, and ask for specific topics and advice. Kat's podcast was started as an extension of *Create! Magazine*, but has since evolved into its own intimate community of dedicated followers.

Since there are already numerous amazing art blogs and podcasts out there, you also don't have to start your own to explore this avenue. See if a podcast you love accepts pitches and write to them about why you think you'd be an interesting guest for them to interview. If you prefer to try blogging, you can do the same by checking how to submit to a blog you enjoy reading. After gaining enough experience from working with *Create! Magazine* and through previous employment, Alicia began reaching out to blogs and other magazines offering to do guest posts. She proposed ideas she had based on their content and has had many successful responses. This has allowed her to continue to build her resume, make new professional connections, and earn additional income.

Continue ›

‹ *Continued*

Podcast/Blog-Post Topic Ideas

- Interviews with other artists and art professionals
- Techniques and demos
- Inspiration
- Travel and residency experiences
- Career tips and advice
- Exhibition reviews
- Your favorite books, galleries, museums, etc.
- Art history research

Think of the communication methods that are most natural to you. Brainstorm how you can share and document your stories and expertise through writing, speaking, or filming. Once you've decided, develop a plan for committing to this new endeavor and get started on the first step, whether it is launching your new YouTube channel or pitching a guest post to a blog.

We hope that these ideas sparked curiosity and excitement for what you can do next in your career. Pick a few of these suggestions and aim to try at least one of them a year, even if it's as simple as writing a thank-you card to a collector or artist friend.

TAKE ACTION

- Think of several people who have impacted your art career in a positive way and ask them for their mailing address. Send them a small postcard or inexpensive gift to let them know you appreciate them.

- Come up with an item for a giveaway to your audience. Decide on what the desired outcome is: more followers, new email list subscribers, or more interaction with your existing community. Create a timeframe, draft the rules of how to participate, and announce your giveaway!

- Research art fairs in your area and see if the location, cost, and reviews make it a good fit for you. Go through your inventory, select which works you would bring to the fair, and begin working on a plan after you read Tips for Surviving an Art Fair as an Artist (page 253).

- Think about small businesses that would be a good match for your artwork and brainstorm unique ways to curate a pop-up show for a mutually beneficial partnership.

- Ask yourself if blogging or podcasting may be the next step in your career. Is there a specific art-related topic you are passionate about? Don't keep your brilliant ideas from the world!

EMAIL MARKETING BASICS

Email marketing can be an effective tool when it comes to making sales and engaging with your clients. To beat the ever-changing algorithms and new requirements of social media platforms, artists absolutely must build their own dedicated email list. As useful and fun as social media can be, we don't own our followers and can lose these contacts at any given moment. We have witnessed large Instagram accounts in our community taken down due to content that "violates community rules" without any further explanation, or those who lose their profile to a hacker. Though this is generally unlikely to happen, it's always a good idea to take precautions and gather information from your audience beyond social media apps to set yourself up with guaranteed contacts that you can access at any time, without relying on social media.

Having a mailing list of existing and potential clients gives you a platform where you can share new paintings, exhibitions, and other exciting news directly with your collectors and fans. If a person signs up for your newsletter, they have given you permission to contact them, which often means a higher probability of an eventual sale. Take advantage of this!

GETTING STARTED

Find a Platform

The first step in email marketing is to research which platform is suitable for you and your needs. We use Mailchimp for *Create! Magazine* and PxP Contemporary, and Kat also uses it for her personal art marketing. The reason we started with this service is because it lets you maintain your list for free up to 2,000 subscribers, so it's perfect for those just starting out. You can then focus on building your list and learning about the platform without having to pay for it. Then, when you are ready to pay for a premium account or have outgrown the free version, you can access additional tools and features. For us, Mailchimp is incredibly user-friendly, with its drag-and-drop templates and contact management system. Alicia has also used Constant Contact at a former job, and although she encountered a few formatting glitches on occasion, it worked well overall. We also know of artists who have used Robly and other platforms successfully.

If you don't have a mailing list yet, we've included a list of suggestions for you to consider on page 141. Ask your peers what platforms they use, compare the prices, and make sure that the one you eventually choose has all the features you will need!

Develop Your List

To grow your mailing list, you need a basic form through which your patrons can sign up to receive your updates. Most platforms offer a simple HTML code that you can embed into your website, or your site may have a content block that can link directly to Mailchimp, Constant Contact, or whichever email app you choose to work with. Be sure that your sign-up form is visible on your website. You may consider linking it on your top navigation menu or the footer of your website, including it on the contact page, or all three. With *Create! Magazine,* we also sometimes use a pop-up banner that offers a free digital issue or store discount when they sign up for the email list. If you apply this to your practice, whether you offer the chance to win a limited edition print or tell subscribers they will be the first to know of new artwork releases, it can help encourage more people to join your list. Some artists even include a link to their email list on their social media profiles—if you've built up a following online, this especially should be something that you include as well.

While it is important to grow your list, remember that quality is much more important than quantity. You don't just want to send messages out into the void to people who aren't actually interested in your content. You hope for your emails to be read, opened, and acted upon, but don't worry if your numbers are low at first. It takes time to learn when your audience is most responsive and what the best way is to present your message to them. When Kat started her list, she only had ten subscribers for her artwork—and most of them were people she already knew. Through networking, exhibiting regularly, and a multitude of media features, she's grown her audience and developed a larger base of those who are interested in her art. Now, several years later, her list includes hundreds of collectors and supporters, and this has resulted in significantly increased sales.

Envision Your Audience

If we were to establish any definite rules for email marketing, one of the most important would be this: craft each email campaign with personality and care. What we mean by this is that when writing your letter, try to speak to your ideal collector directly. Imagine what kind of person they are, what they dress like, where they live, what they do, what they enjoy, and even where they shop. Write to them like you would to a good friend, always envisioning them in your mind. This will not only help you share meaningful content and imbue your words with your individual voice, but also make sure you avoid sounding robotic, therefore increasing your chances of connecting with your audience. It's hard to truly engage with others via a note on a computer screen, but the more you are able to make yourself sound genuine and personable, the more likely people will be to reach out to you.

When you're first starting out, do your best to imagine what type of person would enjoy collecting your art and pretend you are writing to them in your emails, as well as your social media captions. As you grow in your career and improve your marketing skills, you will gain a clearer vision of who your ideal collector is and can adjust your approach accordingly.

Most email marketing platforms allow you to automate the greeting to include your contacts' first names. It is a personal choice to do this, but it can be a nice touch to personalize your message so that it sounds as if it is written to each person individually, rather than a mass, generic audience.

What to Include

You can decide on the tone that feels right for you and your work, but even if you tend to be more informal or casual when engaging with your collectors and followers, we still recommend always starting with a basic greeting. Next, explain what it is that you want to share, whether it is announcing a new show, sale, event, or body of work. Try to be concise, but engaging. Like on social media, you don't have very long to capture someone's attention and get them to interact with your message. Use great images of your artwork, and break up the text into small paragraphs to create a clean visual look—your subscribers may be turned off by big chunks of text that take too long to read. Always put the most important information at the top, since many people won't scroll all the way to the bottom of your emails. Doing so ensures that your audience won't miss the news you really want them to see.

Don't forget to include any relevant details for shows and events, such as the location, date, time, and if it requires a ticket or RSVP. Links are incredibly helpful, so use them throughout your message, both within the text and with your images. Make it easy for clients to purchase your work by linking each artwork directly to your webshop, gallery, or an email message to you inquiring about the piece.

We love concluding our emails with gratitude by using phrases like "Thank you for your support!" People appreciate simple etiquette, and we do too. You don't have to overthink the content in your messages, and to get you going, we've included templates for two typical artist emails on page 139.

Design Tips

Luckily, if you're using a platform like Mailchimp, you won't spend too much time formatting your newsletter. Choose a template that fits your aesthetic—like with your website, we tend to prefer minimalist designs so that the focus is solely on your work and your words. If you don't use a premade template, focus on using consistent images and fonts within the body of your message and in the links. Varying text sizes and styles can be incredibly distracting and difficult to read. We both save time by duplicating email campaigns that have already been sent out and then editing them to add new content. This is an easy way to keep our emails looking consistent, which is an integral part of building your art business. You want people to be able to recognize your signature style, in order to grow your brand awareness.

At this point, you know we're sticklers for high-quality images, but in this case they do not need to be high-resolution. In fact, photos that are too large will take a long time to load, resulting in less engagement with your campaign. Mailchimp is great in that it automatically identifies images that need to be adjusted for optimal usage within an email. Artwork images will likely be the visual focus of your message, but also feel free to add variety with install views, works in progress, and even links to videos. For special announcements, you can include an animated graphic or screenshots of your recent media features. Emails don't have to be boring, so don't treat them like a chore. Instead, think of this approach as another way you get to show off your personality, connect with your audience, and share exciting updates about what's happening in your art career.

Frequency & Timing

Most artists send a monthly, bimonthly, or quarterly newsletter, so as to not contact their mailing list too frequently. These are probably the best options for how often you should send out newsletters, because it's not likely that you'll have a new show or body of work to share every week. However, some artists choose to email their subscribers more frequently. Sending a weekly, or even daily, email is a considerable time commitment and can result in mass unsubscribes from your audience, so think very carefully about if it would really be the most suitable option for you.

Tip:

Most email marketing platforms allow you to automate the greeting to include your contacts' first names. It is a personal choice to do this, but it can be a nice touch to personalize your message so that it sounds as if it is written to each person individually, rather than a mass, generic audience.

It's best to create a consistent schedule you can easily keep up with, hence the suggestion of once a month or every other month. It's okay to send a special email when you get exciting news that you wish to share with your audience immediately. If it is a time-sensitive event or a major accomplishment that deserves its own special announcement, it's fine not to wait to include it in your next newsletter. Consistent frequency in sending newsletters also helps build continuity with your audience, and they will learn when they can expect to hear from you.

Continue ›

‹ *Continued*

We experience the best results when we mail our campaigns during the week, specifically Tuesday through Thursday, and they hit inboxes in the morning, midmorning, or early afternoon. The other days of the week are when people are busier with work or enjoying the weekend, and we find that our audience is less likely to respond.

Doing a quick search online for the best times of the day to send emails will yield various results, and everyone has their opinion. One great thing about upgrading your email service is that your provider will likely offer additional features, such as suggestions for the optimal day and time to send your campaigns based on your audience, A/B testing (where you can split your subscribers into two groups to find out which versions of an email work better), and more. If you aren't able to access these features, you can do some testing on your own to see if certain times of day, days of the week, or subject lines result in greater engagement with your emails.

WHEN TO SEND AN EMAIL BLAST

Need some ideas for what news to share with your email subscribers? Here's a helpful list to get you started!

• To share a new piece, series, or print release

• To promote your upcoming exhibitions

• To link to articles, interviews, podcasts, and other media features

• To provide details about an event, speech, or presentation

• To launch your studio sales

• To invite your audience to an open studio

• To announce a recent residency you completed or award you received

GETTING NEW SUBSCRIBERS

Remember that numbers aren't everything. Anyone would rather have five collectors who buy repeatedly, versus five hundred who never purchase a thing. However, growing your list over time with the right contacts will help bring in new sales and interest in your art. We mentioned previously that you should link your email signup to your other online platforms (i.e. website, social media, etc.) and also consider a pop-up on your site with a special offer. Another idea is to do a giveaway or promotion in which people have to provide their email in exchange for one entry. We see brands and bloggers do this all the time to grow their mailing lists, and sometimes they even team up together for an even bigger marketing event. If there is a local store or brand that might make sense to partner with, reach out to them to ask if they would be interested. It could end up working very well for both parties, and through cross-promotion, everyone wins!

During exhibitions or events, keep a signup sheet in a visible place where people can leave their contact information, which you can later transfer to your email marketing platform. If you choose this option, don't forget to input the analog data regularly. Some artists and galleries prefer going digital from the start and use an iPad with the signup form from their specific email provider to capture new email addresses from potential clients. This goes without saying, but always ask for permission first before manually adding anyone to your list. There are strict regulations about this and your account can be punished for abusing this privilege.

You can also use your social media pages to promote and remind your audience to join your mailing list. If they're a dedicated follower, you know they already enjoy your content. Invite them to subscribe so that they can learn more and get exclusive access to new works or events, and hopefully this will lead to sales in the future.

DEALING WITH UNSUBSCRIBES

Unfortunately, unsubscribes will occur at almost every stage of building your email list. If you are taking the time to craft quality campaigns that speak directly to your collector, and you still notice your numbers dropping, try not to be discouraged. When people leave your platform, it doesn't always mean that you upset anyone or did something wrong or provided no value. Everyone receives a lot of email, so it could simply be that the person receives too many emails already and would rather keep in touch with you in a different way. They can always rejoin later, and if they're interested in your work they definitely will.

When Kat first started growing her list of collectors for her paintings, she made the mistake of messaging too frequently during a crowdfunding campaign. The repetitive emails turned off quite a few audience members. While this experience was an unpleasant lesson, it wasn't the end of the world. She soon recovered and began growing her list again.

NEXT STEPS

Once you set up your list and are actively growing it, what happens next? Our best advice is to practice, experiment with your content, find your authentic voice, and research newsletters from successful creatives in your industry. Subscribe to artist and gallery email lists that you find inspiring and see how they approach this part of their business. While we never want to copy anyone's style, it's okay to write down ideas or techniques they use that you think would also be beneficial to you when communicating with your audience. With time and practice, you will create meaningful letters to your audience and build a list of raving fans!

---

7 "Email Marketing Benchmarks," Mailchimp, https://mailchimp.com/resources/email-marketing-benchmarks/.

SAMPLE NEWSLETTER TEMPLATES EXHIBITION OPENING

[Subject line]

[Simple greeting, such as "hello," "greetings," etc.]
OR
Dear [Insert name automation in your email service platform],

I'm excited to invite you to the opening of my solo exhibition, [Title], at the [Gallery or venue name]. [Include event location, details, dates, and times].

If you are unable to attend but would like to see the works being presented, you can view the collector preview here: [Insert a link to the online catalog or PDF including pricing, sizes, and the medium for each piece].

For questions or to purchase work, please contact me at [Your email] OR [Gallery director] at [Gallery email].

Thank you so much for your support! I am grateful to be able to share my art with you.

Sincerely,
[Your name]

Studio Sale

[Greeting],

As a thank-you for your incredible support of my art, I would like to invite you to an exclusive studio sale of my original work.

EXAMPLE: I am making space in my studio for a new collection and would love for you to own one of my original [Insert art description] at a special price. I am extending this offer to my collectors and supporters for a limited time only [Add dates when the sale will be available].

You can shop the works here: [Insert shop link, PDF of the catalog, or another link to the sale].
[Insert optional perks, such as free domestic shipping, payment plans, discounts, etc.]

[Mention supporting media features, awards, or anything else that may be of interest to your potential collector.]

Thank you again! Please reach out to me at [Your email] if you have any questions about the work, pricing, or anything else. I look forward to sharing my art with you.

Yours truly,
[Your name]

SUBJECT LINES

Subject lines, like choosing when to send your emails, can be another tricky subject, but this isn't something to stress over. In fact, you can easily go overboard by sounding too salesy or gimmicky. Using all caps or a lot of exclamation points at the end can also result in your email landing in your recipient's junk or spam folder. Check out your inbox right now and see which subject lines catch your attention.

Each email subject line should create excitement and a slight sense of urgency so that your audience can't resist opening your message. Do this with smart word choices like "exclusive," "limited," or "first." We suggest keeping a document or notebook full of ideas, and then tailoring them to your events, sales, announcements, and other offers.

Explore a few of the following examples!

New Work or Print Release
Exclusive Preview of My New Collection
New Limited Edition Print Release!
First Look at [Work description]

Event Announcements
Upcoming Art Fair [Include location and perhaps also date]
Exhibition Opening This Week!

Invitations
You Are Cordially Invited to [Exhibition name]
Join Me at My Exhibition [Exhibition name]

Studio Sales
Don't Miss This Exclusive Offer
Original Work [Discount amount]
Build Your Collection at a Great Price
Studio Sale! Take Advantage of [List offer or discount]

TAKE ACTION

- Sign up for an email marketing platform and start a list of your contacts.
- Include links and signup forms on your social media channels and website.
- Determine the frequency of your emails.
- As you start your email campaigns, make sure your emails include important dates, links, price lists, and any other important information for your collectors.
- Reply to emails as promptly as you can, and start building meaningful relationships with your collectors!

HELPFUL WEBSITES & TOOLS

Email Marketing Platforms
- Mailchimp
- ActiveCampaign
- ConvertKit
- Constant Contact
- Robly
- Sendinblue

Design Resources
- Canva.com
- PicMonkey.com

Free Stock Images
- Unsplash.com
- Pexels.com
- Pixabay.com

Growing Your List
- Sumo.com
- Leadpages.net

NETWORKING 101 FOR ARTISTS

Prioritizing and maximizing your studio time, or, if you don't yet have a studio, the time spent dedicated to creating your work, is of the utmost importance to build your career as an artist. However, simply toiling away by yourself, even if you are producing incredible work, will not alone bring you success. Whether or not you enjoy being social, networking should be an essential part of your practice.

When we look back at when we began working in the arts, we sometimes think of the possible connections we might have missed because of shyness. While we each appreciate the paths we took to get to where we are today, who knows if we could have advanced our careers more quickly had we pushed ourselves to be better at networking earlier on. Alicia once had a friend who quite literally had to push her in front of a potential employer at a gallery opening because she kept backing out of speaking to her. She made silly excuses, like "What if she's too busy?" or "What if she doesn't remember me?" Luckily, Alicia found a quiet moment to briefly say hello and mention that she would soon be graduating. Note that an opening is not always the right time to approach a gallery director, as it can be very hectic for them, but in this case it worked out for Alicia because she kept the conversation short and to the point. If she hadn't stayed in touch with this contact, she may not have shortly after landed her first full-time job!

It took Kat a really long time to start networking and to overcome her shyness, especially in the beginning. It took everything she had to start putting herself out there. One of her first experiences was managing a student-run gallery during college. This role forced her to interact with artists outside of the university, speak in front of her peers, and overcome her social anxiety. It took several years after college for Kat to show up to local art openings, volunteer at museums, and push herself completely out of her comfort zone in order to start meeting important members of the art community. But once she finally did, these experiences resulted in friendships, exhibitions, publications, and more.

Hopefully, you don't struggle with this as much as we did (and don't need a physical shove in the right direction, like Alicia!), but if introducing yourself, public speaking, and making conversation at big gatherings aren't your strengths, we completely understand, and that's why we're sharing some of the tips that have helped us. You don't have to become a fast-talking, schmoozing machine, but you should master at least a few essential skills that will help you with networking.

NEXT STEPS

Get out There!

Make it a habit to attend local or regional art events. Become a regular face and, at the very least, aim to greet people you've seen multiple times. Maybe even introduce yourself, since you have something in common. Find little ways like this to make connections at the various events you attend. For example, if you are attending a panel discussion or artist talk, you can ask an interesting question and then follow up with the speaker afterward. If that is too far out of your comfort zone, perhaps ask the question privately after the talk. Even when you can't think of a question, people will always appreciate you coming up later to thank them for sharing their work or mention that you found what they said to be insightful.

We have both been asked to go back and speak to the fine art students at our undergraduate university, and we've been so impressed by the few students who chatted with us after our presentations that we gave them our personal business cards or emails to stay connected. Assuming your conversation goes well, like these students' interactions with us, you can certainly ask to keep in touch and hopefully you'll be given their card or email, or some people may suggest adding them as a new contact on social media.

Bring a Friend

Okay, we get it if you're not totally ready to jump in and put yourself out there quite yet. So why not invite someone to go with you to an event? Like Alicia's earlier example, it was great to have her friend with her at that gallery opening early on in her career so he could encourage her to network. Find a supportive friend to tag along, or ask a fellow artist you know who might also be interested in making new connections.

Honestly, sometimes it is also nice to have a third person to balance the flow of a conversation if there is a lull, and an outside perspective might share something interesting about you or your work that you didn't even think to mention! The only caveat is that you shouldn't put your buddy in the awkward position of being the third wheel. Ideally, go with a friend who can gracefully exit a conversation that's not relevant to them and not interrupt when you're in the middle of speaking with someone important.

Tip:

Another way to make any social situation more comfortable is to take small breaks after you've been engaged in a long conversation or stuck in a crowd making small talk. Constant networking over a few hours can be exhausting! Go refill your drink, step outside for a moment, or compose yourself again in the bathroom when you have a chance. A common joke amongst introverts is that we go to events and seek out the pets or children to hang out with. You won't do yourself any favors if this is all you do, but if it helps you calm your nerves and find a common topic to ease into a conversation with a stranger (e.g. "Isn't this dog so cute? I love seeing pets at openings! What brings you to the gallery this evening?"), then use this strategy as needed.

Set Parameters

If you are getting to events pretty regularly, but find that you tend to talk to the same people or nobody at all, perhaps try setting goals or rewards for yourself. You could tell yourself, "I won't leave this event until I _____ (meet two new people, get one business card, introduce myself to the guest speaker, etc.)," or, "If I make a new contact today, I'll _____ (get that fancy sketchbook I've been wanting)." Use what motivates you most to make sure that it will really get you to step up your networking game and stick to it. If you set a goal, make it happen, and don't allow yourself the reward unless you do. But also don't beat yourself up if it takes a few attempts at first. This is an ongoing process, with unlimited opportunities to try again!

Practice Makes Perfect

You should have a few "elevator pitches" ready to go in case you meet someone like a curator or gallerist who may be interested in your work. Practice both a shorter and longer version to use, depending on how long the conversation goes, and have your friends, family, or colleagues tell you what they think. You can even practice in front of the mirror if nobody is available. Ask yourself (or your friend) if you presented your work in a way that was interesting, concise, and understandable. If not, keep trying until you get to something that works. With numerous public speaking opportunities under our belts now, we're both much better at this today than we were previously, but for longer talks we still like doing a bit of preparation beforehand with notes or an outline so that we're not completely winging it on the spot.

It's not just what you say that matters, though. How you speak, stand, and carry yourself can have an incredible effect on how others perceive and interact with you. Alicia loved learning about this by reading the book *Presence* by Amy Cuddy, but if you want a shortened version of what she discusses, Alicia highly recommends watching Amy's famous TED Talk online. Based on this, you might consider practicing a firm handshake, speaking louder or more slowly, and doing a few "power poses" before your next event so that you can walk in with confidence and poise. When we get excited or nervous, we tend to talk faster, which can leave you out of breath or cause you to lose your train of thought. While it can be frustrating when this happens, just pause, breathe, and then pick back up with your conversation. We're often so concerned with how others are judging us, but in reality many people barely notice our mistakes, if at all. Even if you're nervous, it always helps to smile. :)

In the early days of the magazine, Kat used to schedule a day each month to visit galleries in person. She started locally in Wilmington and Philadelphia, but then challenged herself to visit prestigious galleries in New York City and introduce herself and her publication. She would bring her business cards and a copy of the magazine to show as an example. At first, the experiences were awkward at best, but over time Kat gained confidence and started getting inquiries for ads and requests to feature artists and exhibitions, and she even made friendships along the way.

When it came to her art, Kat used a similar approach by visiting exhibitions on quiet days and introducing herself to the gallery. It's not an accident that many of the places she initially visited and supported ended up inviting her to exhibit her art years down the line. Plant the seeds and trust the process of meaningful, sustainable relationships in your community.

When visiting in person, don't ask anything upon the initial meeting (unless it happens to come up organically). Start by introducing yourself and come from a place of service. People are skeptical of being asked for favors, sales, or exhibitions, so the best approach is to offer a sincere compliment, then briefly share who you are and what you have to offer. Ask if they have a mailing list and sign up. After the in-person interaction, follow up and keep showing up to support the organizations you admire. We promise it pays off.

Remember People's Names & How to Pronounce Them

Unless you have a specific medical condition that makes it difficult for you to recall names or faces (like noted American artist Chuck Close), do your best to remember who you meet. People really appreciate it! There are tons of memory tricks for this that you can look up online, so try a few and use whatever helps. It's not expected that you'll know everyone's name after one meeting, but if you consistently accidentally call people by the wrong name or introduce yourself again, putting in a little more effort can save you from committing an unfortunate faux pas.

Misspelling names can also be very frustrating—with names like Ekaterina Popova and Alicia Bonilla-Puig, we know this firsthand!—especially if their email address includes their name and you wrote that right, but then incorrectly spelled their name in the greeting of your email. Yikes! That can suggest that you weren't paying attention and leave them with a negative first impression. Double-check your spelling before hitting send—and thank goodness for the retrieve function that certain email providers offer. If you haven't yet enabled the unsend feature, we highly suggest doing so.

Warm Up to Cold Emailing!

Sending emails to potential contacts can be intimidating, but it's such a simple way to connect that it's always worth trying. It's free, it doesn't take much time beyond researching the person's email address, and you have nothing to lose. Our suggestion is to mention something notable about the person you are trying to reach. If you read about them on a blog, heard an inspiring podcast episode, or received a referral from a friend, let them know. Give them a sincere compliment about their work or ask a smart, relevant question and tell them how you found them. After that, you can briefly introduce yourself and what you do. If you hope to meet them for lunch or coffee, send them a list of your available times and location suggestions, allowing them to choose what would be most convenient for them.

One of the best tips we can give you for cold emailing is to be very specific with why you are reaching out. We've received countless messages from people asking to collaborate with us in the future, and while we love to work with new brands and artists, it is confusing when they don't explain exactly what they envision in a potential partnership. If you want to do an Instagram takeover with a company that fits your work, be interviewed for a podcast, or set up a coffee meeting, SAY SO in your initial message. The person you're contacting can't read your mind and won't be able to give you what you ultimately want if you don't tell them what it is and provide them with directions on how to follow up with you to keep the conversation moving forward. Don't force them to write back because they need more information, or to come up with ideas about when/where to meet or how to work together. It's a waste of both parties' time and leaves a poor impression.

In addition, being clear helps the person you're contacting quickly identify whether they can indeed assist or support you or if they should refer you to someone else they know instead. This should go without saying, but specificity also means tailoring each message to the individual or company you're writing to. Recycling the same note doesn't feel personal or genuine and will result in much fewer positive responses.

Meet Your New Contacts IRL

Once you start to make these connections online, work on getting people to meet with you in person as well. It's great to have a professional community that you can reach via social media and email, but it's easier to build relationships when you can talk face-to-face, or even over the phone, and really get to know someone. Once others become familiar with you and your work, they can remember or recommend you for future opportunities and give more thorough references.

Don't hesitate to ask a potential mentor or colleague out for coffee. As long as you keep your invitation short and polite, it's likely that you'll get a positive response. Just be respectful of others' time. Depending on who you are reaching out to, they may receive tons of these sorts of requests and simply may not have enough hours in the day to meet or even respond to everyone. If you don't hear back, reach out to someone else in the meantime, and then try again later.

Meeting offline is also important because you never really know how a person may differ from their online persona. What if you realize that their opinions on something you feel strongly about are in contrast with your views, or that what they are working on isn't actually of interest to you? You want to invest time in making and maintaining relationships that are going to be beneficial for both parties. Think of it sort of like a job interview (or a first date—ha!), where you'll likely know pretty early on whether or not you're a match.

One of the most pivotal moments in Kat's career was when she served as a contributor to an online magazine that covered museum exhibitions. Though this was an unpaid position, the ability to attend press lunches and exclusive previews at major museums along the East Coast was invaluable. Kat made sure to exchange business cards with other influential writers and press, and she stayed in touch with them for years to come. One of the exhibitions she covered at the Delaware Art Museum led her to a young curator, Margaret Winslow, who later introduced her to the art community in Delaware. This serendipitous connection ended up linking Kat to some of the most supportive individuals in her life. Meeting this curator also resulted in studio visits, exhibitions, and, most importantly, a strong local community that inspired her to start her magazine.

Follow Up

This is one tip that we can't stress enough! Half the battle of networking is meeting new people, but sometimes the harder half is actually keeping up with everyone. There are two types of notes we like to send to make sure we regularly stay in touch with both new and old contacts—and we suggest the same to you! First, whenever you meet someone new, make it a habit to follow up with a thank-you note. You likely know this one already, so just remember to do it consistently. It doesn't have to be long or overly formal—a quick email will certainly suffice—and it's a nice gesture that people appreciate.

The second message we send to contacts in our network is a professional update when we go through a job change or know that we'll be looking for new employment soon. It never hurts to reach out to former employers to let them know what you've been up to, especially if you will be seeking a new job. It's better to be in contact again first, rather than writing out of the blue to ask for a reference or other favor. For artists specifically, you might think about a curator, writer, or gallery from the past that you had a good experience with. Definitely drop them a line if you have exciting new work to share, a big exhibition coming up, or other noteworthy news.

Following up also applies to initial contacts. Everyone has busy schedules and you never know why someone hasn't responded to your email. What if it got lost in their inbox? It happens! So follow up with a simple note asking if they got your first message. You may also find that some people say "yes" initially when you offer to meet up, but then you don't hear from them for a while. Again, depending on who you are trying to connect with, it may take a little more effort. A friendly reminder or two from you will keep your meeting from being put on the backburner or forgotten. Try not to take this personally and be as flexible as you can. Certain people are simply hard to pin down!

Get Them to Ask You

There's definitely an art to networking (no pun intended!), because ultimately you're trying to get someone else to do something for you: hire you, look at your artwork, consider you for a magazine feature, etc. Because people generally don't like being told what to do, if you ask outright you might meet resistance or get an uncomfortable, passive response. But there's no need for Jedi mind tricks here. Shifting how you approach telling people about what you are doing and are ultimately looking for can yield more positive outcomes.

For example, instead of: "I need a job right now; you should take a look at my work, or share my art if you like it," try, "I graduated recently with my BFA in painting and am seeking opportunities in local museums," or, "I've just completed a new series of (insert your art here) and I'm really excited to begin showing it." Start with something that piques their interest and gets them to ask more questions: What kind of work do you want to do in museums? Can you tell me more about this new series? This keeps the conversation going, and they will be more likely to ask you to send your resume, a link to your website, or whatever else you are hoping for in the end!

Alicia used this approach to land a temporary job when she first moved to Amsterdam before she found something more permanent. Doing a little research on art events in the area, she noticed that the city's annual iteration of the Affordable Art Fair was coming up soon. Knowing that fairs can often be a stressful and busy time for the galleries involved, she simply reached out to the local galleries that were planning to participate, which she found listed on the fair's website. She mentioned her experience working for galleries and at fairs and that she would be happy to help if they by chance needed an extra set of hands for the week. Note that Alicia never said anything about a job (even though she desperately wanted one) or about considering her for anything beyond the fair (even though that would have been the most ideal outcome!). She never heard back from most of the emails she sent, and one said no thanks, but another asked to meet her for coffee and that's who she ended up working with for the duration of the fair.

Timing Is Everything

Like Alicia's experience with her temporary gig in Amsterdam shows, how you approach people is important—equally as important is when. Imagine if Alicia had tried to connect with galleries only a few days before the fair; they'd have been too busy to respond and would not have had time to interview her beforehand. If she had tried to reach out months in advance, they wouldn't know yet whether they wanted help or what kind of assistance they might need. Try to think from the other person's perspective and strategically consider when would be a good time to contact them. Take a look at social media, if they post regularly, to see what's going on for them and if they might be particularly busy or in a more open period.

This is a tip that we used to secure interviews with two major artists for *Create! Magazine*. While these artists might normally have been too busy to respond to our request or taken more time to get back to us, we noticed that both were coming out with books soon, so we figured that additional promotion of their projects incorporated within their interviews would be something of interest. Neither turned down the offer. A win-win on both sides!

In Five Lessons You Learn from Working in the Arts (page 191), Alicia mentions a job she wouldn't have gotten if an employee hadn't recently given her notice, which freed up an opening at the company. The backstory on this situation, however, is that she had recently stopped by to update them that she was looking for new opportunities and considering working in a gallery. Since you can't control anyone else's timing, put yourself in the position of getting your foot in as many doors as possible so that when the right opportunity does become available, you're present and ready for it.

Make It Memorable—in a Good Way

How do you want people to remember you? Smart, friendly, professional, accomplished? All of the above? Think about this, and then make it happen. You can't control what others will think about you, but you can use your personality, the way you talk, and even how you dress to promote yourself as the person you want to be seen as. The biggest part of this, though, is how you see yourself. Start there first, before expecting others to view you in a certain way. When you are confident about who you are, you will exude that and it will influence how others both regard and interact with you.

We have both struggled with how to gain confidence and fight self-doubt, but you have every reason to be proud of your creativity and your career. You are an artist and a unique individual, which means that nobody else can do exactly what you do! Share that with people and you'll definitely get noticed.

There can be a fair bit of negativity in the art world, between jealousy, greed, and a fine line between useful and malicious criticism, but don't get sucked into it. We both remember our interactions with these kinds of people, but not in a way that would ever make us want to work with them. Stay positive and encouraging. Likewise, always put forth your best effort, like Kat did when she was still working her various day jobs. If she had arrived late and acted poorly with clients, she would have burned her bridges and lost those connections. There are so many instances when we've noticed people cut corners or treat others in a disrespectful manner, and it's definitely memorable—but for all the wrong reasons.

> *"Meeting new people will inevitably lead you to even more connections, and your network can grow infinitely from there."*

Use Your Network to Network

While it takes a bit more effort at the beginning, networking does get easier as you progress. Not only will the practice help, but your network itself will begin working for you too. Meeting new people will inevitably lead you to even more connections, and your network can grow infinitely from there. For better or worse, the art world can be pretty small, but this can actually work in your favor if you make a few key connections to start with and then ask those people to help you meet others you might be interested to know.

If you're in a situation where the only person you know at a networking opportunity is the host or organizer, feel free to ask them if they wouldn't mind introducing you to or pointing out someone who might be a good person for you to meet. Try not to hover around them throughout the duration of the event, because they will likely be busy and need to mingle with everyone, but a quick request when you first arrive can help you navigate this scenario more smoothly.

With these new ideas and suggestions in mind, we hope you feel more confident and informed about networking in the arts. Really, there's little reason to be scared or nervous, because the more people you meet and get to know, the faster you're likely to grow and progress in your career. Even if not all of the contacts you make will help you advance professionally, you may meet lifelong friends, and that can be equally as rewarding. We're both so thankful for the network we've created thus far and wish you tons of success in finding your own.

TAKE ACTION

• Identify upcoming networking opportunities in your area, or ones that you're willing to travel to.

• Practice your elevator pitch and make sure that you can say it with confidence!

• Research contacts for cold emailing and draft a few tailored messages as templates. Once they are ready, send away!

• Start making new connections through multiple avenues using some of the ideas listed in the Ideas for Networking & Where to Meet People in Your Industry sidebar, and follow up.

IDEAS FOR NETWORKING & WHERE TO MEET PEOPLE IN YOUR INDUSTRY

Looking for ways to get connected and start growing your network? Here are some ideas for getting started:

• Volunteer at a museum, gallery, or nonprofit organization.

• Apply for an internship or apprenticeship.

• Sign up for a class, workshop, or creative business mastermind.

• Join an online artist community, such as THRIVE Art Studio or The Art Queens.

• Attend an industry conference.

• Visit an open studio event in your area.

• Go to artist talks and stay a little longer to introduce yourself.

• Invite someone you admire out for coffee.

• Check out gallery openings and First Friday events.

• Participate in artist-focused art fairs.

• Become an art blog or online magazine contributor.

• Look for artist Facebook groups to join.

• Start your own blog, podcast, or social media account for artists.

Navigating the Art Business World

THE DO'S AND DON'TS
OF APPLYING TO ART GALLERIES

One of the traditional markers of an artist's success is securing a gallery to represent their work. While it is by no means necessary to have a gallery, especially in recent years with more artists selling directly to collectors online, the right one can lead you to new opportunities that you might not otherwise have access to or would take longer to accomplish on your own. These opportunities may include getting museums to acquire your art, planning solo or group exhibitions, exhibiting at art fairs, and reaching a new set of collectors.

Finding a partnership that works for both you and the gallery is essential. It does take time and a fair bit of research, and the application process can be equally daunting, whether you have already sent out a hundred emails or are mustering up the courage to reach out to your first gallery. But it doesn't have to be overwhelming. Based on insider knowledge from working for galleries and our own previous experiences approaching this task as artists, we've put together the following tips on what to prepare before you submit, how to find the right fit for your work, and what to avoid when applying to galleries.

HOW TO PRESENT YOURSELF

Make a Professional Impression
As we discussed in Your Artist Website (page 9), it is important to use a simple, memorable domain name and email address. You'd be surprised by how many people send applications with websites or personal emails that do not include their names or aren't directly related to their art! Ensure that your first impression makes you look like a professional studio artist who is ready to take the next step and partner with an established gallery.

Showcase a Full Body of Work
While it may be tempting, don't jump the gun and try to submit before you're ready. Make a consistent body of work, at least fifteen to twenty pieces, viewable on your site. These pieces don't all have to be in the same medium, but they should demonstrate that you've put thought and effort into developing an idea, a technique, or a certain subject. Remember that a prospective gallery has to imagine what a full solo show of your work would look like. If you don't have many works posted on your website, the gallery owner might think that you don't have enough pieces to fill a solo exhibition in their space. In addition, showing off more of your work also gives the gallery a wider variety of your art to choose from, making it more likely that they will want to work with you.

HOW TO DECIDE WHERE TO APPLY

Make In-Person Visits

It's essential to research and compare galleries. Ideally, you should visit all the galleries you are interested in and talk to the owner or director in person to get a feel for whom you would be working with. Just like when you're job searching, you want the relationship with your gallery to be mutually beneficial. If you don't like the space or didn't connect with the staff, you'll be glad you avoided applying there.

Consider your must-haves in a gallery relationship. You might want to note if they regularly produce a catalog for their artists' exhibitions, if they are private versus open to the public, and which art fairs they attend, if any. Determine the things that are important to you, and don't waste time on applications to galleries that don't meet your requirements.

Don't be afraid to talk about contracts if your meeting was successful. Get all the important details on how they handle commissions, discounts, shipping fees, and framing costs, and how often they plan on exhibiting you both in their space and at offsite locations like fairs. You want to make sure that you agree with their terms before signing anything.

Tip:

Consult with a lawyer or someone you trust to look over any contracts. Ask your peers what they have experienced in their own gallery partnerships so you know what to expect and can identify anything a potential gallery is proposing that seems out of the ordinary.

Conduct Online Research

For those who can't visit galleries they are interested in, do some solid research online to find the best matches. Learn who they already represent. Visualize a group show with their artists and honestly answer this question: does my work fit the aesthetic? Read their artists' resumes to see where they studied and have exhibited. Do you have similar accomplishments or degrees? If you feel comfortable, ask what a few of their artists' works sell for. Are your prices comparable? You may even consider reaching out to the artists directly and asking for their opinion of the gallery. Of course, it is not likely an artist would bad-mouth the gallery representing them, but they could offer additional insight you would not otherwise find out from online research.

FINDING GALLERIES AS AN EMERGING ARTIST

It can be slightly more difficult—but not impossible—to find a gallery that specifically focuses on artists at the beginning of their careers. Try looking for galleries with a smaller project space or other dedicated area where they are often more willing to show emerging or experimental work. This is an easier way to get your foot in the door than asking to be represented outright. After you've shown with them, assuming it went smoothly, you can broach the subject of continuing to work together. You can also visit art fairs, which sometimes have a dedicated section of booths that represent emerging artists or are newer galleries that have been in business for fewer than five years.

Explore Social Media

Look closely at every gallery's website and social media channels. A quality gallery maintains their online presence using the same standards that they expect of yours: modern, clean, and up-to-date. Irregular posts or no new content for some time may simply be an indicator that they've been very busy, which is a good sign, but finding errors and broken links throughout the site could be red flags. Trust your instincts!

If a gallery is active on social media, it may seem like a good idea to reach out via a direct message or to tag them in your posts, especially if you already have a strong following of your own. But there are a few reasons why this is not recommended. First, many gallery social media accounts are run not by the director, but rather by an assistant or specialized marketing person. If this is the case, who knows who will actually see your message, if it will be responded to, or if it will be passed on to the person at the gallery in charge of acquiring new talent. You could easily be wasting time sending messages that won't help you connect with who you actually need to speak to.

Second, another important thing to keep in mind is that even if the right person does see your message on social media, they will likely go straight to your profile page first, rather than directly to your website. Your website gives a complete, professional overview of you and your work, but that is much harder to maintain via a Facebook page or Instagram account.

Continue ›

Why take that risk, even if you've worked hard to establish strong social media pages? For example, neither Facebook or Instagram makes it easy to share a resume, and it would take quite a bit of scrolling and searching for someone to figure out which works are available. Both of these undesirable issues underscore the idea that you need to put your best self forward on your first impression, which is more easily accomplished by getting a gallery to look at your website first.

Additionally, if the first time a gallery notices you it is because they see multiple posts you've tagged them in to get their attention, they will probably not be interested in working with you.

This comes off as too eager and is distracting. Remember that galleries use social media as a tool to build their brand too! Today, galleries, writers, and curators use Instagram often for scouting new artists, but best practice is to let them come to you. If you find someone you want to reach out to, we highly recommend using email instead of social media.

HOW TO INTRODUCE YOURSELF

Don't Just Show Up

Alicia worked at galleries where, on a weekly basis, artists just showed up with their portfolio. This simply is not the right way to start the conversation. If you arrive unannounced, you catch the staff off-guard and there is no guarantee that someone will be available to meet with you. It's extremely awkward and uncomfortable to have to turn artists away in this situation, so avoid putting a gallery in this position!

Similarly, exhibition openings or the first few days of an art fair are tough times for long conversations with a dealer because they are focused on their clients and closing sales. If you're visiting and notice a lull, however, certainly take the chance to meet them or request an appointment at a more convenient time. This way, when you follow up via email, you can remind them that you've already met. Be sure to always mention when and where you first connected so they remember you.

Look for Opportunities

Besides showing up to gallery openings, do look for other opportunities to introduce yourself. Attend art events in your community and you are likely to meet the people you want to work with organically. Practice speaking to others about your work confidently. Be ready with an elevator pitch that is short (one minute) and one that is a little longer (around five minutes or more) for when time allows for an in-depth conversation. Try your pitch out in front of friends, family, and peers first. Be concise, be memorable, and be confident. Make them want to represent you.

HOW TO APPLY

Don't Submit Unsolicited Applications

After checking out a gallery's website and reading it thoroughly, do not submit an unsolicited application if a gallery's website explicitly says that they are not currently looking for artists. Alicia worked at several galleries that noted they were not actively seeking applications and yet were still contacted by multiple artists each week! Thoroughly read a gallery's website to avoid making this mistake and wasting your time. Yes, the gallery may at least look at your work, but we've never heard of anyone securing representation this way. Not to mention, if their site specifically states that they are not looking, they likely will not even respond to your message. Your time could be spent much more wisely.

> *"Be concise, be memorable, and be confident."*

Galleries do not do this to be rude or because they don't care about new talent. Think about it from another perspective: If you were already represented by a gallery and they continued to take on more artists, you would have less opportunity to show and the gallery would focus less effort on selling your individual work. They only have a set amount of resources (staff, marketing outlets, budget, space, etc.), so wouldn't you want them to use as much of it as they can on you?

Though we personally avoid applying to galleries that aren't looking altogether, if it otherwise seems like the perfect fit for your work, our best advice is to see if you can get a face-to-face meeting with the director. Alicia does know of an artist who did this successfully, so if you're gutsy, go for it! This artist was able to build his case after participating in a few group exhibitions at the gallery, in which multiple pieces of his work sold.

Reading the gallery's website carefully can also help you put together a better application, which improves your chances of a successful outcome. We have received many requests from artists wanting to join the roster of our gallery, PxP Contemporary, since we launched in May 2019. When Alicia has reviewed work from potential new exhibitors, however, she has noticed a handful who submitted art outside our specified price range. This means that the artists blindly applied without even reading through the paragraph on our "About" page. Make sure to note any key details like this so that you don't make a simple mistake that will lead to a rejected submission.

Create & Send Your Application Package

Once you've found a great gallery accepting submissions, read their application instructions carefully, triple-check your materials, and have a friend look for typos or other missing information. If the gallery does not list specific instructions, send a brief email stating your interest with a link to your website, and attach your resume, a ZIP file of images, and your artist statement. For large files, you can use programs like Dropbox and WeTransfer, but be wary of sending multiple emails for the director to open. Ideally, you want to send a complete application in one message. Look on the gallery information page of their website to find the name and email address of the owner or manager so you can send your message directly to him or her.

Here's a template that can be tailored to you:

Dear [Gallery Owner],

I am writing [in reference to the call for artists listed on your website OR to submit my work to be considered for representation]. My current body of work [describe in one or two sentences]. I have exhibited most recently at [name notable exhibitions, preferably solo or two-person] and am part of the permanent collection of [list any notable institutions]. [Also mention relevant awards, recent press, residencies, or other gallery affiliations].

Please find attached my artist statement and resume, as well as a selection of my work. Additional pieces can be viewed on my website: [website address]. If you have any further questions, feel free to contact me at [list email, phone, or both]. Thank you for your time and I look forward to hearing from you shortly.

Kind regards,

[your name]

This example is on the formal side, but it gives you an idea of what to say to keep it simple and direct. Remember to note at the beginning when and where you met, if you had the chance to introduce yourself to them recently.

Be Patient & Follow Up

Try not to get frustrated when your application goes unanswered. Hopefully, a gallery will at least acknowledge your application, but they often do not. Alicia's general rule is that once she applies to something she "forgets" about it, rather than spends countless hours worrying or obsessively checking her email. If she hears back, hooray!—but if not, it doesn't feel as disappointing because she's already working on the next project or opportunity.

There will always be more chances to apply, and it may take time to find the right gallery for you. This doesn't mean that you shouldn't follow up though. It is appropriate to send a message a week or two after the initial submission to confirm if your application was received or if it is being reviewed. If you still don't receive a response, however, then it's time to move on. Feel free to try again in six months to a year, when you have new work to share.

FINAL NOTES

Alternative Models

As you go through the process of seeking gallery representation, we suggest that you also consider alternative models like co-op galleries. Depending on where you are in your career, it might be worth it to exchange a few sitting hours per month for the opportunity to show. Always read their agreements carefully to decide if the exhibition potential outweighs the membership fees and/or working requirements.

While we love traditional galleries, and Kat has experienced success with being represented, we also highly suggest looking into other avenues as well. We'll explore this topic further in Alternatives to the Gallery System (page 166), but it's worth noting that connecting with independent curators, art advisors, and interior designers can help broaden your client base as well. While most galleries sell to private individuals or those purchasing on behalf of an institution, a curator or designer might be looking for art to place in a corporate office, hotel lobby, restaurant, or department store, and some are tasked with finding artists for large-scale mural projects.

Most importantly, never underestimate the power of building your own personal brand! With a strong website and social media presence, you can start to make sales on your own.

Say Goodbye to Fear

Never let the fear of rejection hold you back. When Alicia was still in art school, she found a gallery in Philadelphia that focused on emerging artists. She compared her work to what they were already showing and thought she would be a strong match, but after letting doubt creep in, she talked herself out of submitting an application for a whole YEAR! Luckily, once she finally pushed her fear aside and applied, she heard back shortly after and was asked to bring in a few pieces for a final review. At the meeting, the gallery director decided to take all of the artwork she presented and she signed a contract on the spot. Sadly, the gallery eventually closed, but at the time, despite being overjoyed at the positive outcome, Alicia was a little disappointed in herself for giving in to her self-doubt for so long. Don't let that be you!

Now that you are armed with the necessary tools and information, go apply to amazing galleries and get represented. And tell us all about it when you do!

TAKE ACTION

- Make in-person visits to any local or regional galleries that might be a fit for your work.
- Find and research galleries online and read their websites thoroughly to ensure that they are a match.
- Introduce yourself at events and follow up to share your artwork.
- Put together a complete submission package that you can send to your list of potential galleries.

AIMING FOR REJECTION LETTERS

Yes, you read the title of this chapter correctly! It would be great if we could tell you that there is a secret for getting accepted to every show or gallery you submit your work to, but that simply isn't the case. By sharing the guidelines we set throughout this book, we seek to help you improve your percentage of successful applications. That being said, you will still receive a few—or even a lot—of rejections. Let's talk about why that isn't bad.

We've known too many artists (including ourselves) who see a rejection letter or email as a personal failure, and we have to change our mindset to understand that the two are not the same. Let's say you hear back from a juried show that you weren't accepted to. It can feel disappointing to some or devastating to others, making them feel as though their art isn't good enough or even that they aren't good enough because our art can be so personal and feel like an extension of ourselves. However, there are always numerous factors at play when a juror makes these types of decisions. It is often space that limits how many artists can be featured—whether in a show, a magazine, or a museum—and in this instance, the juror may have liked many artists, including you, but was forced to narrow their selection.

Getting rejected isn't the time to overthink and obsess over why you weren't chosen, even though we know it is easy to fall into this trap. Instead, we encourage you to cultivate a positive mindset that will allow you to keep applying to new opportunities with confidence. When you can do this, it won't matter why you weren't selected for opportunities in the past because you'll already be looking to the future. Not sure how to make this mental switch? We've got six tips for you.

SIX TIPS FOR ACCEPTING REJECTION & CONFIDENTLY MOVING FORWARD

Practice Compassion

Something that Kat often says is good to keep in mind: remember that whoever is making the selection is a person too—someone who has emotions, who is subjective, and who has a different personal and educational background than yours. Just because he or she may not connect with your work does not mean that others won't either.

When you receive a rejection letter, always respond graciously to the person or organization for their time and consideration. Even though your work wasn't right for this opportunity, a juror may keep you in mind for something in the future, so it's nice to leave a good impression. If you are submitting to a magazine or blog, your work may get published at a later time, or the juror will choose to share it on social media. We see this happen with *Create! Magazine* all the time.

Continue ›

Sometimes an artist has to submit up to five times before getting selected, and it's essential not to take your anger or frustration out on those who could potentially feature you. It's almost shocking the types of responses we sometimes receive from artists who weren't selected for the magazine, considering that the guest jurors are the ones who curate the work, not the staff! If you absolutely feel compelled to share your thoughts, carefully consider who you're addressing your message to—but it shouldn't really ever come to this point. Even if you are upset, taking a step back to give yourself a reality check on being rejected should help you realize that it's not worth burning bridges.

Ask for Feedback

If it seems appropriate, you can politely ask if the juror has any feedback as to why your work was not chosen. At worst, you might not receive a response—if you don't, just let it go. On the other hand, you might hear about what you can do to improve your applications or how the curator is already considering you for a future project, even though you weren't a fit for the current one. Most importantly, imagine if you learned that what was holding you back was formatting your images incorrectly or the juror not being able to read your resume. Wouldn't you want to know? Alicia has done this after unsuccessful job interviews, which then helped her land even better roles.

Believe That Better Things Are Coming

If you aren't receiving rejections, are you submitting often enough, or at all? It may feel like carving out time to be in your studio and complete work is the hard part, but putting yourself out there can be just as difficult, if not more so (we say this about networking too!). Don't let that stop you. Keep applying, and continue to seek new opportunities. Even if you have recently received a streak of rejections, stay positive that an even better acceptance will be coming soon.

When Alicia applied to four graduate programs for her MA in art history, she heard "no's" back from three of the schools on Wednesday, Thursday, and Friday of the same week and was also rejected from an internship program she had considered doing as a backup. As a result, she was in a funk all weekend, absolutely convinced that she wouldn't be going to grad school after all, and devastated that she no longer had any idea of what she would do next. Then, on the following Monday, she finally got an email that the last school had accepted her, and that was the turning point that led her to Philadelphia to start her career.

Be patient and trust that things will work out as they are meant to. The only way to break through to your next opportunity, dream exhibition, or media feature is by taking risks and putting yourself in the spotlight.

USE REJECTION AS FUEL

Rejection is often also redirection. Maybe the body of work you created just scratched the surface of what you are capable of and the "no" will force you to push yourself deeper into your studio practice. Having a healthy mindset around your acceptance rate will propel you forward, instead of causing you to shrink back in fear and disappointment. A dose of healthy self-reflection is sometimes necessary to help us grow and improve.

"The only way to break through to your next opportunity, dream exhibition, or media feature is by taking risks and putting yourself in the spotlight."

We've mentioned this before, but pushing yourself toward bigger challenges isn't always about achieving or completing them. Setting a higher standard for yourself automatically motivates you to level up, and even if you aren't accepted, you'll still improve more than if you never tried at all.

Ask yourself the following questions whenever you don't get an opportunity you really wanted:

- Did I put my best work forward?
- Did I use quality materials and photography for this particular submission?
- Did I follow the exact instructions to the best of my ability and apply on time?
- Are the selected works in a similar style to my own or does this organization have a different aesthetic than me?

Trust the Process

Early in Kat's career, she applied to numerous local and juried exhibitions. Even though she got a lot of "no's" in the beginning, a few opportunities emerged because of her willingness to put herself out there. For example, a year after an initial rejection, a curator invited Kat to a local exhibition. This event resulted in a sale and several meaningful connections. The woman in charge of organizing the event said she had kept Kat's work in the back of her mind for future opportunities ever since she first saw it. Be confident that there is a place for your work in the art world, even if you don't get your desired results right away.

Remember to keep your highest goals and visions in mind when you experience disappointment. As crushing as repeated rejection can feel, the more you focus on growing your creative skills, building a community, and making connections with your collectors, the more you will view opportunities as a bonus, and not a requirement for happiness and success. Trust your vision and know that you will eventually arrive at your goals, regardless of whether you experience disappointment, obstacles, or rejection. Release attachment to any outcome, and submit your work confidently to as many opportunities as you can, especially when you're starting off in your career.

Turn to Your Community for Support

Do you have a community of artists or other people who you can turn to for support? Sometimes it helps to be able to share with a friend that you were bummed you didn't get accepted into something you were hoping for. Surround yourself with others who can not only encourage you to continue moving forward after a setback, but also push you to be more resilient. Learn to brush off rejection letters. Better yet, aim to grow from them. If you're getting a lot of them, that's an indicator that you're doing everything you can to put yourself out there, and that effort will be rewarded in the long run. It sure has for us!

We've faced rejection on many occasions and know that those received from the opportunities we expected to get can be very disappointing. We try not to dwell on them for too long, because as many times as that has happened, we've also had other opportunities come up that we never dreamed of. Those pleasant surprises are what should motivate you. Aim for the rejection letters at first—to learn from them, to grow, to practice applying, and to eventually get over the fear of them. Soon enough you will get more acceptances to bigger and better things. You never know where the right opportunity can eventually lead you.

TAKE ACTION

- Make a list of potential galleries, juried shows, and publications you want to apply to.
- Create a monthly budget for opportunities with application or jury fees.
- Put together a list of reputable open calls that you can submit to for free.
- Make a goal to apply to [x] amount of galleries, publications, grants, etc. each month.
- Track your progress in a Google document or Excel spreadsheet.
- Take pride in the fact that you are getting closer to your goals, no matter the outcome!

ALTERNATIVES
TO THE GALLERY SYSTEM

Most of us are very familiar with the traditional gallery model, in which the artist's work is sold by a dealer and the artist is offered a percentage of the sale, ranging from 30 to 70 percent. Countless artists throughout history, and today, have achieved great success within this system, but it is not the only way for you to sell your art. In fact, we highly recommend that you don't rely solely on a gallery. There are several alternatives that can help you exhibit, sell, and promote your art both online and in person. The market is changing, and while many still benefit from selling their work through a gallery, many artists are also claiming their independence and using alternative ways to promote their work.

In this chapter, we offer a few ideas to get you started. If you've previously thought that the only way to succeed is to be represented by a gallery, you may want to consider these options in addition to, or instead of, a gallery. Even if a gallery is your ultimate goal, supplementing your sales by utilizing one or more of the following avenues can help you get noticed, earn more money, and make meaningful connections in the process. Kat experimented with several alternatives for years before she found gallery representation for her work. So don't worry if it takes some time to find your ideal setup.

DIRECT SALES & E-COMMERCE

The most obvious way to sell and promote your art is directly to your audience by opening an online shop through your website or using an app such as Shopify, Big Cartel, or a similar platform. We discuss all our best tips about setting up an online shop in Your Artist Website (page 9), but if you are starting out and don't have anyone else helping you sell your work, we recommend that you take charge of your sales (and success!) and launch a store.

For Kat, this was crucial in the early stages of her career. She offered affordable works on paper and small paintings several times a year. These sales added significantly to her income and helped her begin to build connections with clients who later invested in larger pieces. Our advice to help you make the most out of selling online is to share high-quality images of your art, provide detail photos and installation shots, keep your pricing consistent, and calculate packing and shipping costs in advance.

Be sure to cross-promote your work on social media, via your email list, and by running affordable ads on Facebook and Instagram. Remind people of your available work and create a sense of urgency by defining a limited sales period. This will inspire your buyers to take action. Don't be afraid to gently nudge your audience by posting on Instagram Stories and following up with interested patrons. Only a small percentage of users will see your posts, so let them know what you have to offer more than once in order to reach as many people as possible.

CO-OPS & ART COLLECTIVES

A co-op gallery or collective is a group of artists working together to run an exhibition space. Instead of a dealer or gallery director, the artists make decisions about what to show, how to utilize their space, and the best way to handle marketing efforts — together. These organizations may rent or own a traditional "white box" where they hold their exhibitions or have a space in a communal studio building. Members are eligible to participate in their regular group shows and can potentially pitch solo exhibitions to the board as well.

Co-ops generally require members to pay a monthly or annual fee that goes toward maintaining the physical space. You may also have to sit for gallery hours, assist during exhibition openings, and hold a position, such as director of marketing, treasurer, etc. If you are new to a community or just starting out, co-ops can be a good way to meet other artists in your area and get your foot in the door. Having the support of a co-op can be incredibly helpful for your career, but we always recommend that you continue to promote your work yourself as well.

Several years ago, Kat became a member of a Philadelphia co-op called 3rd Street Gallery. This experience helped her build her resume and exhibit more regularly in the city than she had previously. In the time that she participated in the co-op, she sold several works and made connections with local artists. It was worthwhile to join at that moment in her career.

Art collectives have a similar structure, but in many cases, members share a workspace and often exhibit together. There are now online art collectives that you can join or be invited to that help artists show their work in pop-up exhibitions, share a booth at an art fair, sell work online, and more. You can research local or online collectives based on your style of work, career experience, and other factors to see if this may be a good fit for you.

ONLINE ART MARKETPLACES

Online marketplaces for art have become popular over the past decade. Whether they allow all artists to submit work or have a curation process, these online platforms usually take a smaller commission percentage and handle the shipping logistics for you. The downside to selling your work through a large website, such as Saatchi Art, is that they are huge. Therefore, it's sometimes hard to stand out among the hundreds, or even thousands, of other artists.

Continue ›

If you are fortunate enough to catch the attention of the leading curators and get a feature on a blog or social media, it can certainly give your work a nice boost and result in sales. For Kat, this happened when Saatchi Art included her painting in one of their collections. She ended up selling several works to new buyers. However, we should note that it can be challenging to maintain collector relationships because you don't have access to the buyer's information. That is another thing to keep in mind when considering joining this type of platform.

The upside of selling your work through a website like Saatchi Art is the ability to create on-demand prints and offer this type of product to your collectors without investing any money upfront. An online marketplace could be a way for you to try this out if you have not previously sold prints and want to gauge interest from your audience.

POPULAR ONLINE MARKETPLACES

www.saatchiart.com
www.artfinder.com
www.artspace.com
www.etsy.com

BOUTIQUE GALLERIES

If you are worried about not receiving the proper attention for your work from a large online marketplace, you can look for smaller, private businesses, both online or brick-and-mortar, that will give you more focused attention. New niche galleries have been opening up recently that, although their objective is to sell art, differ from traditional galleries in many ways. For example, we know of galleries that only show women artists and others that, instead of maintaining a brick-and-mortar space, exist primarily online and curate pop-up events.

We saw the need for more quality, curated online spaces for artists, which inspired us to found PxP Contemporary in May 2019. Alicia curates group exhibitions and solo collections on the platform, often selecting work based around a certain subject or within a set price point. Whereas many galleries are still catching up to online sales, we've made it easy for collectors to place orders via our website and we believe that transparent pricing encourages sales among our clients. Other platforms we love are Collective 131, a gallery that shows contemporary women artists and was founded by Cassandra Fiorenza, and See You Next Thursday, a weekly art auction on Instagram run by Calli Moore.

NICHE RETAIL RESOURCES
www.pxpcontemporary.com
www.collective131.com
www.seeyounextthursday.com

INDEPENDENT CURATORS, CONSULTANTS, INTERIOR DESIGNERS & ADVISORS

Through juried exhibitions or becoming more involved in your community, you may start to meet art or related industry professionals who work independently. Working with a curator, advisor, designer, or agent may be a smart option to look into to broaden the scope of opportunities that you're exposed to, especially if you aren't with a gallery yet, or are still weighing your options to determine whether a gallery is the best fit for you. These roles usually take on different kinds of projects than a gallery would, and therefore can promote your work to new audiences and clients. Whether you're able to attract their attention or you reach out to pitch your work, we advise you to make sure that you are working with someone you trust. Ask around for references if you haven't heard of them before.

MIX & MATCH

We encourage you to research and experiment how to best present your work to the world. As you grow and evolve, you may find that working with a gallery no longer serves you, and one or more of the above outlets may be more suitable. If a gallery signs you, they may ask that you no longer sell your work through another gallery or online marketplace. Out of respect for your partnership, please abide by their contract if you agreed to the terms.

Remember that it's okay to move on and change your marketing tactics. You can combine several of these gallery alternatives to promote your art. Don't ever feel pressured to invest money into paid opportunities if you are not ready. Direct sales, co-ops, and online galleries are just a few ways to showcase your work. Remember, you can participate in artist-run art fairs, curate your own pop-up shows, hire an art agent, and host open studios as part of your strategy too.

TAKE ACTION

- Decide what the next step is for your career: do you need to have more physical exhibitions, push sales, or network?
- Research co-ops, online galleries, or other platforms that can help you achieve your next goal.
- Submit applications, if necessary, for co-ops and collectives, or write a compelling pitch about your work if you're reaching out to an advisor or curator.

SUBMISSION SAVVY: HELPFUL TIPS ON HOW TO SUBMIT, IMPROVE ACCEPTANCE RATES & AVOID COMMON MISTAKES

If you are anything like us, you probably apply to numerous opportunities each year, crossing your fingers and hoping to get selected for that dream exhibition in New York or to appear on the glossy pages of your favorite art magazine. Hopefully, you've heard back from a few with positive responses, but if not that's okay. Getting rejected means that you're putting yourself out there.

But what if there was one thing preventing your artwork from being chosen for that dream exhibition or publication? We're sure you'd want to know what it is, right? So we've put our heads together to come up with a few simple things you can do to increase your success rate.

TIPS FOR SUCCESSFUL SUBMISSIONS

From working in galleries and curatorial positions, and especially in our work with *Create! Magazine,* we see hundreds of art submissions each week that we would publish in a heartbeat, but often there is something that stops us. Double-check that you aren't unknowingly following habits that deter curators, publishers, and bloggers from featuring your work.

If you are having trouble getting your artwork noticed, fear not! Use the following basic tips and watch those acceptance letters multiply.

Tip 1: Use Great Photography — and No, It Doesn't Have to Be Expensive
This is the easiest mistake to fix! We spend so much time, energy, and resources making our work that it's a disservice to show less-than-perfect images of it. Nothing is more frustrating to a publisher or curator than seeing an incredible work of art captured with poor photography. They may love your piece, but they can't publish or won't exhibit it because of this issue. If there are tons of submissions to go through, they won't have the time to follow up with you and ask for a better photograph. Make sure you get it right the first time around so this one simple thing doesn't cut your chances of being selected. Here are a few solutions:

Get a professional's help. Hire or ask if you can trade a product you make or a service you offer with a photographer friend to get the best images of your work. Reach out to any alumni groups, if you went to college, to see if your colleagues are offering a good price first. Kat has personally traded works to pay for part of a photography package or worked out a payment plan during financially difficult times. Ask your friends and community for recommendations for the best value and quality! People around you are usually willing and happy to provide you with advice.

Invest in a camera and take the photos yourself. If you are unfamiliar with photography there may be a learning curve, but if you are eager to DIY, there are plenty of free videos and resources online to get you started. Kat uses a Sony Alpha a6000, which has been her favorite camera for the price. It is user-friendly, even if you are not a photography guru, and takes amazing quality photos of art, her studio space, and references. Explore other options and ask other artists in your peer group what they use to find the best price and quality for your needs.

Use your smartphone. Several artists that *Create! Magazine* previously published use their phones to take amazing photos of their work. With the camera technology in smartphones undergoing immense improvements over the last decade, you may opt not to spend money on a DSLR or other high-quality digital camera.

If you decide to use your smartphone, adjust your settings to the highest resolution and take photos during daylight hours or using a daylight lamp to get the best results. Remove any additional objects in the background if you're shooting a 3-D piece or installation image, and check that there aren't any distracting shadows or uneven lighting that will take away from your work.

For the majority of two-dimensional art it is best to crop your photo to the edge of your work when finished so that it is a clean image of your piece. If your work requires installation views and detail shots, make sure they are equally crisp and focused solely on your art. With the proper lighting and environment, you should get pretty strong photos of your work. If you know how to use photo-editing programs, you can also adjust your images to make them as close to reality as possible if your shooting conditions were less than ideal. Look specifically at how the colors, textures, and other details are depicted and compare them to the "real" thing to see if they match. Not only do you want your audience to see the most true and accurate representation of your art, but it can also save you headaches with unsatisfied clients or disillusioned curators if you put forth the effort to both take and present only the best-quality images.

Tip 2: Give Context by Including Basic Information

We can't tell you how many times artists have simply sent us an image or a selection of pieces with no descriptions, contact information, or a link to their site! More times than we can count, we would have loved to feature the piece, but had no way of reaching the person. Since we never publish or post an artwork image without credit, our hands were tied. Don't let this be you! Always write a polite greeting, include a brief introduction, and mention a way that the person you are writing can reach you if they need more details. Make it super easy for the person to follow up to increase your chances of a positive response.

Much of this issue specifically relates to artists applying via social media messages, which has become an increasing trend among young and emerging artists. We understand that it is much easier to shoot a simple DM to a gallery or publication you wish would feature your work than to look up their email or try to connect in person, but if you want them to take you seriously, it won't happen by sending an informal note on Instagram. (We explore better networking strategies and how to approach galleries in The Fine Artist's Guide to Social Media & Marketing section, beginning on page 99.)

Tip 3: Follow the Rules

When filling out application after application, the temptation to be lazy and recycle the same submission package is sometimes too great to resist. Don't give in! If the organization asks for the images to be labeled a certain way, do it! Ignoring their requests is an easy reason for them to nix

> *"Make it simple for whoever is reviewing your submission to want to feature your work."*

your application without even taking a proper look at it. Sometimes organizations use their directions as a test to see if people are paying attention and taking the opportunity seriously.

Make it simple for whoever is reviewing your submission to want to feature your work. We are all busy, so we all appreciate it when someone respects our time. Submission guidelines and rules are not there to make the process more tedious for you. Many systems that companies use require a specific labeling method or file format, so if they ask for a jpeg, send a jpeg, and don't reach out asking if you can send a png instead.

Follow the directions to the letter and only follow up with a question if something about the application process is truly unclear. Remember, if you can't bother to read and abide by their submission guidelines, why would they feel compelled to want to put their time, money, effort, and resources into supporting your work?

Tip 4: Be Part of the Community

This is especially helpful when it comes to local organizations and events—being a familiar face is always a good idea! Even simple gestures, like commenting on Instagram, reaching out to someone you admire for coffee (when it's appropriate), or showing up to art openings, increases opportunities for YOU to be involved in the future. The best practice is to do this with people and organizations you genuinely enjoy, instead of trying to get something out of it, because people can tell when your intentions are forced. By nourishing these relationships, online or in person, you inevitably plant the seeds to be considered for future opportunities.

We hope these simple tips will help you get more yeses and propel your art career forward!

THE ONE MISTAKE THAT KEEPS YOUR ART FROM BEING FEATURED

We've seen it happen time and again, and artists have asked us about this when considering what to submit to *Create! Magazine* or our gallery, PxP Contemporary. Think that including images from multiple series of works will double or triple your chances of being selected for that juried show, publication, or gallery you've dreamed of showing with? Well, unfortunately, that's not likely the case. We know that it's tempting to show off the range of your style and creative ability, but here's why we think this isn't the time to do so:

You want to demonstrate to the juror that you've taken the time to really develop an idea, push yourself, and stick to it!

When you focus on one subject for a while, you get a much better idea of what works and what doesn't, and this helps you build your creative voice. Always keep in mind that submitting your work is like leaving a first impression. If you submit pieces from two bodies of work it can give off the vibe that you don't quite know who you are yet as an artist or that you're not yet confident enough in either series to commit to it fully. You should focus on sharing work that excites you! Which paintings, drawings, sculptures, or (insert what you create here) are you most proud of right now? Those works are what you should be submitting!

If you are equally satisfied with several bodies of work at the moment, we still recommend only applying with one, or at least one at a time. The biggest issue with not doing so is that you leave it to the curator to fill in the blanks, assuming that they can or will. How is someone who is not familiar with your work supposed to imagine what the rest of the series looks like when they've only seen a few pieces from it? You know that a whole group of works exists that is as great as those you've submitted, but the curator does not. If they have to go through hundreds, or even thousands, of artist submissions, they won't always have the time to go looking through your website or Instagram account to see if you've made others like the one or two that they liked. Don't take that risk! Make it simple from the get-go and include a strong, cohesive body of work or do multiple submissions for each series you wish to be considered.

Sometimes, it's purely practical. For publications especially, it is difficult to consider an artist if they wouldn't be able to put together a consistent spread of their work. Each book, journal, or magazine has a distinct aesthetic, so make it easy for them to know that you are the right fit and to want to include your work. The same applies to a gallery, which has to make sure that your pieces could fill their space and look professional. No gallery would want their clients to walk in and be confused about whether the artworks on the walls were actually done by the same artist.

The gallery's job is to look out for its collectors, who come specifically for their curatorial expertise. Rather than show an interested client all the available pieces in the hopes that they end up buying something, a good dealer will work with them to find the one or ones that they love from a narrower selection of art based on their interest and budget. Showing a potential buyer too many options at once runs the risk of overwhelming them and losing the sale. Collectors do often want to see a variety of works, but their interest will be in a particular theme or style, so make sure each of your collections stays within those parameters.

Sometimes when you're excited about a new body of work you want to start submitting it right away. If you're wondering if you should start putting it out there, make sure you're ready by considering the following: Do you have enough work from this collection completed and photographed? If not, what's the rush?

Avoid submitting one or two new works with a few old ones—there will always be more opportunities to apply to. You can continue to submit entirely from an earlier series for now, if you want to keep building your resume and if there is no restriction from the organization on how recent the work must be. On the other hand, sometimes it's nice to simply allow yourself the time to fully dive into this great new idea and finish a solid collection of artwork before thinking about exhibition or publication submissions.

Of course, none of this is to say that you have to stick to the same thing forever. On the contrary, it would be hard to have repeat collectors if your work never changes. Your gallery, if you have one, and your collectors simply want to see you continue to grow and will support you along the way!

So, if you're making abstract sculptures, but have always wanted to try painting birds, go ahead. Ultimately, you have to DO YOU. But when it comes time to apply to that next opportunity, we hope you'll consider the provided tips and give yourself the greatest chance of being selected!

SUBMITTING TO BLOGS, MAGAZINES & OTHER MEDIA OUTLETS

Have an important solo or group exhibition coming up or another exciting event that you want to promote? In an ideal situation, the gallery or venue that you're working with will handle the majority, if not all, of the marketing related to the show, but you should also make the effort to help create buzz and raise awareness for your art. Getting featured by the media can have many benefits, aside from getting visitors to a show. The more marketing you do beforehand, the more likely you are to make sales, meet potential clients, and have influential press coverage. Both the galleries and the collectors that end up buying your art love to see that you've been featured in the media, as it validates their investment in your work. Even if it's a small blurb in a local newspaper, take pride in the acknowledgement and don't be shy about announcing it to your network!

How to Connect with and Pitch to Media Outlets

Using the following simple guidelines, we'll help you navigate when, where, and how to pitch your story or event to a variety of media outlets. There's never a guarantee that you'll get a response, but following these tips will ensure that you're setting yourself up for the best chance of success.

When to approach media outlets:

- To announce an exhibition or event
- To promote a new body of work, collaboration, or project
- To share that you've won an award or grant
- To discuss a meaningful residency experience
- To mention that you've been purchased for an institutional or corporate collection
- To build your resume

Tip:

If you're an emerging artist you might not have awards or shows to promote yet. Not to worry! There are tons of blogs, newspapers, and magazines that are happy to feature artist interviews, regardless of where the artist is in their career. Simply focus on outlets that have highlighted newer artists in the past and include a unique perspective about why they should be interested in your art in your pitch.

Examples of media outlets to send your information and images:

- Blogs covering art, culture, design, interior design, and creative business
- Magazines about similar topics, or think outside of the box to come up with more! Sometimes artists are featured in fashion, lifestyle, and architecture magazines too.
- Local newspapers
- Art podcasts

You can find many of these outlets by searching online. Look for the contact or submit page of each publication or podcast and take note of whether they have any specific directions on what to include with your pitch. If not, you can reach out to the general email address, but do try to find a name to address your message to.

Another way of locating these press opportunities is to pay attention to where other artists in your community or on a similar career level have been featured. Mine other artists' resumes and peek at their press sections to find out which blogs and magazines have written about them. You can also search social media hashtags to find additional media outlets you might not yet be aware of, or art writers to reach out to.

The most important thing to remember is that you need to make it very simple for PR organizations to share your work. Always tailor your cover letter. At *Create! Magazine*, we can tell when we get one that is generic, and it doesn't usually result in a positive response. Make sure that you've read at least a few previous articles or listened to old podcast episodes to really confirm that it is a fit for you! You're wasting valuable time if you apply too broadly or don't bother to learn about the media outlet you are submitting to beforehand.

What to include in your pitch:

- An introduction to your work and interesting summary of why they should feature you, including:
    - All important dates and locations, if you're pitching an event
- A press release, if you chose to create one, attached as a separate document
    - Look for templates online if you're unsure of how to write one
- A selection of high-quality and high-resolution images
    - Organize an image folder in Dropbox, Google Drive, or WeTransfer and link to it in your message
- Your contact information for where you can be reached

Follow up after a week or more if you have not heard back, but keep working on new opportunities in the meantime and don't obsess over the outcome. Programs exist that let you track whether your emails have been received and opened, but we think it's better to forget about it once you've submitted, rather than worry over if and when you'll get a response. Your time is better spent on sending more pitches or making great work!

As your art develops and you get the hang of putting together excellent submission packages, you will get featured more and more. One article or podcast interview might suddenly snowball into three, five, or ten additional media requests.

> *"As your art develops and you get the hang of putting together excellent submission packages, you will get featured more and more."*

We have been fortunate to experience incredible PR opportunities for both our individual artwork, the magazine, and the gallery in the past decade precisely because we've used these steps. The key is to not give up and keep putting yourself out there!

If you're still feeling a bit lost, we've created two submission pitch templates to get you started. Adjust these templates so that they are specific to your own work or event. Also make sure you're writing from the heart, and only apply to organizations you genuinely respect and where you'd be thrilled to be featured to achieve the best results.

SUBMITTING TO BLOGS, MAGAZINES & OTHER MEDIA OUTLETS

[SUBJECT LINE]

Dear [name],

My name is [name] and I [web link + a short description of what you do]. I am a big fan of your organization and love [include something specific you admire or a past event you attended].

I would like to invite you to [exhibition or event] if it is of interest to you and your team.

The show dates are: [exhibition date, time, and location].

Please find a press release for the event attached below, and you can view images from the show here [link to Dropbox or a webpage].

If you have any questions or would like to conduct an interview, feel free to contact me at [website, e-mail, and phone number].

Thank you so much for your time and consideration!

[Signature]

Submission Letter for Blog or Magazine Pitch

If you see that the media outlet you're applying to specifies that your message should begin with a certain subject line, don't forget it! This will help them easily see your message and may even be a small test to make sure that you were paying attention to their directions. Otherwise, the subject line shouldn't be something you stress over. Keep it simple with a phrase like "Introduction to the work of [your name]" or "Abstract sculptor interview pitch." Trying to be too catchy or using all-caps can hurt your chances of the recipient seeing your message as email providers may flag it as spam and automatically reroute your note into the junk folder.

[SUBJECT LINE]

Dear [name],

My name is [name] and I [web link + a short description of what you do]. [Share your brief bio + why their audience would love your work], so I thought you might be interested in my recent series [insert an interesting fact about your new work] for [blog or company name].

I've included a selection of images for you to review [include your website and a link to Dropbox or a place where they can easily download your work] in addition to my artist bio and statement, which are attached below.

Please let me know if you need anything else. Thank you in advance for your consideration!

You can reach me anytime at [website, e-mail, and phone number].

[Signature]

WRITING EMAIL SUBJECT LINES

Crafting a subject line that ensures your email will be opened can be challenging. Many people's inboxes are flooded daily with excess messages. You want to be sure that your email is easy to spot and identify. Remember to keep your subject lines succinct and informative.

Here are a few examples of subject lines you can adapt to your own needs, depending on the situation. Please be sure to review submission guidelines for each organization to make sure you follow any rules regarding subject lines and email content.

Exhibitions and Events

Opening (Tonight, Tomorrow, This Week, etc.): [Your Exhibition Name and Brief Description]
You Are Invited: [Your Exhibition Name and Brief Description]

Introducing New Work

Exclusive Collector Preview: [Medium or Description of Work] by [Your Name]
New Print Release: [Description]
Collection of [Work Description] Inspired by [Travel, Event, etc.]

Request for Blog or Media Coverage

[Editor's Name], Might you consider covering [Event or Exhibition]
[Your Name and Exhibition or Event] Press Release

For General Submissions

Artist Submission: [Your Name] [Medium]
Introducing Work by [Your Name]

Examples of media outlets to send your information and images:

- If you're not already, get active in your community! Start interacting with artists, galleries, and companies you admire on social media, and attend art openings to start building relationships and creating opportunities to show your work.

- Make a list of where you will submit your art and note any details about each application's requirements.

- Draft letters and templates for media pitches to save time, but always tailor each submission to the specific blog, podcast, or company you are applying to.

FINDING & BUILDING RELATIONSHIPS WITH COLLECTORS

The second most important part of making art sales, after having great work to offer, is being able to find your ideal collectors. We know that this can feel like a major challenge, but if you've already committed to creating a strong and consistent body of work, priced your art fairly, and begun promoting yourself online as well as through exhibitions and media features, you are well on your way to building a prospective client list.

IDENTIFYING YOUR AUDIENCE

Who Is Your Audience?

Having a strong body of work, pricing your art fairly, and promoting yourself are the first steps, but in order to take it to the next level, start thinking about the specific people who may be interested in your art. If you aren't starting from scratch and have built up a small following online and with an email list, look through both and see if you notice any similarities, such as where these people live, their ages, estimated income level, and any interests or hobbies that they enjoy besides art. These are incredibly valuable bits of information that you can then utilize when you do targeted ads on social media.

Let's say you find out that a sizable portion of your audience also enjoys something like cooking—you may also consider pitching your work to culinary blogs and websites or reaching out to ask about their advertising packages. There are plenty of trade magazines you could also try to have your work featured in, or try to think about any local boutiques specializing in home goods where you could potentially mount an exhibition. Consider doing a brand collaboration or giveaway promotion. Focusing your marketing efforts on art publications, podcasts, and blogs will help elevate your status within the industry, but allow yourself to think bigger too. There are many art lovers who have never set foot inside a gallery. Find creative ways to make sure that the people most likely to be interested in your work will see it.

While it is great to work with clients who are already seasoned collectors, artists need to be more proactive about reaching new potential buyers. Be excited about the opportunity to teach them about how they can ask for pricing and payment plans or consult you on framing options. Having a great sales experience with you will help them fall in love with the process and then hopefully they will continue making new purchases, whether from you or other artists in the future. Think about it like paying it forward. For clients who come to you already having bought art in the past, they continue to do so because of their positive experiences from artists who worked with them before. Make sure you continue that trend so that everyone, even if not you directly, will benefit from it in the future.

Tip:

If you are brand new and don't know your audience yet, ask yourself who you think will connect most with your work, and start promoting yourself with that response in mind.

Where Does (or Would) Your Audience Buy Art?

This seems a rather obvious question, but thinking about it may actually spark a few new ideas. Perhaps you've made most of your sales from a few gallery shows, your website, or inquiries on social media. Are there other similar galleries in your city, in other cities, or online that might reach a similar client base as those who have expressed interest and bought your work before? Are there other websites that might help you connect with your ideal collector, including artist directories like All She Makes[8] or art marketplaces like Saatchi Art? Finally, after reading the chapters on social media in the The Fine Artist's Guide to Social Media & Marketing section (beginning on page 99), have you identified ways to expand your outreach on Instagram, Facebook, and other platforms?

As mentioned before, you should also try to think of as many other options for where you can sell your artwork as possible. These options can be art-related, such as hiring an agent, hosting an open studio, or applying to a fair, or it might be something different, like showing in a restaurant or cafe!

Why Do They Buy Art?

Artists often do not consider the motivations for collectors to buy art as much as they should. The more specific you can get on the reasons why your clients choose to purchase your work, the higher chance you have of finding other people like them. We all love the art-buying regulars who have a romantic view of collecting and buy because they truly enjoy supporting contemporary, living artists and couldn't imagine not having art surrounding them in their home. These people are likely more traditional clients whom artists reach by working with galleries, advisors, and, if they are comfortable buying from artists directly, through a polished website and social media presence.

Other collectors are interested in aesthetics and design because they want a certain look for their space. Seek out interior designers, architects, and home decorators whose portfolio shows residences, hospitality, or office areas where you think your artwork would be a great fit. Perhaps include one or a few professional digital mockups of how your pieces would look on the walls, if you have the skills to do so and feel confident enough that they are indeed a strong match.

8 *All She Makes* is a curated directory for women artists worldwide: www.allshemakes.org.   *Continue ›*

Some people buy artwork when it is related to a charity they are passionate about. You probably won't make a lot of money this way, so only do it sparingly and with causes you believe in too, but see if you can donate to any benefit exhibitions or auctions. Even though the client who purchases your work via one of these events will get it at a discount, you'll be reaching a new audience, and this collector may come back to you again down the line.

Finally, if you pay attention to auction and art market news, you'll know that the investment potential of art is a major driving force for numerous collectors. You may not encounter this very much through selling your work on your own, but it is not unheard of for some people to ask why your work is worth what it is and if you think its value will increase over time. These collectors tend to buy primarily at auction, through an advisor, or high-end galleries, but you may run into them by attending upscale art events. Try not to pass up the opportunity to go to a charity gala, gallery cocktail party, or major museum exhibition opening if you can afford it. Sometimes having friends in the industry pays off and you'll be given a free invite! Don't be shy about politely inviting anyone of interest to your studio, as long as you're not pushy about it and give them the opportunity to decline.

What Kind of Marketing Appeals to Them?

Have you spent enough time tracking which kinds of ads or marketing have been most successful for you? If not, take time now to do so. You may find that you need to focus on more Instagram ads or email campaigns, because those usually result in new sales or inquiries for you. When you are starting out, try multiple options at a time to see which avenues work best. As we have discussed before, if your audience skews younger, they're more likely to find your art online on your website or through social media platforms. Older clients tend to prefer Facebook and emails, and they also read print magazines and newspapers. Especially in the beginning, don't discount any form of marketing until you try it. From postcards and stickers to flyers and banner ads on blogs, you never know what may work best for you.

You should also never underestimate the power of referrals. Having even one or two of your clients tell a friend about your work can lead to sales, new opportunities, and more. Help this process out by spending time each month networking and meeting new people both in the arts and in different fields! Revisit Networking 101 for Artists on page 142 for tips and advice.

COMMUNICATING WITH CLIENTS

Once you've located your ideal collectors, you'll naturally want to initiate conversations with them on social media, via email, or in person—and they will as well. For clients you meet in person at art fairs, studio visits, and other events, the same simple steps from networking apply: Be professional, confident, and polite when discussing your work and negotiating a sale. Try to gauge interest by how intently the other person is listening to you and if they are actively participating in the conversation. If they seem excited, then keep moving your discussion along and suggest that they look at specific pieces more closely or ask if they have a budget in mind.

When you receive inquiries via email, try to respond as soon as possible. Dragging out the process of closing a sale can cause the client to lose interest. Even if they only sent a one-line note asking about the price of a specific piece, it never hurts to send back a reply with a proper salutation and a "thanks" or "kind regards" before signing your name. We also highly suggest asking if they'd share where or how they found out about your work.

Depending on what the inquiry was about, make sure to answer it fully, and try to imagine any other related questions they may have and proactively answer those as well. Being one step ahead can save time, help close sales, and demonstrate that you are an experienced and savvy seller. To help clients who are interested in your work in general, you can ask about their budget or any size, style, and color preferences they may be searching for. If a potential buyer asks about a particular work, focus on that one by sharing any noteworthy news, awards, and exhibitions or what inspired it. Only share additional works if they are similar or would go well with this piece.

Either attach a document with images and information about your art or include the details about the work(s) in the body of the message itself, and then attach the images to your email. You should include at least one primary view of the full artwork cropped to the edges, and if you have a few detail shots you can share those too. It is sometimes helpful for the client to visualize the work in a space, so if you have a rendering or Photoshopped image of your painting or sculpture in an interior space or an install view from a gallery exhibition, send that along! Alicia has closed many sales by creating a mockup of what a piece would look like in the desired space with a photo provided by the client. Feel free to offer this service if you think it will help!

Once a customer comes back to you expressing that they are seriously considering a work, discuss framing or other display options for three-dimensional art, how you handle shipping and insurance, which forms of payment you accept, payment plans, certificates of authenticity, or any other sales-related questions they may have.

Clients on Social Media

You can certainly go through the full process of making a sale through social media, but we urge you to try to move the conversation to email as early as you can. You want to collect this valuable information so that even if the person doesn't make a purchase at this time, you'll still be able to reach them later on. Much of the same rules as communicating via email apply. Keep your messages concise and include all necessary and relevant information, but stay friendly and don't get too discouraged if the other party doesn't respond. Usually, buyers who reach out to you via email are more serious than those who contact you through a Facebook or Instagram message, though that's not always the case!

The Biggest Secret to Closing Sales

Life happens, and as interested as someone may be in your work, other things may come up that distract them. You absolutely have to follow up with potential buyers in order to make more sales. Some people may be waiting for another person to agree on a work, a new house to be finished, or their first check to come in from a new job, so don't automatically assume that if you don't receive a response from your first email that they are no longer planning to buy from you. At the same time, don't get too overzealous here. Send a first friendly reminder between a few days to a week later—you can make the excuse that you simply want to make sure they received your previous message. You can follow up again a week or two after that, but we don't suggest reaching out again after that.

Tips on Negotiating

There are clients who are direct, know what they want, and will buy right away, while others need a bit of convincing. For the latter, consider how you want to handle negotiating in advance so that you're not fumbling on the spot and end up giving up more than you are comfortable with or losing a sale that you could have saved. Simple things to offer include a 10 percent discount, free shipping, or framing if you can afford to handle those costs. You can also be flexible if a client is purchasing more than one work at a time.

Because we spend a great deal of time and energy creating our work, it can be especially frustrating when a client is stubborn about accepting your quoted price or a sale falls through, but try not to take it personally. You may have also heard "your work is too expensive." If you receive a comment like this, here are a few responses you can use! We created this list based on one from a free downloadable PDF from Artwork Archive called "An Artist's Guide to Pricing Consistently & For Profit."

1. Have you purchased art before?

Don't always assume that someone is being rude when they tell you your work is too expensive. As we noted earlier in this chapter, take advantage of the opportunity to teach new art buyers when you can.

2. Would you like to know more about my process?

If you use expensive materials or your work is detailed and a lot of time goes into making each piece, explain that to the client so they can better understand your pricing.

3. I have been in the business for X years, and my prices have been raised over time to follow the progression of my career.

Especially if you are young or look younger than you are, others might incorrectly guess that you haven't been making art for very long and be confused by the rates you charge. Share notable accomplishments, awards, media features, and more to give a fuller picture of your successful career as an artist thus far!

4. My pricing structure is based on X and Y.

If you used the pricing formulas we described in How to Price Your Art (page 54), you can talk about this and how exactly you come up with the amount you sell each piece for.

5. You could easily break this down by paying in installments. Would you like to set up a payment plan with me?

Spending $1,000 at one time can be a lot of money for your clients, but spreading it out in two payments of $500 or four of $250 could be much more manageable for them. Explain that they can make deposit and then split the remaining balance evenly over the next two to six months (or more) depending on their preferences.

6. Can you share what your budget is? I'd be happy to try to work with what you have available to spend.

Knowing what they are willing to spend will help you find a piece that is within reach and that they won't feel uncomfortable buying.

7. Thank you!

This may seem like an odd reply, but it may surprise your prospective buyer in a good way. It shows confidence, and that will earn you respect—even if it also results in a skeptical look.

8. My prices are firm. I have less expensive (sketches, prints, etc.) if you're interested in seeing those instead.

In some cases, you just won't be able to come to an agreement on the original work of art the client was interested in. Try to redirect the sale to something they can afford.

Can you think of any other ways to respond?

WHAT TO REMEMBER WHEN MAKING SALES

Hearing that a client has agreed to purchase a work from you is always very exciting! So what should you do next? First, make sure that you have all necessary information from them, including their full name, email address, and ideally a phone number. Also make sure that you know the final price agreed upon. When you are selling online, you'll put together an invoice and have them pay in whatever method you accept and they prefer. If you are making a sale in person, you likely won't have time to create an invoice on the spot, so write down their contact information in a place you'll be able to find it again later and take the payment. You can tell them you will follow up with an official invoice later, unless they say they don't need one. We recommend making one for your files anyway, even if that is the case. Don't forget to charge them any taxes or additional shipping and framing costs.

Once payment has been finalized, you can wrap the artwork for them to carry home or pack it securely for shipping. Try to have the piece shipped out in a timely manner, and send the client the tracking number, as well as which mail carrier you used, so that they can check on the status during transit. Ask if they have any special requests, such as if they need it to arrive before they leave for vacation or if they would like it with or without a signature upon delivery. Always remember to add insurance!

Tip:

If the customer is paying in installments, it is common practice to wait until the piece is paid in full before sending it to them. However, this is up to you. If you feel that the client is trustworthy, you can send it after they have paid a deposit or at least 50 percent of the sale price.

Finally, you'll want to check in when the piece has been delivered to make sure that it arrived safely and that they love it. You can also ask for photos when it is hung. If you haven't done so already, add them to your mailing list so that they can stay informed of future exhibitions, new works, sales or promotions, and other events.

If, for some reason, the collector does not end up liking the work, you should already have a set protocol in place. Generally speaking, neither Kat with her own art nor Alicia with our gallery offers returns or refunds (unless the work was damaged or lost). However, we are very clear and upfront about this from the beginning, and if you want to operate this way, you must be too. Perhaps you offer credit toward another work instead, which is what we would do. If you are willing to accept returns, you should also make sure the client is aware of who is responsible for the cost of shipping the piece back to you. Hopefully, this situation won't happen to you or will only rarely occur, but when it does, try to navigate it professionally in order to remain on good terms with your client.

USING CUSTOMER EXPERIENCE DURING SALES

We all know that giving collectors a great experience when they work with you is crucial for growing your business and maintaining relationships with them over time. Can you remember the last time you had a really positive interaction with a company? It might take a bit of thinking, but you'll likely be able to more easily recall a bad experience. Keep that in mind as you negotiate and make sales. One wrong move can leave a bad impression and you could lose that client for life. This is not meant to scare you, however—most people are reasonable and will forgive mistakes. That being said, strive to always have excellent sales from start to finish so that you can ask them for testimonials for your website or referrals to other potential clients, and, of course, so that they become a repeat collector.

HOW TO STAND OUT

Here's a list of ideas for how you can stand out and provide a great experience that will leave people wanting to work with you again!

• Be friendly and professional in your interactions.
• Offer special discounts or deals on occasion.
• Ship as quickly as possible, and consider upgrading shipping speed.
• Invest in quality packaging that adds personality.
• Add a handwritten thank-you note.
• Email them afterward thanking them again for the purchase.
• Solve any issues that may arise in a timely fashion.
• Make the overall process easy for the client.

MAINTAINING LONG-TERM RELATIONSHIPS

One of the most rewarding aspects of being an artist is finding a person who becomes a supporter of your work for many years. They may start with a smaller work, then invest in more expensive pieces as time goes on. Make sure that you express appreciation for them. You can do so by sharing your accomplishments and staying active on social media. These clients will be excited to see that you have continued to grow and develop your career, both for you personally and also because it adds value to the art they purchased.

Also, remember to send out updates via your email newsletter. You might consider doing specialized content for previous collectors only that shares "VIP" sales, limited discounts, and invitations to events, such as artist talks or open studios. Always forward information about your forthcoming shows so that they can reconnect with you and see your new art! Even if they are not local to where you are exhibiting, they may want to suggest that a friend attend, or the most dedicated fans may be willing to travel there anyway. Alicia's favorite tip is to follow up individually if you are really excited about a new piece that you think would go well with what they purchased before or that they would like. It takes courage to do this, but being bold can pay off!

Share your gratitude for your collectors in other ways that you think are appropriate. They allow you to keep doing what you love to do! We both also write regular thank-you posts on social media and give hugs when we finally get to meet our clients in person. Do what feels authentic to you—we're sure your clients will love it!

TAKE ACTION

- Define your audience and ask yourself questions like: Where do they buy art? Why do they buy art? What kinds of marketing appeal to them?

- Respond to client inquiries in a timely fashion and include all relevant information. Try to anticipate their needs and be proactive about answering questions.

- Don't forget to follow up!

- Decide how you want to handle responding to "Your artwork is too expensive." Use one of our sample replies, or come up with your own.

- Make a plan for smoothly executing sales, and brainstorm ideas that will help your customer service stand out from the rest.

- Express gratitude to your clients so that they remain loyal customers and hopefully repeat collectors over the years. Ask for testimonials and referrals from those who had a positive experience buying art from you!

FIVE LESSONS YOU LEARN FROM WORKING IN THE ARTS

ADVICE FROM ALICIA

From galleries and museums to art fairs and an auction house, I've experienced a lot in my early career in a diverse assortment of jobs within the art world. I've seen the good, the bad, and the very bad (to borrow from one of our favorite contemporary art critics Jerry Saltz), but I also know that I wouldn't trade it for anything.

I've learned some important lessons over the past ten years, and the following five are some of the most valuable. While working in the arts as basically everything but an artist is a completely different experience, I'm sure you'll find much that relates to your own creative career path.

Lesson 1: Value the Journey over the Destination

I was certainly fortunate to have had a really supportive mother who encouraged me to pursue my interests, study fine art in college, and work in the arts despite not being familiar with this industry at all, or certain that I would find job security. Yet, I also dealt with my fair share of naysayers and skeptics who were sure I'd never make any money and questioned what I could do with an art degree.

Nowadays, I think this perspective is slowly beginning to change as more people choose to start their own businesses and become creative entrepreneurs, but there is often still a limited view of what an artist is versus what they can be. I'm glad, looking back, that I realized I didn't have to define myself according to these beliefs. I knew that I wouldn't be stuck in one job forever if I didn't like it. Even if I wasn't fully aware of it at the time, I always had a variety of opportunities available to me and, more importantly, the chance to make new opportunities happen for myself.

It might seem crazy to have jumped from web and social media management to ecommerce at an auction house, or from collections work for museums to art consulting for a major arts media company. However, the skills that I learned along the way were almost always transferable to subsequent roles and have also become invaluable for my current work. Though I struggled at times, occasionally juggling two, three, or even four different jobs to make ends meet, it was worth it to persevere. Along this nonlinear path, I found out what my strengths were and what I most enjoyed doing, which ultimately led me to where I am today.

Lesson 2: It's Not Always What You Know

Of all the positions I've had, fewer than three were ones I got from simply applying to a job posting online. I've been connected to the vast majority of new opportunities through referrals or networking. It makes sense, as companies prefer to work with people others have recommended, or that they've had a good experience with previously. This can make looking for a job a bit more difficult, but not impossible. So, first and foremost, don't give up if this is the career you really want. Smaller museums and galleries may not list open positions online, so it's especially crucial that you meet people in your community and share what type of work you're interested in doing so that if they hear of a great open position they can both put in a good word for you and tell you about it!

"Who you know" also refers to maintaining your professional relationships as much as making new ones. Try not to burn bridges, unless the situation absolutely necessitates it, and seek positive mentors to help guide you and advise you on your next steps. Sometimes it only takes meeting one person in your career to change your life. I've had several very influential teachers, professors, and employers throughout my career who I have been able to turn to not only for professional advice, but also sometimes personal guidance.

Lesson 3: Expect (& Effectively Deal with) the Unexpected

You've heard it before and have likely experienced it firsthand: expect the unexpected. When something goes right, you don't get any credit, but if something goes wrong, you get 100 percent of the blame. When working with big clients or important curators, there are often high expectations. While you want everything to go smoothly, of course, nothing is perfect and mistakes happen — whether or not it is your fault or you could have done anything to prevent it.

In a few of my first jobs, I used to dread having to deal with "fires" at work. I would feel overwhelmed and afraid of inevitably getting yelled at. While it isn't fun and I hope you don't have to deal with others who resort to this means of expressing their feelings, I now know that I was taking everything too personally. Sometimes anger may be directed at you even when it's not about you, so learn to brush it off and get back to the task at hand. Luckily, as I matured professionally, I began to realize that tackling big problems on my own wasn't scary, and solving them was really empowering! Even if you aren't thanked for successfully dealing with a tough situation, celebrate your victories. These are the moments when you really grow, develop new skills, and become a stronger person. Cheers to that!

Lesson 4: Make Your Own Definition of a Hard Day's Work

A big part of people's uncertainty about what artists are and what they do is underestimating how difficult being a creative or working in a creative field can be. When you are actively making art, it is likely as physically taxing as it is mentally and emotionally draining. But outwardly, people only see that you work in a studio or at home, have the freedom to start or stop whenever, and don't have a boss breathing down your neck. What they don't see is that as an artist, you're simultaneously acting as the CEO, Director of Marketing, Social Media Manager, Customer Relations Associate, Shipping Coordinator, Accountant, and more of your own business!

We often feel pressured to take on too many additional responsibilities and accommodate others because our schedules are more flexible, but don't let others make you feel like your work isn't important. When doing creative work is your profession, set aside certain times where it is always the priority. Despite common conventions, you don't have to put in eight hours a day in order to be productive. Sometimes spending four solid hours in the studio, or varying your hours on different days is more effective.

Another crucial part of this lesson is that you deserve breaks! Anyone else guilty of checking the clock and realizing that it's somehow 3 p.m. and you completely missed lunch? Oops! Trying to do everything, all of the time, will lead to burnout. I used to do this, and as a result would get sick frequently. Take mental health days, go for a walk, meditate for ten minutes, listen to your favorite podcast, or read a book for fun. Feel free to do whatever you need to do to clear your head and get refreshed, whether it's a little break during the day or a longer vacation from work. Often, the time when I can unplug is when I find new inspiration!

Lesson 5: Timing Is Crucial

There was one job early on in my career for which I sent in my resume, but heard back from the employer that someone with my experience wasn't what she was looking for at the moment. I went on vacation right afterward and upon landing and checking my voicemails, I had a message asking if I was available to come in for a trial period the following week! As it turns out, shortly after I left for my relaxing travels abroad, one of her employees had put in her notice. Sounds lucky, right? Well, sort of. Going back a little further, I had already been an intern for four months the previous year, and I made sure to stay in touch. When I was looking for a job, I mentioned that I was starting to search (never asking directly to be considered), and she told me to send along my resume.

Like in this case, I think there are many times when you have to do some legwork beforehand to make sure that you'll eventually end up in situations that work out in your favor. Being in the right place at the right time isn't always by luck.

Likewise, you never know when a great, new opportunity might present itself. Hopefully, it's when you're ready and available to accept and dedicate yourself to it. Oftentimes, however, it's not. We are definitely in an industry that can feel like it's "feast versus famine" and you could not have any work or sales for a few months, but then suddenly have a ton of upcoming shows and commissions on your plate.

Continue ›

When you're younger, or in the earlier stages of your career, I suggest saying yes to as many projects, collaborations, or other professional opportunities as you can, even if they are all happening simultaneously, to continue to network and open doors. More connections now can lead to more and better opportunities in the future. That being said, there are two caveats to this: First, be honest with yourself about how much you can handle at once. Second, make sure that whatever you are working on does still align with your interests, or pays enough to be worth your efforts—ideally both!

In the same way that you might unexpectedly find new opportunities, you can also create them, even if the timing doesn't at first seem right. It's rarely the "perfect" time for anything. We're always going to be busy and have a lot going on, but as Kat would say about leaving her day job to commit to her creative career full time, there are times when you just have to go for it!

While it feels crazy and scary and overwhelming all at once, one of the best parts of this industry is the people I've met, who have become some of my biggest supporters during times of change. I hope you've also had the chance to experience the power of this community and how exciting it can be to be a part of it.

TAKE ACTION

- Despite the ups and downs, I have enjoyed my path so far overall and am grateful for the opportunity to share it with you. Take a moment now to sit and reflect on what have been some of the biggest lessons or takeaways in your career. Looking back helps us appreciate our past experiences and focus our minds on what we envision for the future.

HANDLING COMMISSIONS

Commissions are a great way to form meaningful connections with your collectors and patrons. A commission gives you the chance to work more closely with a client and offer them customized artwork based on their vision, style, size requirements, and/or budget. It can also be a way to earn additional income. Artists often use commissions to support themselves financially, while simultaneously working on or building up their personal art portfolio.

Kat started offering commissions as early as high school when her abstract floral work caught the eye of one of her teachers. The word quickly spread, and others became interested in the decorative works she offered at the time. Her paintings were priced very affordably and barely covered the materials and time spent on them, but it was a valuable experience that informed how she would handle commissions later in her career. We all have to start somewhere, and we often learn aspects of our creative business through mistakes early on.

Once she graduated and was a few years into her career, Kat partnered with real estate agents to create pieces for families who wanted to commemorate their homes. She made colorful interiors for clients and others, based on their requests. This is a great example of how, as your work and interests evolve, you can adapt by offering a wider range of services to your patrons.

Though working directly with clients comes with its own set of challenges, we hope this chapter gives you the tools and insight necessary to make commissioned work an enjoyable and exciting process!

PRICING STRATEGY

You'll likely start selling your art and charging for your time at lower, more modest rates, but these will soon increase as you gain experience and expertise. When you put yourself out there early on and market your work, it gives you the confidence and skill needed to continue growing and eventually charge more for your work. Be sure to check out How To Price Your Art (page 54) for helpful formulas to set you up for success from the start. We recommend charging a premium fee for custom work, because you will inevitably spend more time planning and revising each piece.

Artist Erika Lee Sears gives excellent advice in one of this chapter's highlight interviews (page 197) to be proactive and prepare price lists with the type of commissions you offer. Be sure to include sizes, medium, prices, and the approximate time it will take you to complete each kind of work.

GETTING COMMISSIONED WORK

To book new clients, you should proactively advertise the fact that you offer custom pieces. Include a section on your website and show previous examples, if applicable. Post regularly on social media, announcing that you are accepting new commissions. The holidays are a great time to take advantage of the fact that people will want to give or get customized artwork, but be sure to plan this at least a few months in advance so that you don't have to scramble to complete all of the pieces before the shipping deadlines. Since you should know about how long each commission will take, only accept the number of new clients you can complete in time. Even though you might be tempted by the additional income of more commissions, you wouldn't want to burn yourself out, especially around the holidays when you want to focus on enjoying time with loved ones! You can also utilize the tools you learned in Email Marketing Basics (page 132) to let your collectors and supporters know that you are open for business.

IT'S OKAY TO SAY NO

Custom work is not for everyone. As Kat's paintings evolved and she moved away from abstract decorative pieces into expressive interiors, it became less exciting for her to work with clients and was no longer a practical fit for her career. In the beginning, she continued to take work, but once she branched out to create other revenue streams and could afford to say no, she moved away from commissions.

Remember that you have options, and there are other ways to earn income if this type of work is frustrating for you. If a client contacts you with a request that you know you will not enjoy creating, it's okay to thank them for the opportunity and politely decline. If you don't find pleasure in the project, it will be challenging to put forth your best work and will require more effort than the money is worth.

IDEAS FOR COMMISSIONED WORK

Not sure where to start with commissions? Here's a list of ideas to consider!

• Portraits
• Pet portraits
• Work in your style and subject matter, based on client's color preferences
• Depictions of a specific item, house, landmark, or landscape
• Murals
• Size-specific works
• Create your own!

We've covered the basics of commissions, but we want to share more in-depth knowledge from artists in our community. Read the following interviews with Erika Lee Sears, Alonsa Guevara, and Chambers Austelle to learn their advice about booking, completing, and getting paid for custom work.

ERIKA LEE SEARS
www.atinyrocket.com

At what point in your art career did you start offering commissions?

Even in the beginning of my career, I have always been open to commissions. Creating artwork is an extremely special experience and a commission is an even more intimate process because you aren't just creating, but also making it for your collector. To me, commissions are such a compliment that a collector is so deeply connected to your work that they want you to make something especially for them.

What is your process for working with clients? Do you prepare contracts and ask for a deposit?

Once a client asks for details about commissioning a piece, I let them know about the materials I use and the timeframe for the entire project. I do ask for 50 percent up front for time and materials, and the rest is due upon completion. I also have a prepared price sheet, but I let them know if they want another size, I can have one made custom for them. After they pay the deposit, I do a series of sketches for proportion, vision, and sometimes color. This takes time, as often there are revisions that need to happen with subject matter, layout, and overall idea. Then it's time to make the artwork.

Continue ›

It doesn't happen often, but after a piece is completed, a client sometimes asks for changes. Maybe the color wasn't what they envisioned or something was just a bit off. If it's something simple, like toning down a color, that's easy and then I change it. If it's something more complicated that once I make the change, I can't go back, then I let them know. Or, if it's a change that will affect the quality of the work, I won't do it. It doesn't happen too often, but be prepared and don't be defensive about them having an idea of what they want the painting to look like. This is part of the customer experience.

Share a few tips for artists to help them price their work to make sure it's a profitable venture and a positive experience.

Know when to say no. If it's not the right fit for your artwork, then it's not the right fit. Sometimes clients ask to copy another artist or want you to replicate someone else's artwork. In general, don't be afraid to say no to a commission.

Do not work for free. You are doing a disservice to your artwork by doing it for free. If the client is serious about wanting a commission, they will pay a deposit.

Pricing is difficult, but create a price sheet. Know that you have to make a profit in order to live. In the beginning, you'll have to start at one price, but as you gain experience your pricing will increase. Here are some additional factors to consider when establishing a pricing sheet: quality of materials, time, shipping, and consider pricing per square inch.

Provide exceptional customer service. Be polite and respond to emails in a timely manner, usually within twenty-four hours. Your client is spending their hard-earned money on your artwork. Make it a memorable and unforgettable experience.

Creating artwork is deeply personal, but you are working together with your client. If they have critical feedback, don't take it personally. If it's a challenging scenario, think about trying to provide excellent customer service.

What are some typical requests you receive for commissioned paintings?

I get a pretty wide array of requests because I have several different series, but I am always open to my client's vision. Some want a similar painting to one they have seen. Others want to commission a birthday, an anniversary, or a wedding gift. Every now and then I do get pet portraits, which I always have a soft spot for.

How do you market and promote this service?

On my main webpage, I have a section that indicates that if you are interested in a commission to please email me. When a client inquires about a painting that has been sold, or maybe they want a different size of a painting, I talk to them about a possible commission. Every season, I will post on my social media and newsletter that I have available spots in my commission schedule.

ALONSA GUEVARA

www.alonsaguevara.com

Visit:

https://annazorinagallery.com/wp-content/ uploads/2016/07/PRESS-RELEASE-CEREMONIES.pdf to learn about Alonsa's series of paintings that depict imaginary rites performed to honor various stages of life.

Tell us about the kind of commissions you offer. When did you feel ready to do this type of work?

I started taking commissions a long time ago, even before I graduated. I did a lot of portraits of family members and landscapes, and I also made money by teaching private classes for young people and adults. However, I took a long break from doing this type of work when I moved to the US because I was busy studying.

I began retaking orders not that long ago when I started doing the ceremony paintings. I take a lot of other requests, too, and I even collaborate with big companies. I am very open to working in different ways, especially when it relates to the things that I want to do. When I get an offer that doesn't match my work or isn't something that I'm interested in, I don't accept it. But if the project is related and gives me a bit of freedom to create art or express myself, I take it on.

Right now, I am taking orders that are related to the ceremony paintings. The process changes slightly, depending on the project, for example, some clients want me to paint them inside this bed of fruit, covered with their favorite fruit, their favorite flower, or something that is symbolic to them. They pose for me, and then I make these paintings.

I also have clients that want me to make pregnant portraits for them. Since a lot of my work is about fertility and life, I have women asking me to create a work of them while pregnant. Some customers want portraits with a baby. They give me a lot of freedom to do what I want, but they choose the fruits and the colors, and then I'm free to do whatever. Recently people have been requesting ceremony paintings, but I am open to other projects too.

Do you have a system or process for communicating with clients in the early stages to ensure they are happy with the result?

Yes. I do. In the case of the ceremony paintings, first, I take pictures of the client. Because those are nudes, I want to meet them first. I want to make sure they understand the process. We talk about how it's going to work. My husband, James, helps me take the pictures, so I let them know that there's going to be a male in the process of taking pictures. I want to make sure they feel comfortable with the fact that they will be nude in front of him. I ask them about what they want: what kind of fruit, what kind of flowers, the feeling of the painting, etc. And then, after that, we communicate by email. Sometimes they want me to be more in charge of decision making, which is easier for me.

Continue ›

After that, we do the photoshoot. A few weeks after, I edit a few of my favorite pictures, the ones that I think are the best in composition, feeling, and color. And then I send them about five options. The client chooses their favorite, and I ask them to please be as honest as possible and tell me every single detail they don't like or wish was different. The picture is going to be my guide for the painting. Of course, things change later on. I move things around. I create more volume, more contrast, different things, but I'll use the photo as a reference, so if something bothers them, I want them to tell me in advance. For example, making a leg smaller is easy, but changing the position of an arm would make me have to repaint the entire work.

I make the requested changes in Photoshop. When the client is happy with the image, I go ahead and paint them. The more information the client gives me about what they want, the easier it is for me to create the best painting for everyone involved. Communication is the most important thing for both of us to be happy because there can be a lot of misunderstandings if you don't make things clear at the beginning.

How did you figure out the pricing of your commissions vs. your available paintings?

A long time ago I would just charge whatever, but now I have a specific price for my paintings. The commissions are a little higher. Let's say my large paintings are $20,000. (The ceremony paintings—which are about 80 by 32 inches—are $20,000.) A commissioned piece is $25,000. The difficulty of the work is reflected in the price. Some of my collectors have asked me to make a new ceremony painting for them, but they give me a lot of freedom, so it's more like I'm creating another one of my own paintings, so the price doesn't change. For portrait commissions, the price will be a little bit higher.

I charge more for custom orders because they involve a lot more work than one of my paintings, which I can make the way I want and at my own pace. When you're working on a commission, you're always talking to the client, making sure they like it, so it usually takes a little longer. Commissions also always come with a deadline, so you have to charge a little more.

Have you ever had a negative experience? How did you handle it, and what did you learn from it?

I don't know if I ever had a negative experience, but I definitely had uncomfortable ones. One example would be when I make a portrait of a client and he/she doesn't completely like the way he/she looks. Then I realize that they have a different perception of themselves than what I see in their picture, so what I do is I fix it and always try to remember that they're paying for their painting, and I want them to be happy. The clients have expectations, so I try my best to reach them.

Sometimes I've realized during the process of making a painting that I charged too little because the project is taking longer than expected, or I have other kinds of work at the time (I also teach and have different demands). Sometimes you have to figure it out and make a note of certain things, so you know better for next time. These experiences are feedback that naturally comes up along the way.

Share a few tips for artists who want to get more clients for commissioned work.

It depends. Are you a beginner? Are you a professional painter that wants to do commissioned work? Have you ever done it before? Do you know your timing? Do you know how long it takes you to do a portrait or whatever commissioned work you are going to do?

Of course, the most important thing is to let people know you are doing commissioned work. Whatever media you use to get your work out there (whether it's online or word of mouth), you need to let people know. Put it on your website or Instagram. Also, if you have never done a commissioned work before, make a few for free, either for someone else or for yourself. If you want to do portraits, do one of your mom or a friend. Then you have an example, so when people ask to see your work, you have something to show them. First, get it out there. Tell people.

Second, have an example that you can show, one or two. The more, the better.

Third, something I did a lot before, is be strategic about the timing and think about a good day to start your commission work. In my case, I did it before Christmas. I began offering commissions to people in September. I would say, "I can make commissioned work from this size to this size. You can choose three different sizes, like formats. And this is the cost. I just need you to send me a picture, and this is an example of how I can paint it."

Choose a strategic time and offer to people one-on-one. For example, you can even say, "Hey, your husband's birthday is coming up..." or something like that.

And number four is to start by communicating this to your friends and family. This way, you have someone you can trust: they love you, so if you mess up at the beginning, it's okay. That way, you can have some examples, things to show future clients.

Also, number five is always to know that people have ideas of what they want their commissioned work to look like. Their ideas might differ from yours, but that's okay. In my opinion, the best way to do commissions is to show the painting to the client a little before it's finished so they can change anything they want to change before you finish it. Always expect client changes. This way, you won't be shocked when you receive a huge email with all the things they want to change.

CHAMBERS AUSTELLE

www.shopchambersaustelle.com

Tell me about what kind of commissions you offer. When did you feel ready to do this type of work?

The commissions I accept are in the style of my usual work. I don't know how often you ever feel prepared for something, and many times I think you should avoid using that as a gaging point, because comfort comes with time and experience. I started taking commissions early on mostly out of financial necessity, as I feel is similar to most artists I've spoken with.

Do you have a system or process for communicating with clients in the early stages to ensure they are happy with the result?

I usually speak with them about the general direction and components that are prevalent in my pieces. If we are working from a photograph (if the piece will be of them or a family member), I help choose the image that will work best for the piece. Some clients are completely open to letting me have full artistic discretion, while others are less confident or more apprehensive about the end result. When this is the case, I'll either set up a time to chat with them over the phone or will create a digital mock-up or sketch. I prefer letting most of the decisions organically happen throughout the painting process, but in some cases having a set and direct layout is the best option for the collector.

How did you figure out the pricing of your commissions vs. your available paintings?

I price my commissions the same as other originals, but ask for a 50 percent deposit as well as a $150 custom fee.

Have you ever had a negative experience? How did you handle it and what did you learn from it?

Some experiences have been smoother than others, but that can be expected with any customer service interaction. I've learned that for me, it's sometimes best to do all you can within reason to ensure that they're happy with the result. Afterwards, you can reevaluate how everything was handled and make adjustments if necessary. Basically, you learn as you go.

Share a few tips for artists who want to get more clients for commissioned work.

Think about how you market or what platforms you use and let them work to your advantage. You want your collectors to be able to get information quickly and easily. My main platforms and marketing strategies are Instagram, my website, my newsletters, and influencers. I usually make announcements twice a year that I am accepting commissions. I usually fill commissions slots six months to a year in advance. So for example, around June of 2019, I announced openings for 2020. For Instagram, I'll post the announcement to my feed and stories, add it to my profile, and might work with an influencer to help share the news. Using examples of completed commissions and installations is a great visual aid to pair with your announcement. For my website, I'll add the news to my header with a link to more information, so anyone who visits my site immediately has that information available. And lastly, I'll send out a newsletter. Once I have a better idea of what my schedule looks like for the following year, I'll make a second announcement to fill any new slots I might have added.

TAKE ACTION

- Create a price sheet listing various sizes, media, and styles you offer, including tentative timelines for your potential collectors.
- Announce that you are accepting commissions on social media and through email marketing, and list this service on your website.
- Create a list of upcoming holidays or events that may be a tool for promoting your custom work.
- Look up contract forms for commissions and customize one to fit your needs.
- Decide on what type of payment methods you will use (PayPal, Shopify, check, bank transfer, etc.)
- Once you book a client, ask for a 25 or 50 percent deposit on your work.
- Remember to only take on clients you can manage without too much stress.
- Have fun and provide exceptional customer service so you can ask for testimonials and get referred to new clients!

ART-WORLD ETIQUETTE

In our fast-paced and ever-changing world, it can feel difficult to keep up with emails, social media, and more, in addition to creating your best work! While we never want you to sacrifice spending quality time in your studio, there are small things you can do to make sure that you stand out on the administrative and business side of your creative practice. Using the term "etiquette" might seem antiquated, but as you make contacts and develop relationships, the more you can do to leave a great impression and build your reputation, the better off you will be in the long run.

If your goal is to become a professional artist, we recommend following these simple, unwritten rules when interacting with fellow artists, curators, press, and galleries online and in person. If you have not followed these guidelines in the past, don't worry. We want to give you the tools to empower you to show up as your best self and help you land that dream opportunity going forward. When in doubt, use The Golden Rule of treating others as you want to be treated.

THE UNWRITTEN RULES OF ART ETIQUETTE

Follow Instructions

As time-consuming as it may seem (although this usually only takes a few extra minutes), when you are submitting an application or hoping to get featured by a big Instagram account, read the requirements and follow the directions. If they have taken the time to outline specific application requirements, it is because there is a certain way that is easiest for them to review your work. Be respectful of that and don't make it hard for them to review your application or submission—not to mention, those who don't follow instructions may simply be ignored or discarded. Abiding by the outlined requests demonstrates that you value their time and organization, and are also worth investing their efforts in.

With *Create! Magazine,* we advertise the submission process on our website in multiple places, as well as on the highlights section and bio portion of our social media profiles. Yet we've received hundreds of emails and messages on social media with missing information, zero context, informal language, no greeting, or vague requests. Since we try to be as helpful as possible, we take the time to respond to everyone, but we end up having to repeat what's already readily available on our website over and over again. Of course, we are happy to assist when there is a valid question, but can you imagine how frustrating it is to share the same information every day? Do a little bit of research whenever reaching out to someone to see if they have a protocol. They will be so grateful you did, and your chances of success will increase as well.

Give Thanks

After you submit your work, reach out for a business opportunity, or get featured by your favorite blog, be sure to send at least a quick thank-you email to the person in charge. Whether they respond isn't the point here. Genuinely acknowledging the hard work of others is something everyone appreciates and has the added benefit of making you memorable. If you can mail a handwritten card or note to someone you met for coffee or include a small gift in the package to a new collector of your work, we encourage you to do so. When your work gets featured, share a link and tag the organization to let them know you are supporting them as well. Little gestures like these can go a long way in the art world.

Introduce Yourself

This can feel a little awkward at first, but, for example, if you made a connection with someone online or were featured in a juried show they curated, next time you see them in person, go up and introduce yourself. Tell them who you are and how you know them and give them a genuine compliment about what they do. Or, if you love a fellow artist's work, tell them! Smile, say hello, and let them know that you admire what they do. This doesn't have to take long and isn't much effort on your part, but it definitely makes an impact.

Maintain Your Personal Brand

When visiting art fairs, exhibitions, or networking functions, present yourself in the best light. Wear your favorite outfit, style your hair, and practice good hygiene. There is nothing wrong with expressing your personal style, and we encourage you to always stay true to who you are. Fashion can be an extension of your art practice, but make sure your clothes follow basic rules of professionalism, even if your look is sporty or avant-garde. It's essential that you feel good about yourself when networking or attending art-world functions and for us, a nice outfit helps add a boost of confidence! If the event calls for a specific dress code, follow it to the best of your ability, out of respect for the organization.

TAKE CARE OF WHAT YOU HAVE

If you are wondering how to get new collectors, grow your social media following, and elevate yourself as an artist, the answer is this: by taking care of what you already have. Reply to any comments or compliments on social media, try to promptly respond to purchase inquiries, send thank-you notes to your collectors, and be available to your community. By being a polite and caring person, you will eventually get referred to others, and your circle will expand.

Avoid Copycats—and Being One

As you develop your artistic voice, you'll likely look to many artists for inspiration and references. This is fine, but if you borrow something directly from another artist you must always give credit where credit is due. Unless appropriation is part of your practice and you are doing it legally, we highly encourage you to keep pushing your work until it is distinctly your own.

That being said, there are probably hundreds of thousands of artists who paint landscapes or make sculptures of animals. Some crossover is bound to happen. If you discover that another artist has stolen an idea or image of yours, be absolutely certain before you make any formal claims. This is a very serious accusation, and you shouldn't bring it up with them if you can't fully back it up with proof. Try to reach out directly and come to a resolution rather than announcing it publicly, which should only be used as a last resort. Luckily, we don't see this happening very often between artists. Instead, our experience is that artists have had this occur with larger companies stealing their work for profit. There are numerous resources from which you can learn more about copyright for artists. If this is an issue you are having or would like to learn more about, we recommend looking into the Artists Rights Society (https://www.arsny.com/copyright-basics) and seeking professional legal advice. You can learn more about the importance of developing your unique style in an interview with painter Kestin Cornwall on page 316.

Concise Is Key

These days, everyone gets many more emails and messages than they have the time to deal with on a daily basis. If you want yours to stand out, get your point across quickly. If you've sent more than a few back-and-forth emails, a call may be more efficient. When you want someone to meet with you, suggest specific dates and times in advance so that you don't have to spend two to three additional messages to land on when it is convenient for you both. Try not to send multiple emails in a day if it isn't urgent, and give your recipient at least forty-eight hours before following up, especially if that time includes the weekend. Don't assume that everyone is keeping tabs on work duties on their days off. Everyone deserves a break!

Set Up Auto Responses

We both like to be proactive about responding to messages in a timely fashion. Alicia does this on business pages on Facebook by setting up auto responses. This shows any potential client that even if we don't reply right away, we will get to it as soon as we can. Kat does the same with her general email for *Create! Magazine*. You don't just have to use away messages when you're on vacation. Set one up during busy seasons so that people aren't worried if they don't hear from you immediately. That being said, even if you don't respond right away, do try to at least skim your messages regularly to see if there are any that are important enough to necessitate dealing with sooner rather than later.

Follow through with Your Commitments

We can both name instances where we have recommended artists for certain opportunities or invited them to be in the magazine with no result. While there are some we'd give the benefit of the doubt that the message never reached them for whatever reason, there are others who simply backed out or never followed up. Not many people have the time to keep reaching out to you if you forget to stay in touch about an exhibition they wanted to include you in or write back about a potential article feature. It's especially unprofessional if someone else has used their personal connection to make an opportunity happen for you to not to go through with it, unless you have a true reason for not doing so. It doesn't just reflect poorly on you, but can also give a bad impression of your personal connection, and they may not be interested in helping you again.

Celebrate Others

If you are attending another artist's opening, refrain from making your visit all about you. There is nothing wrong with introducing yourself, but if it's someone else's big event, don't pitch your work, try to get employment information, or openly discuss gallery representation. If you eventually want to work with the star of the show, support them and follow up at a later date. You can even use your attendance as a conversation starter in the future!

Remember That the World Has Enough Critics

Fortunately, this doesn't happen very often, but sometimes an artist will share something negative on social media or leave a rude comment on a post of someone else's work. There is nothing wrong with having an opinion or speaking your truth if you don't agree with something, but try to focus on and celebrate the work you do like. Because the art world is very small, you want to be sure you are noticed for your art and not your criticism. Rude comments stick in our memory in the most vivid detail, and we definitely have no desire to work with someone who leaves these unpleasant surprises in our world in the future. As David Nicholls said, "No-one ever built a statue of a critic."

Handle Conflict with Grace

There have been times when we have received difficult emails from art-world professionals who are our peers. Having someone else, especially those who you thought were friends, pick fights or accuse you of doing something wrong when you didn't can immediately put you on edge and make you feel uncomfortable. We always reach out to each other when this happens to discuss how to best respond to these messages together and take the time to craft polite yet firm responses if there is a need to reply.

When Kat was going through a rough time with her first business partner, it was challenging to respond to harsh messages and threats of lawsuits with poise and professionalism, but thankfully she didn't give in to her emotions. Alicia did the same when a former employer delayed and then refused to pay her contractually agreed upon salary. Rather than write back angrily, she simply sent irrefutable proof of all the hours of work she had completed.

When you experience conflict, don't react right away. Call a friend or a mentor and share the context of a situation. An outsider's perspective can help you see the issue differently and give insight you wouldn't think of otherwise. Even if you end up being in the wrong, take some time to think before hitting the reply button. Apologize if you need to and arrive at a solution that comes from a place of kindness and confidence. Attackers often act out of their fears and insecurities and are looking for you to overreact to validate their own beliefs.

Make & Accept Apologies

You will inevitably make mistakes throughout your career, so get used to the fact that you'll have to say sorry. When you are honest and upfront about your transgressions, the more likely it is that you will quickly be forgiven. If you are the offended party, do your very best to be forgiving. That being said, if someone has hurt you, you also have every right to say that you are no longer interested in maintaining a professional relationship with them. Cut toxic people from your life as soon as you can. The same may hold true for those for whom you'd rather take the blame and apologize to than be in a fight with. If they are otherwise very important to your career, it might be worth it to salvage the relationship, but be wary of people who you always feel forced into apologizing to.

We've also noticed that many people, women especially, use "sorry" in situations that don't warrant it. If you don't respond to an email right away, unless it should have been time sensitive, you don't have to apologize for the delay. Artist Dani Donovan (@danidonovan) made a printable "E-mail Like A Boss" guide that she shares on her Instagram profile. For instance, instead of "Sorry for the delay," she recommends saying, "Thank you for your patience." Along the same lines, if you have valid criticism to share about something, you don't have to apologize beforehand. Don't apologize for having an opinion. It's your voice—use it.

Write Like It's a Letter

Even when conversing via social media, or with someone you have worked with previously, be careful with informal language. For at least the first few emails to another person, don't forget to include a greeting. You don't need to use "Dear," but at least include a "Hey" or "Hi." Then end your message with something like "Kind Regards," "Best", "Cheers," or whatever you prefer. We don't see this happening as much recently, but also leave text-speak (e.g. c u = see you) for your text messages.

Give Someone Else a Hand

We're always open about the fact that numerous individuals have helped us along the way. While there was a lot that we had to learn and do on our own, there were also difficult times we never would have made it through without kindness or advice from others. Whenever we can, we try to support emerging artists, other peers, friends, or even family members. Don't discount small acts like sharing someone else's artwork on your social media page. They are often greatly appreciated. We aren't suggesting quid pro quo, however. You should genuinely want to help without any expectation of getting something in return. We love the idea of paying it forward, and it brings much-needed positivity into our community and beyond!

Most of these unwritten rules are professionalism basics that don't just apply to the arts. We're sure that this was mainly a refresher for you, but it's always good to be reminded of how important your reputation and your relationships with others are, especially in your work environment. Our connections are everything to us. They've helped lead us to new opportunities, supported our businesses, celebrated our wins, and cheered us up after our losses. No amount of sales, exhibitions, or media features can compete with that.

TAKE ACTION

• Think about your career thus far. Has there been a time when you were confused about how to act professionally? Based on our suggestions, what do you think was the best way to handle the situation? Is that what you did?

Developing
&
Growing
as an Artist

DEFINING YOUR UNIQUE STYLE

Having a distinct style is the cornerstone of your creative practice. Developing it will guide your various bodies of work, even if they shift between a variety of subjects or media, and set your artwork apart from the masses of other artists active in the contemporary art market. For many collectors, one of the biggest selling points for buying a piece of art is that it is unique—an original that nobody else can own. So while it is imperative for you to define your personal style, be aware that it is a process that usually takes artists years to undergo, not a matter of months.

We are always learning, growing, and changing. Therefore, aiming to settle on a specific type of work that you create permanently shouldn't necessarily be your goal. Instead, embracing your natural inclinations toward particular colors, shapes, themes, or subjects is the best way to become recognizable in the art market. Trust that your audience of clients and art lovers will be interested in your story and evolution as an artist, rather than sticking to rigid, self-imposed rules in order to achieve a consistent body of work.

For Kat, the search for her artistic voice has taken many years. As a high-school student, she explored various imagery and subject matter in her work. Initially creating art that was observational, she later experimented with surreal images, and then abstract florals, before eventually finding her way to painting memories from her childhood. Years later, her practice evolved into finding beauty in everyday scenes. This led her to her biggest series as of writing this book, which included paintings of homes, interiors, and intimate spaces in dream-like colors. Had she not experimented with multiple themes and various styles, she probably would not have arrived at her most successful work to date. Even now, you can see elements from her early paintings, such as florals, specific colors, and mark-making unique to her, appearing in her newer work.

Kat's work stands out because of her use of color, which often includes shades of pink, purple, and teal. She frequently utilizes contrast, incorporating light and dark into her paintings. Her work is expressive and rooted in realism, but is not restricted to explicitly defining her subjects, as her work also has abstract elements. Because of the longevity of Kat's bedroom series, people frequently recognize her work, even when she introduces other subjects. Her brushwork, imperfections, color choices, and unique vision is what makes the work memorable. If Kat creates a painting in an entirely new palette, she often hears comments about how her paintings are "pink." Repetition and consistency will make viewers recognize your art, even if they can't articulate how.

So, how do you find your voice without feeling restricted in your art practice? There are several ways to uncover your unique style as an artist.

HOW TO UNCOVER YOUR STYLE

Do the Work

The first and most important rule is to have a strong commitment to your work. It's not glamorous, but the longer you experiment, study, and create art, the more prominent the elements that make your work unique will be to you and your audience. Looking for a shortcut will only rob you of the gems you will discover along your journey. However, you can still be a successful exhibiting artist, even as you grow and evolve.

We recommend sticking to a series and creating at least ten to twenty pieces. It is likely that not all of these will be masterpieces, so just allow yourself the opportunity to test things out. You can only discover whether you enjoy something if you give it time and immerse yourself in it. You have to be willing to be bad initially in order to eventually get better. It takes courage to start something new and muddle through those rough first drafts, but you'll inevitably improve and this will motivate you to keep going. Even if you don't end up loving your work, you will learn new skills, pick up new elements to add to your visual vocabulary, and learn from the experience.

Create What You Know...

If you crave expressionist movement and flowing forms when you create, you'll likely drive yourself crazy if you try to force yourself to make tight, carefully calculated representational art. It seems obvious, but many artists get hung up on what they think they should be making, rather than what they desperately want to make, because they believe they'll sell more, easily secure gallery representation, or amass more followers online. But this is simply not true — we promise that there is a niche for everyone. Create art that is authentic to your personality, background, education, or whatever else you believe defines you. Your audience is much more likely to respond to your art when it is genuinely a representation of you.

Think about who you are as a person. What are some of your hobbies? Important relationships? Things that inspire you? Write these down and then see if it feels natural to incorporate them into your art. Not everything about your life will make it into your work, but something will, even if it is very small.

...Or Learn about Something You Don't

Some artists are driven by curiosity. If this is you, take advantage of it and dive into a subject you've always wanted to learn more about. Head to the library to find books to read or visit a museum, even one that isn't art-related. You may very well find that something you learn during this time sparks an idea for a new series that helps you gain clarity on your creative voice and style.

Explore, but Don't Overstay Your Welcome

At a certain point, you may outgrow a theme or style and want to journey into something new. Trust your gut and your soul's calling when you feel bored or uninspired by your current series. For Kat, this happened after almost four years. She was enjoying her collection of bedrooms and interiors, until one day it just didn't align with her vision anymore. Sometimes boredom can be solved by pushing your subject matter even further, but in other instances it's an indicator that it's time to move on and try something else.

Pay Attention to What You Love

Noticing what you love about the work of other artists is one way to begin honing in on your aesthetic. It's a great idea to keep a journal or a file on your phone or computer where you collect art, color palettes, patterns, textures, and anything else that piques your interest. Being inspired by other artwork doesn't mean that you are copying or settling for something that already exists. As long as you are not stealing another person's image, you can borrow elements and ideas from the work of other creatives and reinvent it using your own story, vision, and aesthetic.

Go Back to Art School

If you are a brand new artist or desire to change your art, you can always experiment with sketching other artwork in your spare time. Throughout our art instruction, multiple teachers and professors encouraged us both to copy the work of other artists to discover what elements could be adopted into our own work. It's a common practice in traditional art education to reproduce art by classical masters to improve your skills, and it's something that you can easily do yourself by visiting museums in your area. These sketches are good practice and will inform your future work, but they should not be part of the series of original artwork that you promote and sell. Never claim to be the author of copied works.

Tip:

Try not to get stuck in this "copying art" phase for too long. This learning tool is strictly for research, and you should move on to making your own unique creations once you've begun to identify a style you want to pursue further.

It's likely you won't work in one specific style, medium, or subject for the rest of your life. You are welcome, and even encouraged, to evolve and change as often as you need. You are the visionary behind your life and career, so make it fun! Sure, if you choose to pursue a traditional gallery path, your work is expected to have a certain level of consistency, but that doesn't mean that you can't explore other types of work on the side, especially for your enjoyment. Who knows . . . maybe your secret projects will become your best work yet! Read more about finding your creative voice in an interview with artist Kestin Cornwall (page 316).

Read more about finding your creative voice in an interview with artist Kestin Cornwall (page 316).

BOOKS TO HELP YOU UNCOVER YOUR STYLE

Find Your Artistic Voice: The Essential Guide to Working Your Creative Magic by Lisa Congdon

Steal Like an Artist: 10 Things Nobody Told You About Being Creative by Austin Kleon

Creative Block: Get Unstuck, Discover New Ideas, Advice & Projects from 50 Successful Artists by Danielle Krysa

Art & Fear: Observations on the Perils (and Rewards) of Artmaking by David Bayles and Ted Orland

TAKE ACTION

- Think about who you are as a person. Write down personality traits, interests, and anything else that you may be able to incorporate into your work to make it authentically you. Experiment with using some of these qualities in your art and decide which feel natural to keep.
- When you find an idea or style you want to explore, commit to making at least ten to twenty pieces to see if it is a fit.
- Try copying works of other artists if you ever feel stuck, but move on when you're ready to pursue a new idea.
- Be honest with yourself if you want to move on from a style, medium, or subject matter you've held on to for some time. It is okay to change and evolve!

FINDING OPPORTUNITIES FOR YOUR ART

Identifying quality opportunities to showcase your art in public spaces and a variety of media outlets should be an essential part of your career development. Because artists working today do not necessarily have to be represented by a gallery or exhibit work in traditional ways, we can take charge of promoting our work to the world and finding patrons who support what we do. The art market is slowly broadening, and we now have many options on how to approach this aspect of our careers. We don't have to limit ourselves to the traditional gallery model, which gives us the power to be more creative with our sales and marketing. Utilizing social media, networking, pop-up events and exhibitions, and artist-run fairs as tools to help you move ahead in your art career will help your work get noticed by those who matter.

For Kat, having traditional shows is no longer a requirement to sustain her studio practice, though they are an excellent opportunity to connect with collectors and supporters in person. Before a gallery signed her, she was selling her work through her Facebook and Instagram accounts, as well as online gallery platforms such as Saatchi Art. Having an art dealer often provides her with unique opportunities, such as participating in bigger art fairs and being listed on Artsy or 1stdibs, but these are more of a bonus than the foundation of her career.

When Kat was fresh out of art school, she dreamed of having a fancy art gallery and thought this was the secret to thriving financially as a painter. Now, instead of relying on outside opportunities for sales and credibility, she participates in exhibitions, competitions, and juried shows to give her collectors more confidence about purchasing her art. She celebrates media features and awards as affirmations that she is on the right path in her career.

Being behind the scenes of *Create! Magazine* has allowed us both to witness the curatorial process firsthand. It has shown us that the jurors' tastes and interests are valid, but they're not always a reflection of the quality of the rejected works. Sometimes curators simply run out of space, and therefore have to pass on featuring artworks they truly like. Kat frequently receives emails from guest jurors asking to include artists in future issues because of how impactful their work was. So these days, when either of us gets a rejection letter, we view it as a "not yet." For submissions that required an entry fee, instead of thinking of it as money lost, we simply feel good for having supported the organization running the open call. You can learn more about our philosophy on how to handle rejection in Aiming for Rejection Letters (page 161).

> *"Even the smallest opportunities will give you a reason to celebrate and inspire potential collectors to invest in your work."*

When you are starting out or trying to get traction in your art career, you must put yourself out there as much as possible. Even the smallest opportunities will give you a reason to celebrate and inspire potential collectors to invest in your work. By sharing what worked for us, we hope to equip you with the knowledge that will help you get exhibition opportunities, press, awards, and more.

HOW TO FIND OPPORTUNITIES

Start Small

In Kat's experience, applying to local opportunities that are geared toward emerging artists is the best way to start building your artist portfolio. When a competition is limited geographically, your probability of getting accepted increases because it likely will attract fewer applicants. In the United States, most regions have an art council, art association, or other similar organization that lists opportunities for local artists. Be sure to periodically check their websites to see if there are any relevant calls for art or grants you can apply to. If you are brand new, a great way to start your exhibition track record is by having a show at a nice coffee shop or restaurant. Be sure to include your contact information and price list if you do.

When Kat moved to Wilmington, Delaware, after graduating, she was geographically near Philadelphia, but not close enough that she felt connected to the art community. She spent hours researching opportunities that eventually led her to join the New Wilmington Art Association, a nonprofit founded by her friend Michael Kalmbach. She joined the organization and ended up volunteering during exhibition openings and more. This allowed her to meet other artists in her area and, eventually, she got invited to participate in local shows that gave her the confidence to keep going. Do research on any local art groups or networking organizations you can join to help you get connected and discover opportunities.

Alicia used this same tactic early on in her career as well. She joined the Chester County Art Association in order to be able to exhibit in their open exhibitions and apply to their regular juried exhibitions. In one of the first shows, she displayed a nocturne painting. Despite it being a small exhibition, she framed it professionally and asked her family to join her when she went to see it on the opening day. You can imagine the pleasant surprise when Alicia arrived to find it marked with a little red dot! It was her very first sale to someone she did not know and it would have never happened if she hadn't decided to join this local arts organization.

By Word of Mouth

One of Kat's first exhibitions out of school happened because of Alicia, who introduced her to a gallery in Lancaster, Pennsylvania, called Red Raven Art Company. The gallery was about an hour away from our university and exhibited a mix of established and emerging artists. At the time, they had a "highlight wall" for new artists, on which Alicia had exhibited previously (and heard of through another Kutztown art student!). The high-quality environment, beautiful art, and cozy small-town atmosphere was the perfect place to start leveling up with our exhibitions. Kat ended up selling multiple pieces and receiving the largest check she had ever earned for her art.

Tip:

Be generous with sharing relevant opportunities with your friends, and they will return the favor. This is a good time to remember how important networking is. The more people you can introduce yourself and your work to, the more likely it is that opportunities will find you, rather than you having to seek them out. Of course, this is all contingent on leaving a great impression! We provide tons of tips on how to speak about your work and make new connections in Networking 101 for Artists (page 142).

Look for Credible Websites

We both have a list of call-for-art websites, which we will share at the end of this chapter. We use these sites to look for exhibitions, juried shows, publications, and competitions. We also have a shared Google document with our favorite websites that allow us to list the open calls for *Create! Magazine*. It's a good idea to spend a few hours each month scanning these platforms for opportunities that may be a good fit for your work. Create a document or spreadsheet with your favorite call-for-art resources, both local and national, to help you find opportunities. While you should always be cognizant of any shipping fees or other costs, eventually branch out to searching for international exhibition or publication open calls as well.

Read Blogs & Publications

Art magazines, blogs, podcasts, and other media outlets often share calls for entry or competitions for artists on their websites. Several organizations have asked us to promote their call for art because we reach such a large audience of artists through *Create! Magazine*. Search the navigation bar or footer for an opportunities section and scroll through the listings to see if there is anything worthy of your time.

If you want to submit directly to a certain media outlet, look for a page that describes their application process and follow the directions carefully. If you can't find that, do your best to locate a general email address or the contact information for an arts editor to whom you can send your materials for consideration.

Remember that getting your work in print doesn't have to be limited to a fine arts publication. Alicia had her art featured in several literary journals, and even a printmaking supplies catalog, before ever having her work in an art magazine. As long as these are respectable outlets, it shouldn't matter if the publication is strictly related to fine art or not. It is 100 percent still a valid way to market yourself—plus, it adds to your resume!

Use Social Media

We also recommend following the Instagram tags #callforart, #callforartists, or #callforart[current year] to find opportunities. There are also a few accounts that post calls for entry, such as @artopencalls. Be sure to research the website and look into any previously featured artists before applying to any call for entry.

Private art-focused Facebook groups are another great place to search potential shows and calls for entry. These groups may require you to join and become a member. Be courteous and follow the code of conduct if you choose to use this tool. A few that we use are:

- Art Opportunities, Jobs, and Advice
- Open Calls/ Residencies/ Opportunities for Artists
- Open Calls
- Open Call for Artists

But there are many more!

Join Email Lists

National and even some local organizations may also offer a weekly newsletter that highlights a selection of the calls for art or other opportunities from their website. This can be an easy way to make sure that you're regularly seeing new calls for art. By signing up to receive emails from an arts organization, you won't even have to spend the time seeking out endless call-for-entry websites—a curated list will come directly to your inbox. Choose to sign up for a newsletter that provides listings for shows near where you live or, if not specific to your region, shares opportunities that best fit your artwork.

Create Your Own Opportunities

If you have a great idea for an exhibition, event, new blog, or podcast, we absolutely recommend that you just start it yourself if you don't find that it exists already. Even if someone else has created something similar to what you imagine, as long as you aren't copying directly, we're sure you can put your own spin on it so that it becomes truly your own. Like Kat with *Create! Magazine* and Alicia with running PxP Contemporary, we both saw gaps in the art industry and had ideas of how we could better serve the emerging artists in our community. Don't be afraid of cold emailing to pitch a potential project or set up a meeting to discuss it in person or over the phone. While this takes time away from making and promoting your art, you inevitably meet so many new contacts and can also be introduced to different kinds of opportunities, both of which may help your career as a studio artist as well.

MAKING THE MOST OF ART OPPORTUNITIES

Check Your Inventory

One mistake Kat made early on was to apply to opportunities while not having enough work ready. This situation was stressful, because there were a few times when she was accepted but had nothing to send to the gallery. Not being able to participate when the organizers had selected her work out of a large pool of applicants was always a disappointing experience. Try to apply only when you are ready, so that if you get a "yes," you are prepared. There may be times when a single piece gets multiple acceptances at once and that is fine, as it is sometimes simply impossible to avoid crossover. If you can, try to negotiate with the gallery to see if you can swap the chosen work(s) for another or other pieces, instead of having to miss out on the exhibition.

Act Like a Pro

When you get accepted into a show, treat it with the respect and professionalism you would if you were having an opening in your dream gallery in New York or London. This approach may seem over-the-top, but pretend you are practicing for the biggest event of your life—even if you are in a small, local space. You never know the connections you will make and what they will lead to down the road.

For example, Kat had an exhibition at the same gallery that she showed with right after she graduated. The curators had been following her journey and offered her space in a show with one of her favorite artists. Had Kat been unprofessional or careless the first time around, she may have never had this opportunity or the sales this show brought her.

Alicia made a few incredibly embarrassing mistakes that taught her about professionalism when exhibiting with galleries. She once was so excited to show a newly finished piece to a dealer that she brought it to a meeting, even though it was still wet! The gallery owner smiled politely as she walked off to the bathroom to wash oil paint off her hands, but this situation could have easily been avoided. When Alicia didn't frame a work correctly, a different gallery director went to pick up her painting and the canvas fell out and onto the floor. The dealer looked up at her in shock. Luckily, the painting was fine, but Alicia immediately knew she should have checked that her artwork was fastened more securely. Finally, at a group exhibition for which she had forgotten to send in her artist information on time, Alicia had to ask the artist showing next to her if she could use a printout of his artist biography to write down her information to give to a prospective client she had spoken to that evening. Thankfully he was happy to help, but she should have definitely been more prepared with her own business cards to hand out and not have missed the deadline to submit her info to the gallery.

Continue ›

Hopefully you read the last paragraph and thought, yikes! But these cringeworthy experiences were worth it in the end to learn crucial lessons about what to do and things to avoid when you start out with exhibiting. After getting past these growing pains, Alicia began showing regularly and more successfully, so that by the time she graduated, she had been included in more than fifty shows both throughout the United States and abroad.

Make It Easy for Collectors

Once you land a new opportunity, make sure you have business cards or postcards, a mailing list signup, a price sheet, and your basic contact information ready. It's better to be over-prepared, even in the smallest local exhibitions, than to miss out on a great connection. Make it effortless for interested buyers to contact you or even just follow you online.

Celebrate Your Victories

We talk about the importance of celebrating your accomplishments throughout the book, but whenever you get an acceptance letter, have work featured in an exhibition, or win an award, tell the world about it! Your circle will cheer for you, and your potential collectors will be excited to see you making progress in your career. Post your good news on social media, send a newsletter, and be sure to invite your supporters!

WHY HAVE AN ART EXHIBITION?

The purpose of having art exhibitions or features should not be about competition, even though it may feel like that on a particularly tough day. The way we look at it, art shows can be a great way to build your confidence, find collectors, get new ideas about future work by having meaningful conversations, and expand your community of supporters.

When we apply to opportunities and put ourselves out there, we inevitably send a message to the world that we are ready for our work to be seen. Not getting your dream opportunities right away may be agonizing at the time, but even rejection, if we approach it with a healthy perspective, can be used as creative fuel to make us try harder and keep going. Of course, there are so many aspects of the art world that are out of our control. Exposing our work to another human who has emotions, moods, and evolving tastes means that you can almost never guarantee that you'll be accepted. But that's okay!

We find that putting ourselves out there gives us inner peace and supports the idea that we are doing everything we can to grow our career, promote our work, and reach out to a larger audience.

WHICH OPPORTUNITIES TO APPLY FOR

So how do we know what opportunities are worth our time, considering many art and nonprofit organizations require a submission fee? Applying to shows can be costly, but as long as you are clear on what your intention is, you will be able to filter through opportunities easily and only select the ones that will bring the most value to your art practice.

Here is a list of questions that we ask ourselves before applying for any opportunity, paid or free:

Can I envision my work there?
Did you notice any previously featured work that is similar in style, media, or aesthetic to yours? For example, if you are a photographer but the listing primarily shows sculpture, save yourself time and money and keep searching.

Does the brand look professional?
Even if the open call promises cash prizes or a show in Manhattan, pay attention to the quality of their website, including spelling, images, and the overall design. Unfortunately, businesses with the intention of scamming artists out of money do exist, but you can easily avoid them by scanning the site or searching for reviews of their organization online. If you are unsure, ask a few artists in your circle or post about it in an artist Facebook group to see if they have heard of the gallery, magazine, etc.

Would I be proud to share this?
If the gallery looks cheesy or run-down and has an overly outdated website, it's probably best to skip it. There are plenty of quality opportunities for emerging artists that will make you and your community proud, so keep looking. Just because it's an art opportunity, it doesn't mean it will bring any attention or sales. Trust your intuition before applying or agreeing to participate in anything.

Are there hidden fees?
A red flag for many galleries is if they ask you to pay for the exhibition. We don't mean small contributions to cover marketing or catalogs or a submission fee, which is often normal—we're talking about thousands of dollars' worth of expenses. There are a few art organizations that do nothing to promote your work and charge you large sums for participating. It would be more of an investment to pay for a booth at an art fair, buy Facebook and Instagram advertising, or take a new workshop. It is true that many galleries and magazines are self-funded and ask for small financial sums that range anywhere from $10 to $200, but beware of scams.

Tip:

There are artists who believe that if an opportunity requires any fee at all, it is a scam and not worth your time. If you agree with this view of not wanting to apply to "pay to play" juried shows or publication opportunities, that is fine. However, we urge you to keep in mind that doing so will vastly limit the number of opportunities available to you. Many art organizations simply do not have the funds to cover all expenses. Try to think of a submission fee as an investment for your future, whether you are accepted now or sometime down the line.

What value will this bring me?
Deciding whether something is worth it is very personal. Be honest with yourself when choosing to participate in a show that requires you to spend money on shipments, travel, or other expenses. Artists are not guaranteed to make money back or break even when investing in exhibitions, and sometimes it's better to pass on an opportunity than find yourself in financial hardship because of it.

Kat had multiple opportunities to show her work overseas when she first graduated. Every time she calculated the shipping costs, it felt unreasonable, given her low price range at the time. On the other hand, when she was presented with an opportunity to show her 6-foot painting in New York years later, Kat invested in an art mover because she wanted her larger work to be seen by a new audience. While this investment was scary at the time, she trusted the gallery and because she was familiar with the art fair, she decided that even if she didn't sell her work, it was worth it for her career. Follow your intuition, discuss the opportunity with your peers, and always pay attention to any warning signs.

Alicia once was wary about spending the money to have a painting framed and making the long drive out to a museum to drop it off for jurying. What if it didn't even get selected? After a little encouragement from her mother — along the lines of "you have to invest in yourself in order to succeed" — she decided to go for it anyway and hope for the best. Not only was the work selected, making it her first piece included in a museum group exhibition, but it also sold!

Sometimes It's Just Not Worth It
Once in a while, an opportunity comes along that may not cost you much financially, but can waste hours of your time. A few years ago, Kat was accepted to a juried show in Brooklyn, New York. This show was her first exhibition in NYC, and she was thrilled. The challenging thing was, the gallery did not accept shipments. This requirement wouldn't have been a problem if Kat was local, but living in Delaware meant that she had to take a bus trip with her work (she didn't have a car at the time) and figure it out from there. We should also mention that she did not yet have a smartphone, and navigating the subway system, as well as the city streets, was a nightmare.

After hours of walking around the city in the rain, with three paintings under her arm, she finally arrived at the gallery on the verge of tears. The experience was beyond frustrating, and even though the gallery was professional enough, the work didn't sell, and it was a massive waste of Kat's time and energy. Sometimes the opportunity just isn't worth it, no matter how prestigious it sounds. Decide what's important to you personally before agreeing to participate in any show or event.

Continue ›

One on occasion, an administrative mistake caused Alicia to accidentally be notified that her work had been rejected when it had actually been accepted. She had already put the exhibition out of her mind when she got a second email reminding artists of the upcoming deadline to have the artwork arrive for the show. After she called the gallery to clear up the initial miscommunication, she rushed to get her drawing framed and shipped off to Georgia. Enticed by the idea of exhibiting in a new state, and not wanting to disappoint the show organizers, Alicia cut corners on the shipment packaging in order to make sure the piece arrived in time. As a result, unfortunately, the artwork arrived damaged and was not able to be shown at all. It would have been better if she simply politely declined the opportunity after she had heard about the acceptance mistake. Scrambling to meet an almost-impossible deadline cost her time and money, not to mention, it ruined a piece she loved. It clearly was not meant to be!

We hope our experiences and tips give you more clarity on how to find opportunities — and which ones to skip. Before applying to anything, do your research, trust your gut, and go through a mental checklist similar to the following.

Submission Checklist

- You have high-resolution, labeled images of your available work and an edited, professional bio/statement ready to go.
- The opportunity is an excellent fit for your work and aesthetic and will connect you to new collectors and curators or will boost your online traffic.
- You researched the venue or know people who have previously worked with them.
- There are no red flags that make you question the credibility of the opportunity or institution.
- For online features: the fee is reasonable (the average rate in the market is between $10 and $100), and the website and social media profiles are active with engaged followers.
- For physical exhibitions: you are able to ship your work or travel by car or public transit without issues.
- You would be proud to share the opportunity with your community.

ART OPPORTUNITY RESOURCES

www.transartists.org
www.artjobs.com
www.artopportunities.org
www.theartguide.com
www.callforentries.com
www.collegeart.org
www.wooloo.org
www.artdeadline.com
www.artandartdeadlines.com
www.chicagoartistscoalition.org

Tip:
Explore your local opportunities by searching for your region or city and "call for art" or "call for entry."

TAKE ACTION

- Find and join a local art council, art association, or similar organization in your area, and periodically check the website for relevant calls for art.
- Share any relevant opportunities with your art friends—and ask them to return the favor!
- Create a list of call-for-art websites and spend a few hours each month searching these sites for opportunities.
- Actively read art magazines and blogs and listen to art podcasts to learn about calls for entry or competitions for artists.
- On Instagram, follow relevant hashtags, such as #callforart, #callforartists, etc., to stay abreast of opportunities.
- Consider joining one or more private art-focused Facebook groups.
- Subscribe to national and local organizations to receive regular newsletters that highlight a selection of calls for art from their website.
- Before applying to an opportunity, be sure to complete the Submission Checklist on page 224.

STARTING OVER: FOUR WAYS TO MOVE ON & MOVE FORWARD

ADVICE FROM ALICIA

We all know that big changes in life are inevitable. Sometimes we're happy about them and ready for them, while other times we're not. But starting over definitely doesn't have to be something you fear. From a smaller endeavor, like starting a painting or an entirely new body of work, to a potentially major upheaval, like beginning a new job or moving to a new city, taking little steps to ease the transition can help make these shifts feel less overwhelming and more exciting!

I've been fortunate to be able to continue working with *Create! Magazine* while living in multiple cities over the past few years. If you had told me five years ago that I would leave Philadelphia, where I attended grad school and got my first full-time job in the arts, to move to Chicago and then live abroad in two different countries (the Netherlands and Costa Rica), I honestly never would have believed it! I'm lucky not only to have had these experiences, but also to have thoroughly enjoyed them. That being said, I certainly had to put forth the effort to make sure that these changes worked out for me. I can't say that they always went smoothly, and looking back, I'll admit that I did my fair share of worrying. But a little bit of anxiety (just a little!) tends to help me push myself to be prepared. Additionally, I try to accept the fact that there are so many things I won't be able to account for or control. Read on to discover a few things I've learned about starting over that I'd like to share with you!

Begin with Research

We say this often through this book, because it works! Kat and I are huge advocates of doing our best to never enter a new situation without trying to educate ourselves about it first. Before she started her first magazine, FreshPaint, and then her podcast, Art & Cocktails, I remember Kat telling me about the various business courses or online tutorials that she was taking to familiarize herself with these topics that she'd never focused on previously. There is such a wealth of information available these days — and much of it either for free or at an affordable cost — that it doesn't make sense not to take advantage of it.

Personally, when it came time for my first international move to the Netherlands, I had to do a ton of research to prepare and make sure that everything, from visa paperwork and temporary housing to cat vaccinations and much more, was all settled before hopping on my one-way flight! In addition to the many calls and emails to the Dutch embassy to sort out the most pressing questions, I found local blogs and expat websites useful for getting a better idea of what life in Amsterdam would be like. I also heeded the advice of a friend who suggested that I check Facebook for groups where I could connect with others who had moved there from abroad. What an invaluable resource! Through these groups, I met incredibly friendly people who were more than willing to give suggestions on anything from apartment hunting and social activities to where I could find the best apple pie in town or get a good deal on a used bike.

If you're starting a new artwork, sketching can be a form of research, and so can visiting galleries or museum exhibitions and reading books about artists working in the same style you're interested in pursuing. Make notes of what you see and what inspires you. Is it certain colors and forms, or perhaps certain patterns or a layering technique? Back in college, staring at the blank canvas and wondering where to start was always one of my biggest struggles, and the same often happens when I write and see the blinking cursor at the top of the screen. Rather than freeze at the sight of the vast white space, look back to your preliminary drawings or at the ideas you jotted down to help you overcome any mental roadblocks and get your creativity flowing.

Say Yes

Specifically with moving, the first few weeks living in a new place are such a great time to explore and figure out your new routine. I love finding out if local museums or other cultural organizations have free days and activities for residents. Ask friends who have visited before for their recommendations, if they haven't offered them already, and follow through on as many as you can. Better yet, if a friend or family member has connected you with someone in your new city, always make it a point to contact them, even if they are older, younger, working in a different field, etc.! You never know what kind of insight that person may be able to share with you, whether you only end up meeting once or you are lucky enough to make a new, lifelong friend.

Maybe try out a part-time, volunteer, or temporary job as a way to meet people, network, and hopefully earn a little extra cash. When I lived in Amsterdam, I worked a short gig at a local art fair, donated my time as a web manager for a women's expat group, and picked up a part-time job at a fitness studio. The first two experiences were beneficial for making connections within the local art community and helped me land a more permanent position at a gallery, while the gym was nice for meeting people my age and earning a little extra income (while being able to take exercise classes that I enjoyed for free!). I had a very similar experience in Chicago, where I worked temporarily for the city's major annual art fair before securing my

Continue ›

full-time role at an auction house.

I think this same "yes" mentality applies to artmaking. Try a totally new medium, make bigger or smaller sized pieces, or work on a canvas shape you're not used to. Experiment, make mistakes, and start over, but keep going! Don't let the pressure of making something "great" on the first or second or fifth try get in the way of fully letting yourself explore. When you do hit your stride and start making new, amazing work that you're happy with, don't forget to share it!

Pushing yourself to get to the next level in your art career can sometimes feel like starting over. You might consider challenging yourself in a new way so that you grow professionally. For example, you could draw every day, apply to a new opportunity to show your work every week, or attend an art event and make one new professional contact. Perhaps "say yes" to practicing good habits, like budgeting or time management. It is always a good time to invest in yourself and build a solid foundation for your future and your career! Who wouldn't want to say yes to that?

Build an Active Social Network

I can't advocate enough the importance of having not only supportive family members and friends, but also professional peers and mentors. It was great to meet so many new people, from finding each other on Facebook or being introduced via a mutual contact, after each of my moves. If I hadn't connected with the various groups that I found in Amsterdam, it would have been impossible to find temporary housing for the first month after I moved and much more difficult to get an art-related job. I've had such nice experiences with other expats in both Amsterdam and Costa Rica who were willing to help and offer advice. When you know what it's like to be the new person in a new place and have someone help you out, it motivates you to pass it on.

If you're at a new job or just rented a space in a new studio building, try to meet people during lunch or coffee breaks, and see if there are any weekly happy hours you can attend. You can even be bold enough to suggest a new social event if one doesn't exist. I once had a colleague ask: "You don't meet every new person thinking that they could become your best friend?," which really made me reconsider how I tend to approach social interactions. Honestly, she was right. What if we were all a bit more optimistic? This doesn't necessarily mean that you need to make tons of new friends fast, of course, but rather that if you are attending an opening at a gallery you've never been to or meeting a friend of a friend for a drink to help you get acquainted with your new city, keep an open mindset that you might really connect with someone. If there's one thing I've learned, it's that you never know the incredible places new relationships can eventually lead you to!

Finding a creative community will help you stay grounded, wherever you are. While it is great that we can stay so connected online via social media, emails, and video calling, if you're away from "home" it is especially important to have people you can see in person regularly. As an artist, it is always nice to have peers with whom you can share ideas, ask for advice, critique each other's work, or attend art events. As we also mention in Networking 101 for Artists (page 161), making new contacts in the industry is one of the most powerful (and free) ways to find new opportunities to build your career. Put effort into building your network and it will soon begin to grow organically.

> *Failing at something does not make you a failure.*

Let Go

In some cases, we have to start over after a failure or mistake, which is a tough situation because it is hard to not feel disappointed about the former job, relationship, artwork, etc. not panning out. Rather than beating yourself up over why something didn't work out, or replaying in your mind what you could have done differently, work toward simply allowing yourself to let go. We discuss this in the chapter about rejection letters (page 142), and I'll reiterate it here: failing at something does not make you a failure. Read that again. Pick yourself up, dust yourself off, be grateful for the experience, and get back at it! Just putting yourself in the right mindset can help you move forward again.

Unless you reuse older or unsuccessful works to create new pieces, don't hesitate to get rid of or throw away works that you don't love (although we do hope that you'll be as environmentally conscious as possible in this process). If you can't think of a good reason to keep pieces around your home or studio that don't represent your best work or have meaning to you, then it doesn't make sense to hang on to them, right?

Continue ›

REUSING & RECYCLING OLD ARTWORK

Works made of reusable materials should be recycled, but we also suggest thinking about how you can incorporate older works into new pieces. For works on paper, for example, perhaps you can experiment with collage or papier-mâché to create textures and layers. Old canvases can be painted over, and any works you're ready to let go of can be sold at a discount or donated. Find a local art center or ask art teachers in your area if they could use any of your materials. As they don't often have the funds for endless art supplies for their students, they are usually happy to accept donations.

Letting go creates room for all of the wonderful things coming your way—in your life, in your creative career, and beyond.

Writing this book, and expanding on the concepts and ideas from *The Smartist Guide, Create! Magazine,* and our personal experiences, felt a lot like starting over. Sure, we know our audience and what we intended to write about, but we wanted this to be so much bigger and more in-depth than our first book. Rather than let it become this big, intimidating project with deadlines and expectations, we both have been so excited about all of the possibilities. Ultimately, we all have to remember that the biggest part of starting over is hidden in the phrase itself: start. You have to just start and start now. Even if it is something small, do at least one thing today that will help you begin, whether it is for your life in a new city or a new body of work or another endeavor.

TAKE ACTION

- Consider what makes starting over most difficult for you. Identifying what it is and what you can do to address it will help you face your new changes and transitions with less fear and apprehension.

ESTABLISHING SMART GOALS

From a variety of professional development workshops and books, Alicia has learned the incredible value of periodically taking a few minutes to write down a list of things that she envisioned for her life (she now does this at least once a year). It doesn't matter if they are big or small, career-related or not. Whether she hoped to travel to Finland, learn another language, read one book per week, get a dog, or make a certain salary per year, what was important was to generate an unfiltered list of what she wanted. After making the list, she thinks about the estimated timeframe she needs to achieve these goals. Is each goal attainable within a few months, one year, or will it take two years or more? While this last act may seem simple, don't skip it! Without this step, you may miss out on a crucial aspect of goal setting: clarity.

Knowing what you want is important, and working toward that is an equally significant part of getting there, but take it a step further by actually writing down your goals, defining exactly what they are, and deciding how long it should take to achieve them. Trust us that this makes all of the difference.

At the beginning of 2019, Alicia sat down and wrote her yearly goals in her Moleskine notebook. She thought about what she really wanted to focus on and make happen in both her personal and professional life in one year's time. Some people like to look at their list every day or on a weekly basis, but Alicia would read hers about every month or so and cross off any goals she had completed. Just seven months after making her list, she realized that she had already achieved all of them. Kat had a similar experience in 2018, setting goals and looking back in December to realize that she had accomplished everything she really wanted to.

When we are clear about what we desire, it becomes easy to spot opportunities that may lead us to the final outcome. This practice will also help refine your intuition so that you can make decisions based on your vision, rather than impulse, and filter through opportunities that may not serve you in the long run. For example, when Kat left her day job, she wrote down that she wanted to get a car, work from a studio in the city, and book exhibitions in London and New York. She had to take massive action with these goals in mind in order to achieve them, but two years later, she has checked all of them off her list.

So, how did we do it? There's definitely not a trick, but part of successful goal-crushing is to establish SMART goals:

Specific

Measurable

Achievable

Realistic

Timely

WHAT DO SMART GOALS LOOK LIKE?

This acronym is commonly used in business, but you can adopt it in your art career too. Let's say, for example, that you'd like to earn additional money from art sales. The first step is to get specific. Instead of saying, "I want to sell more sculptures," you'd specify, "I will make $2,000 per month from selling my sculptures." The more clearly you define your goal, the easier it will be to make it happen. Using this same example, if your pieces are priced at $250 each, you will have to sell eight sculptures per month to reach your target. You should then think about how you can do this, whether it is by

Continue ›

finding more exhibition opportunities, hosting studio sales, boosting your posts on social media, having a booth at an art fair or arts festival, or securing gallery representation. Two thousand dollars is a lot of money and may feel like a big leap if you haven't been selling consistently yet, but it won't seem so out of reach once you break down your goal into smaller, simpler steps.

In this example, the measurable aspect is pretty self-explanatory. Each month as you progress toward your goal, you can see how close you get to $2,000. Making consistent sales takes time, so don't expect that you'll start closing major deals in your first month of trying. (Although, who knows? You might!) The point is to keep tracking your sales regularly so that you know when you're improving and, of course, when you finally do make it to your ideal outcome.

For your goal to be both achievable and realistic, make sure that it is something for which you have the resources to make it happen: the time to commit to it and the desire to put forth the effort. We're not saying that if you're only selling your art for $50 right now making $2,000, $20,000, or even $200,000 is out of reach. We always want you to think big and agree with the words of Ellen Johnson Sirleaf: "If your dreams don't scare you, they're not big enough." However, we also know that rarely does an artist become an overnight success, with their work suddenly exponentially increasing in value. Most progress happens incrementally over time. Set a goal now that you can reach within a few months to a year, perhaps two at the most. This way, you'll be more motivated, see yourself actively making real progress, and not feel disappointed by how long the process could take.

Finally, set a timeline for your goal to give you that extra push to take action now. If your goal doesn't have an associated deadline, set one you think will work for you. In this case, it could be getting to $2,000 in a year. Perhaps even set up smaller deadlines throughout the next twelve months to give you even more structure.[9]

WHAT'S NEXT WHEN YOU MEET YOUR GOALS —OR DON'T?

So, you get to the deadline and have achieved your goal—amazing! Now what? Go back to your goals list and choose what you want to focus on next. Start planning and make sure that it is a SMART goal.

But what if you didn't make it happen? That's totally normal. We both have set goals for which we came up short, and while we know it's not the best feeling, don't beat yourself up over it. Another major shift happened for both of us when we realized that making bigger goals for ourselves isn't always about actually achieving them. It's about setting an intention to expect more from yourself. You'll likely naturally evolve and upgrade your life and career, even if you don't reach the original goal. Also, just because it didn't work out the first time doesn't mean that it never will. If you truly want something, reevaluate, establish a new timeline, and try again.

One aspect that the SMART mnemonic doesn't cover is mindset. If you've listened to our Art & Cocktails podcast or read some of our online articles, you'll know that we are huge fans and believers of manifesting. Writing down your goals, repeating them aloud, keeping them on your phone screen or desktop, and sharing them with your friends, family, or peers absolutely helps make them a reality.

You won't achieve goals that you don't believe in. Fully embrace what you're working toward and start believing that it's not only possible, but will happen.

Hopefully, you noticed in our example goal that we said "I will make $2,000 per month from selling my sculptures," not, "I want to," or, "I hope to." Don't let doubt creep in. Using active rather than passive language when talking about your dreams is part of making them happen. You won't achieve goals that you don't believe in. Fully embrace what you're working toward and start believing that it's not only possible, but will happen. Be grateful that your goals are already in the process of happening for you. Without getting too spiritual, we both have faith that a higher power is there listening, and the universe can feel the energy that you put out into the world.

Alicia recently had an experience in which she was thinking about finding an additional source of income, and she set an intention to start working on securing one. Just a few hours later, she received an email offering a new freelance gig, without even having to reach out to anyone. It's more than serendipity. When you are passionate, excited, and secure in your goals and believe that they will work out in your favor, they do.

9 *"SMART Goal," Corporate Finance Institute,*
https://corporatefinanceinstitute.com/resources/knowledge/other/smart-goal/.

STARTING WITH A VISION BOARD

Thinking about and writing down your goals can be a difficult task early on or when you're trying to level up, because you may have so many ideas or expectations for yourself. If you find that you aren't able to come up with goals that abide by the "SMART" rules, take a step back. Consider starting with a vision board instead, where you'll pull images, phrases, colors, travel destinations, and anything else that you would like to see in your life and career. Putting these in the form of a digital or paper collage that you can visually reference can help you narrow down your ideas to specific, concrete goals that you can start working to achieve. Keep this in your studio or another place where you'll see it regularly for inspiration.

TAKE ACTION

• Do a brainstorming session to create a list of your goals right now.

• Think about and assign a timeline for your goals.

• Pick a few goals from those you want to prioritize in the next year and turn them into SMART goals.

• Start planning the steps you'll need to take in order to achieve them.

GOOD VIBES ONLY: NEGATIVITY IN THE ART WORLD & HOW TO FIGHT IT

The more we put ourselves out there, the more people will share their opinions of us and our work—both good and bad. It's amazing to have people express interest in your art on social media, and even more so in person. We hope that you appreciate the encouragement, internalize that you are deserving of the positive support, and enjoy returning the compliments as much as we do. Interactions that started as friendly messages online have often resulted in new friendships for us and helped us build the community we are immensely proud to have created.

But as they say, "it's not all sunshine and roses." You've likely encountered negativity in the art world, and it can be challenging to be at your best when the attitude of others doesn't match your own. Even when we develop resilience to negative feedback and unsolicited advice, such experiences can still leave you with unpleasant emotions. In the following pages, we've broken down a few everyday scenarios to identify and overcome these unnecessary sources of drama!

IGNORING THE "STARVING ARTIST" STEREOTYPE

"So what are you going to do with that?" was a question Alicia often got from people when she told them she was studying toward a BFA (and when she was in grad school for her MA in art history too!). Her response was almost always met with a look best described as halfway between puzzled and concerned. After working in the arts for the past ten years, however, she feels empowered in this field, now more than ever.

For example, while there is still a ton of progress to be made, we are seeing more women and people of color taking charge and making their way into the roles and institutions that were previously out of reach. Choosing to pursue a creative career shouldn't feel like limiting your options. From exhibiting nationally and abroad to working for galleries and art fairs, museums, and nonprofits to starting a business, writing a book, and more, it isn't what can an artist do . . . it's what *can't* we do?

Even though Kat's parents were always encouraging of her art practice, she personally always felt pressure to follow a career path that would earn her money. Being a first-generation immigrant made her feel like she needed to pursue the "American Dream" and study in a field that would help her earn more money and eventually provide for her family. Growing up and experiencing intense financial struggles made her feel like it was a waste of an opportunity to be in this country and pursue art. After being told by her guidance counselor that her only option was to study international relations, due to her knowledge of a second language, she felt discouraged and hopeless about the future. Luckily, she listened to her intuition and followed that gentle inner voice that said: "You should give art a try anyway." Even though

Continue ›

the journey hasn't been easy, the more she learned about the art world and all the possibilities within it, the more confident she was that one day she would be able to help her family financially by doing what she loved.

It took us both quite some time to arrive at the realization that our possibilities are not limited by what others think artists are capable of, or by how artists have achieved success in the past. Just because it hasn't been done before doesn't mean it's not possible to create new opportunities and pave the way for others as well. While it can be disheartening that not everyone will be 100 percent supportive of your goals, you don't need anyone else's permission to follow your passion. When you put yourself in the mindset that anything can happen, things can surprise you in the best way!

> *"Just because it hasn't been done before doesn't mean it's not possible to create new opportunities and pave the way for others as well."*

MINDING YOUR PS & QS

When we went to Miami Art Week one December, what stood out was the incredible variety of art that we saw (at over ten fairs!). This diversity is one of the things that we appreciate most about this industry: the art world is big enough that everyone can find their place in it. Not everyone will be represented by blue-chip galleries or exhibit in museums, but you do not need to do either of those things to find supportive collectors and share your work with people from around the world. With this in mind, push yourself to be a savvy networker: keep business cards with you, have a memorable elevator pitch ready to go, and don't be afraid to speak up about your accomplishments.

Here's an example:

We stopped at a booth to admire a piece we liked. A man walking by paused next to us to introduce himself as the creator of the work, explain a bit about it, and, as he was on his way to do something else, quickly ended the conversation by saying, "Thanks so much for looking at my work. Here's my card. Please keep in touch!" Keeping your business interactions professional and polite ensures that you leave a great impression.

The art world is excellent for making new connections and finding your niche, but be very careful about burning bridges. It is so unfortunate that for as much good as social media has done for artists, it has also given some people the false notion that they should use it to criticize others. Whether it's posting disrespectful comments or even trying to preface a remark with, "I don't mean to be negative but . . ." engaging in that kind of behavior online guarantees that the other person will not want to work with you.

What if, down the road, they are the link to a big opportunity that you would have loved to be a part of?

It is a huge personal pet peeve of ours when people start a comment with, "Sorry to be the one to say this but . . ." because it's never from someone who writes criticism as their profession. This is a cheap way of putting aside their guilt when they know that the second half of what they're going to say is unnecessary and negative. Remember that it is highly unlikely that any person with a valid reason for being critical of something would apologize for it. If someone leaves a comment like this on your profile or says it to you in person, just ignore it or delete it.

The same goes for overreacting to not being selected for a gallery or exhibition. We know that it is disappointing and frustrating, especially if you've applied more than once. We've been there! You send your best work and hope that it will be picked, but sometimes it just doesn't happen. Our best advice is to stay positive, try to be gracious, and move on. Something better is coming! We give more tips on how to handle rejection gracefully in Aiming for Rejection Letters (page 161).

DEVELOPING A THICK SKIN

We strongly believe that artists should support artists, rather than get sucked into competing with or comparing themselves to others. It's especially disappointing that even today, we still see artists putting down other artists. Remember that everyone is on their own path, and even if another creative is finding success, that doesn't mean that you never will. Jealousy will only distract you, so keep working hard and be patient, knowing that your time will come when it is meant to.

It's also important to remember that people rarely post about the hard times and struggles that they go through. If all you see are sales and exhibitions, it may seem like an artist achieved "overnight success," when in reality, they had to put in blood, sweat, tears, and years of effort. Use jealousy in a positive way by admiring what the person has accomplished and believing that if it's possible for one human, it's possible for you too.

Negative feedback or unsolicited advice (not actual constructive criticism) can feel annoying at best and devastating at worst. Because your initial reaction might be defensive, first ask yourself if it is even worth it to continue a discussion with this person before responding. If you do feel the need to respond, do so concisely and politely, but don't expect anything in return. It's up to you to tune them out, delete their comments, or even block them. We have heard a quote related to this that resonated with us, which says something along the lines of, "Nobody doing more than you will criticize you, only someone doing less." The people who go out of their way to bring you down are simply dealing with their own feelings of insecurity. While it's unfortunate that they take out those insecurities on you, focus instead on the awesome people who are genuinely there to encourage you and what you do!

Continue ›

‹ *Continued*

When Kat started experiencing measurable success in her art career and the growth of her Instagram account, the comments started flooding in. In particular, right before she began to sell her work actively and signed with her first gallery, a gentleman left this comment under her painting: "This is hideous, don't quit your day job." It was unpleasant, but real milestones in her career proved his words were irrelevant. Sometimes people can sense our momentum and try to stop it with negative comments and pessimism because they are jealous or intimidated. Practice compassion, and remember that happy people would never write something like this. Focus on those who support you, and don't engage with this type of behavior from those who don't.

We pride ourselves on the fact that our community is a positive place for artists to share, connect, grow, learn, support, and inspire or be inspired by one another. We know this isn't always how it is and that it can be difficult not to let the fear of facing negativity interfere with or stop you from putting yourself out there. But if it is your dream to be an artist, we encourage you to do it anyway.

TAKE ACTION

- Identify sources of negativity in your life related to your art practice. Are you dealing with "trolls" online leaving negative comments or family members and friends who don't approve of your career?
- Come up with solutions on how to deal with these people. Can you block them or delete their messages? Should you see less of them or not interact at all?
- Confide in a friend whom you trust for additional advice. You don't have to figure this out on your own, and you'll be grateful to have the extra positive support!

IT'S NOT LUCK (& OTHER REASONS WHY CREATIVES NEED TO BE MORE VOCAL ABOUT THEIR ACCOMPLISHMENTS)

You've been accepted to a juried show, received a prestigious award, had an incredible review written about your work, or made a major sale. Congrats! It's one of the best feelings in the world to know that others are supporting what you do. So why are we often hesitant to share the joy that we experience? Perhaps you're shy and don't want a lot of extra attention, or think that being open about your accomplishments is boastful. We can't insist enough that you do it anyway!

We're going to share with you a few key reasons why creatives, and especially women artists, need to be more vocal about their achievements.

THE IMPORTANCE OF VOCALIZING YOUR SUCCESS

We're sure many of you have fallen into the trap of brushing away compliments. Rather than thanking someone for congratulating us on selling a painting or landing a gallery to represent our work, we'll come up with an excuse to make the accomplishment sound like less than it is. "Oh, I got lucky," or, "It's not really a big deal," you might say, but that's not true! Too many of us operate under the strange, outdated notion that it is more polite to negate a compliment than accept it. Even if the circumstances surrounding a particular moment of success were serendipitous, YOU played an active role in making it happen for yourself. You made great work that was recognized by the juror, curator, gallery, or collector, and you put yourself out there by applying to the opportunity or perhaps through networking and being active online. So stop giving anyone or anything else the credit. It's not luck, it's you.

It is important for your peers to know about your achievements. Why? Because you

"Even if the circumstances surrounding a particular moment of success were serendipitous, YOU played an active role in making it happen for yourself."

never know who can introduce you to your next big opportunity, and it may only take one new connection to catapult your career to the next level. Success in the arts often occurs like a domino effect: one person finds your work and from that, another will share it, and then another, and it keeps going from there. It's almost as if the tastemakers in the industry have "FOMO" (fear of missing out), and if one magazine or curator is featuring a certain artist, others feel they should too. Of course, they want to try to find

Continue ›

the "next big name" first, but once one influencer has identified a great new talent, others often soon follow. You can help this process along for yourself by making sure that your community knows when you've been featured in a magazine or exhibition so they can help share it too, and potentially build buzz and momentum.

Making others aware of recent accomplishments also helps with name and face recognition. For instance, Alicia's husband, a creative director in the advertising industry, was attending an award ceremony after starting a new job. When his team was honored with their first trophy of the evening, he opted not to join the group onstage and when his colleagues asked why he didn't, he cited the feelings of not needing the attention or wanting to look too proud. But then he realized, it's not just an opportunity to celebrate with his team, but a chance for everyone else in the room to see who produces high-quality work for their clients. If they see the same person going up to accept multiple awards, they'll start to recognize them, associate that person with being great at what they do, and maybe want to work with them in the future!

So, try not to be shy about sharing that you've won awards or been given other important recognition. You should want your personal, and especially your professional, contacts to remember you for all of the great things you've done and continue to do.

Most importantly, however, you need to vocalize your successes because if you don't, nobody will know about them. This sounds obvious, of course, but we often don't fully realize the consequences of not sharing good news. Alicia once had a boss who started giving her fewer shifts than her two other peers. Confused, she confronted her about what she might be doing wrong or could be doing better. Her employer didn't have anything negative to say. Instead, she simply told Alicia that the other two girls spoke up more often about the projects they were completing on a daily basis, the sales they had made, or that they wanted additional hours. Alicia was so surprised to hear that she wasn't actually doing anything wrong. Even though she was selling just as much (or more!), keeping up with all of her work, and often staying late to do a little extra cleaning or to take on additional tasks, this one simple thing was holding her back.

Around this same time, Alicia also read a quote that stated that believing you'll get recognized just from keeping your head down and working hard unfortunately isn't true, and it's women who tend to suffer the most from this misconception. With that in mind, it made more sense. As her boss usually worked from home, rather than in the office, how was she supposed to differentiate Alicia's sales and projects from what the other girls were doing if she didn't tell her specifically? So now, even if Alicia still sometimes feels a bit reserved about "tooting her own horn," she tries to think of it as an integral part of promoting herself and pushes herself to do so in order to keep her career moving forward, instead of being stuck in the same place.

Posting about your achievements via social media or sharing them with your community in person at an event or during an artist talk is an additional way of attracting new collectors. We've mentioned this previously, but a prospective buyer isn't just investing in a piece of art, they're also putting their money into supporting your career. Sharing that you've been given some form of validation from the art world, whether through juried awards, solo exhibitions, or previous sales, helps convince them that you are indeed someone they should feel comfortable spending on. This is not to say that you need any of these things for your work to sell. When you're new, it takes time to build up your resume, and even collectors understand that. But it really does help to solidify your sales and marketing strategies when you can use these references to show that you are working hard to maintain a successful, professional art career.

Kat noticed the positive impact of sharing her successes and wins early on. For example, whenever she shared that a piece got into a juried show or won a small award, someone would message her and ask about the price. Over the years, announcing press coverage, exhibitions, and any other features, no matter how small, tended to correlate to sales or at least inquiries. For a potential collector on the fence, seeing the artist gain attention for their work is a factor that often encourages them to finalize the sale. You should keep your sold works listed on your website and share them again on social media once you have sent a piece off to a new home. This gesture reminds potential buyers that the artwork they are thinking about might not always be available and gives them confidence that others are investing in your work as well.

Finally, even though it might feel a bit awkward at first, it's very likely that your artist community really wants to celebrate your successes with you. There will always be negative people and those who struggle with jealousy, but your core support group will stand by your side. Just like they will be there for you when you've been rejected or are having a slow period, they also want to be a part of your high moments, especially if you're going to pop that champagne. Cheers!

We all go through highs and lows and it's a powerful thing that more artists, and people in general, are being authentic about when they're not having their best day. We don't always need to see perfect lattes and curated travel photos. But part of being real is sharing when good things happen too, even the little victories. If you're starting out, having a small show at a local cafe or selling your first work are totally worthy and incredible accomplishments. Share them! Not to brag or try to make others think that you're this great, successful artist (you already are one and don't need anyone else's opinion to prove it). But rather, to share something that you're genuinely proud of and that excites you, which your followers and those who support your work will truly appreciate and celebrate too!

TAKE ACTION

- Practice accepting compliments without negating them, if this is something you struggle with.
- List all your accomplishments not only on your resume and CV, but also prominently on your website.
- Share exciting press features, awards, and other news on your social media channels and with your mailing list.
- Regularly share your achievements with your superiors (mentors, bosses, etc.), so that they know you are growing and progressing in your career.

THE GRASS ISN'T GREENER, BUT SOMETIMES IT'S OKAY TO CHECK

Alicia once interviewed Philadelphia-based designer and digital artist Jeff Manning, who told her that his advice to his younger self would have been to focus more on competing against himself rather than his peers. This idea really connected with her and got her thinking about the bigger idea of how often we compare ourselves to others in so many more aspects of our lives than just our careers. It can be detrimental when taken to the extreme, but sometimes it can actually be not just useful, but important to do so. When it seems like everyone else is making more sales, having bigger exhibitions, or getting better exposure, it's difficult to not unfairly or unnecessarily judge ourselves against others' successes—and even more significantly, to not let jealousy get the best of us! So, let's take a moment to identify the productive ways we can use comparison to keep us moving forward rather than stuck in the fearful, self-doubt stage we often mask with envy.

WHEN COMPARISON IS A GOOD IDEA

When You Need Inspiration
One of the best times comparison can be beneficial is when you don't know how to do something or want to do it better. Time for an upgrade on your website? Not sure how to package your artwork in a way that stands out from the rest? Looking for a creative way to design your website or other marketing materials? Look around and see what other artists are doing. You shouldn't have to start from zero. Ask for tips and let yourself be inspired, but do always make it your own.

When Pricing Your Work or Negotiating Your Pay

Like we discussed in How to Price Your Art (page 54), remember that looking at other artists who are in the same stage as you and making similar work (in terms of size, materials, and time spent per piece) is a great way to estimate what you can be selling your art for. Pricing has been kept such a mystery in our industry for so long—a trend fostered by feelings of competition and scarcity between galleries and artists. But luckily, attitudes on this are finally beginning to shift. Whereas collectors of the past might have been intimidated to make an inquiry at a traditional gallery, today potential buyers can see prices listed online, or even contact artists directly via their website and social media channels. We encourage you to not only be aware of how your peers are pricing their work, but to be open to sharing this with other artists if they reach out to you, and, finally, to keep tabs on larger trends in the industry.

Along the same lines, if you are working in the arts (in a full-time role or in addition to your studio practice), get to know what your colleagues are being paid. Hopefully, you saw the salary spreadsheet that was initiated by a curator at the Philadelphia Museum of Art in 2019. It went viral online, with thousands of people who work in museum, gallery, arts administration, and education positions adding their wages to the list. Knowing what others make will help you better negotiate your pay and ensure that you are being compensated fairly within your company. This can, of course, be an awkward conversation at first, but again, the more transparent we all are with each other, the better off everyone will be in the long run.

When You Want to Work with a Gallery

When you are looking to start working with a gallery, check out the artists who are already represented by those you are interested in. Don't miss this critical step! Compare notes on their resumes and websites to make sure that you're really a strong fit. It can actually come in handy when it comes time to putting together your application. Through this research, you may notice similarities between the gallery artists and yourself that you can then mention as evidence to support you joining their roster.

When You're Ready for the Next Step

Let's say that things have been going well for a while. You're making sales and showing in quality exhibitions and now you're wondering what to do in order to take the next step in your career. *How do I show in museums or art fairs? Is an artist residency right for me? What can I do to successfully apply for grant funding?* This is another time when checking in with other artists is a good idea. It is likely that you may already follow or know someone at the next level and can simply ask. But if you don't, there are lots of additional resources to tap into, such as podcasts, books, blogs, workshops, and more. A little bit of networking at the next gallery opening or art event also might help you meet artists who can provide this type of advice.

Continue ›

‹ *Continued*

We hope that these tips will help you recognize when comparison can be a helpful tool, but if you ever find yourself negatively affected by looking at what others are doing, then stop. Unfollow or mute those on social media who aren't serving you, or take a break from it completely. Step back from personal relationships that may be putting added stress or pressure on you. Sometimes we don't realize how profoundly we are being affected, and it can grow into unhealthy feelings of anxiety that are hard to manage. Try to spot the signs early, and proactively separate yourself from what is causing it. Don't let anyone else dictate where you should be or make you feel bad about where you currently are in your journey. Always remember that it is exactly that—a journey. Something that takes time, effort, and consistent work!

"Don't let anyone else dictate where you should be or make you feel bad about where you currently are in your journey."

We have both definitely been sucked into these ideas on occasion, thinking that we should be further along in our careers. But then we remember: what is the rush? We think of those who found success later in life, like Jerry Saltz and Lisa Congdon, and realize that we are exactly where we need to be. We both agree with Jeff Manning's advice. You are the only person you should be comparing yourself to, and if you've grown or progressed or learned something new since last year, last month, or even last week, then you're definitely on the right track. If you're in this creative life for the long haul (like we've mentioned in previous Art & Cocktails episodes!), this is the type of mindset to maintain in order to ensure that you'll remain focused on your own path for years to come.

TAKE ACTION

- Honestly think about times when you compare yourself to others. Are these productive moments for you? If so, write down other instances where this might be useful for your practice. If not, what steps can you take to make sure that it does not become an unhealthy distraction? Should you cut back on social media? Are there relationships that you should reconsider?

- If you are feeling envious of another artist or creative, break down what you are specifically jealous of and turn it into motivation. Come up with an action plan for how you can have a similar experience in your life.

- Make a list of things you are proud of in your life and art career. Single out what you want more of and create a list of new goals based on your unique gifts and vision.

NAVIGATING ARTIST RESIDENCIES

ADVICE FROM KAT

Traveling has been an interest of mine since I was young. Growing up in Russia, I was raised by a single mom who freelanced as a translator. I was lucky to have the chance to tag along as she worked throughout Europe, which sparked my imagination and made me long for more adventures. Unfortunately, when my mom and I moved to America, our financial situation no longer allowed it. I dreamed of exotic places and hoped that one day I would be able to experience the world again. Envious, I watched my classmates go on family vacations or expensive class trips. I didn't get these opportunities early on, so I frequently imagined myself sketching in Paris or taking gorgeous photos of rural landscapes. After a while, I let go of the possibility that travel would ever happen for me, but I still included it in my goals and created Pinterest boards with my wanderlust dreams. I even started to design affirmations specific to my love of travel and imagined myself enjoying future adventures.

At one point, something inside me began to shift. I was starting to experience more success with my art, as well as with *Create! Magazine*, and the possibility of travel became real again. My positivity and commitment to a thriving art career started to pay off.

I remember coming across a listing for an artist residency on a Greek island. Not knowing how I would pay for it or what this experience entailed, I followed my intuition and applied. A year later, I was packing my bags and experiencing my first solo trip and residency.

Before I jump into the details of how I made it work and what my experience was like, I want to mention that you don't need an artist residency for your career, just like you don't need to travel to "find yourself." However, I genuinely believe that if travel is something you keep thinking about, then you should undoubtedly go for it. You will figure it out as you go along.

Another thing I want to mention is that after traveling, I did not have any epiphanies or revelations about my art. Visiting new locations did not impact my art directly, however, I made some lifelong friends, expanded my community, and gained more knowledge and understanding of our beautiful world. I also miraculously still felt at home in some of the furthest places I could get to on the planet. I learned so much from artists who came from all parts of the world and who were working in very different disciplines. I got to meet new parts of myself, experience life in extreme weather conditions, and so much more.

If you frequently fantasize about what it would be like to travel or attend an artist residency, I wrote this chapter for you. I had so many questions before my own residency. I always felt like I wasn't good enough, that I could never afford it, or succumbed to other fear-based excuses that prevented me from doing it. If millions of people find ways to travel (it doesn't have to be an official residency—you can create your own experience), you can surely figure out a way as well.

If travel or a residency is on your bucket list, read on as I share parts of my adventures in each place I visited, how I paid for them, and tips to help you plan your own.

What Is an Artist Residency?

I have been able to participate in three different residencies, and each of them could not have been more different from the last. Each experience varied in terms of the structure, curriculum (or lack thereof), facilities, and, obviously, the location. The one thing that united these experiences is how they each beautifully bring together artists and creatives from every career level, walk of life, and place. In my experience, the more diverse the group is, the better. I love the

SOLO TRAVEL

Traveling alone can feel intimidating, especially as a woman. Alicia remembers being nervous when she took her first solo trip to Iceland, because she was in charge of everything: planning her itinerary, paying for all of the expenses, figuring out where she'd stay and what she'd do, and how she would get around the country, since she didn't want to rent a car. A smaller piece of her even wondered about her general safety, as she knew she'd be walking around alone most of the time. Of course, you must be smart and aware of your surroundings, but as long as your eyes are not constantly glued to your phone, you don't dress too extravagantly, and you research where you're going, as well as common routes to get there, it's not likely you'll be bothered or get lost in an area where you feel uncomfortable.

Despite Alicia's initial hesitations, her experiences traveling by herself have been some of the most fulfilling and empowering. One tip she recommends, however, is to stay in touch with family and friends throughout your travels to make sure others are updated on your whereabouts—and to help ward off any feelings of loneliness. You can also tap into your community to discover tips or advice from people who have already traveled to where you are going. This is often how she finds the best restaurants to go to or activities to do!

idea of learning from one another, regardless of our creative disciplines, age, and nationality.

Residencies typically are a more affordable way for artists to travel and network; they usually offer free or subsidized housing, depending on which one you attend. The programs I chose were diverse and included various types of accommodation, such as individual rooms and shared living spaces (Iceland), bedrooms in a giant mansion in the countryside (France), and a private studio apartment overlooking the Aegean Sea (Greece).

Each experience was unique and valuable in some way and taught me so much about myself as an artist. No trip turned out quite the way I expected, and the work I created always surprised me. As with anything, it's essential to do your research and even reach out to a few people who participated in the program you are considering. A great way to do this is to use Instagram hashtags to see if you can find artists who went before so you can ask a few questions. For instance, if you are looking to network, it's best to research and make sure the residency you are attending has a large group of artists. If you want solitude and space to reflect on your art, seek a more independent or even isolated program. If you require specific equipment, such as a pottery wheel or a printing press, make sure it's available. Sometimes it's interesting to try a new medium when you are outside of your usual environment to break yourself out of familiar patterns. I also cannot emphasize how important it is to trust your gut. If something feels off, it probably is.

RESIDENCY EXPERIENCE: SKOPELOS FOUNDATION FOR THE ARTS
Skopelos, Greece

Skopelos Foundation for the Arts was my first residency, and also my first time traveling solo, so I was equally excited and nervous. Skopelos is a remote island in the Aegean Sea, and to get to it, one has to take a ferry or fly to a neighboring island from Athens. Luckily, the directors provided comprehensive instructions on how to do so, and the experience was seamless— other than the strikes that were happening in Athens during this time (May 2017).

I met up with a few of the girls who were also a part of this experience for dinner in Athens, and we chose to take a flight the next day. You can't go wrong when it comes to meeting up with fellow artists, exploring a new town, and enjoying delicious Greek food and wine. We spent a few hours climbing up gorgeous cliffs, shopping in small stores along the water, and enjoying the turquoise sea before heading to our final destination. I remember even before I reached the studio, overlooking the sea and thanking myself for having the courage to take myself here. It was an emotional and profoundly empowering experience.

The studio itself was on top of a big hill overlooking the deep blue sea. It had everything an artist could ever want, including a stocked art supply closet, pottery kilns, and printing presses galore. We were visiting during the off-season, so there was no schedule, and we had 24/7 access to the facilities. I chose to explore the town and visit the beach as often as I could (who could blame me?). The other artists and I were lucky to be able to meet a few of the locals, including owners of a family ceramic studio and a beekeeper.

Residency Takeaway: Don't Overpack

One thing I learned from my first trip is that, often, less is more. You don't need to bring all of the art supplies you own, as tempting as it may be. I would have taken smaller luggage on this trip if I had done my research on the materials that would already be available. You probably won't make as much work as you think, depending on how long you will be there, so be realistic about what you need to bring. Many places have art stores you can shop at or order from, so find out those details before you travel. I made the mistake of bringing a large suitcase filled with paints, which I then had to drag up the steep hills and over the bumpy, stone streets of the Greek island towns that I visited. You get the picture. Practice a bit of minimalism and be creative with versatile outfits, supplies, and other items.

RESIDENCY EXPERIENCE: NES
Skagaströnd, Iceland

Traveling to Iceland had been a dream of mine since I discovered the band Sigur Rós in high school. Cliché, I know, but after many Google searches and seeing how epic the landscape and nature in this country was, I couldn't get the place out of my mind. I started to look for residencies once I became self-employed and applied to one that looked promising, NES. I will never regret this decision, because when it was finally time to travel to the remote town of Skagaströnd, I needed this experience more than anything.

NES was different from my previous residency in Greece because it was set up to include a large group of artists. The program has multiple houses, which include individual rooms and a shared kitchen and living space. The art studio was an open floor, so it required me to be surrounded by others while making art. I spent very little time in the studio and made a point to walk around and find solitude in the winter wonderland. (Just do a quick search for Icelandic landscapes online to see why this was a priority!)

I bonded deeply with my roommates, both filmmakers, who showed me ways to see our world I hadn't considered before. Though I felt reserved at the time, being in a large group disarmed me and inspired my work in many ways.

One of the essential takeaways from this trip was the healing power of nature and the incredible landscapes that exist on our planet. Of course, I could have easily taken a tourist trip to see Iceland, but having meaningful artist connections and conversations contributed more to my life and art than I could have come up with on my own. Because of the extensive group program, I made some impactful friendships that I'm grateful for to this day.

Residency Takeaway: Learn from Others

On this particular residency, the highlight (aside from the mind-blowing landscapes) was being around artists who worked in all disciplines. Being a painter is fantastic, but it was really inspiring to see the world through the lens of dance, film, ceramics, and more. Even though I may not utilize any of these techniques in my work, I formed a strong appreciation for and understanding of how other artists work. Not to mention, the friendships we made on that trip are still a warm memory, and I keep in touch with many of the artists.

RESIDENCY EXPERIENCE: CENTRE POMPADOUR

Abbeville, France

This residency was a feminist retreat in a gorgeous chateau in Northern France. It was a pretty independent experience, aside from a communal dinner with wine at the end of each weekday. This experience gave me room to think and consider the next steps in my art career, while having important conversations with female artists from around the world. I was educated about feminism, got to share my story, and connect with women of all age groups and walks of life.

I was initially attracted to this experience because of my love of interiors, and what better way to study gorgeous indoor spaces than to live in a chateau?

Residency Takeaway: Plan Your Travel Arrangements

If there was a downside, I would say that traveling to and from the mansion was very challenging without a car. Most European cities I visited had frequent transportation, but this rural town did not. Biking and taxis were the only methods of transit. Luckily, Alicia met me in Paris after this residency so I could continue to explore France and spend some time in the city after having been in a remote area for the previous two weeks. Researching and figuring out the details of your stay before you travel is essential!

FUNDING YOUR RESIDENCY

My residency experiences required artists to pay a fee, which is typical for most organizations. I had wonderful experiences and used several methods to pay for each trip. If you feel unsure of the value a residency will bring you, ask around, and listen to your intuition. Many of these programs are established by artists and have limited funding, but the stay and studio space are very affordable. Research free or grant-based opportunities if you are not willing to pay out of pocket, or apply for grants.

Grants

I funded my first residency partly with a small grant from the state of Delaware. The Delaware Division of the Arts had an opportunity-based award for which anyone who lived in the state could apply. I did my research, entered my best submission, and got approved. The funding only covered a part of my trip, so I calculated how many paintings I needed to sell to raise the rest of the money and promoted my work to make that happen. It was a big plus, however, that my residency in Greece was affordable in terms of the cost of living.

The Icelandic residency was also partially funded by a state grant. Still, I had to cover a lot of the expenses out of pocket, as the cost of living in Iceland is tremendously higher than in Greece. Before you travel, look at average prices so you can plan in advance for how much it will cost you to eat and travel for the duration of your trip. Budget in a little extra whenever possible for miscellaneous or unexpected costs that will likely come up.

Crowdfunding

A few friends of mine traveled by raising money through crowdfunding campaigns. If you are not familiar with how this model works, two popular examples of companies that do this are Kickstarter and GoFundMe. Essentially, you ask the people in your community to pledge a certain amount of money in exchange for a small thank-you gift based on the amount they give you (e.g. a print, an original piece, or something else that you create). Visit both websites to read about all the details and best practices for launching a successful campaign on each respective platform. Search for artists who have reached their crowdfunding goals, especially for traveling, and ask for tips on how they did it to see if this would be a good option for you.

Studio Sales

Clear out your inventory and see if you can have a big sale to help you save up for your trip. I sold a few medium-sized paintings, which was more than enough to cover two of my trips. You can also plan ahead and make smaller, more affordable works, and let your collectors know that the proceeds will go toward supporting a fantastic opportunity that will potentially elevate your art career.

Continue ›

‹ *Continued*

Some residencies offer stipends and grants as well, so read the "about" section to see if this is the case and learn how to apply or ask for them.

You might still have hundreds of questions about artist residencies, but I assure you, every program you attend will provide a guide to travel and local resources for you to read through before applying. I never felt utterly lost because I always followed the given directions. If you're worried or traveling alone for the first time, link up with another artist who will be attending the same residency to make your travel more fun!

If traveling abroad is something you keep thinking about for your art career, visit the Residency Resources websites listed here and start planning your perfect opportunity. I wish you the best on your new art adventures. Bon voyage!

RESIDENCY RESOURCES

www.resartis.org
www.transartists.org
www.nyfa.org
www.collegeart.org

TAKE ACTION

- Make a list of travel destinations you think would inspire your art practice in some way, and begin researching artist residencies in these locations.
- Search the hashtags for artist residencies on social media or do a Google search to see which opportunity would be a good fit for you.
- Brainstorm ways you can fund your trip based on our suggestions.
- Start working on applications, including grants if needed.
- Celebrate your acceptance and share your travel plans with your community!
- Arrange your travel and housing.
- Be smart about packing! Decide what materials and clothes are absolutely necessary to bring and leave out the rest.
- Get excited and be open to all the possibilities of what you will learn and gain from your residency experience!

TIPS FOR SURVIVING AN ART FAIR AS AN ARTIST

In recent years, art fairs have undoubtedly become staples in the art economy. Each year more events are popping up all over the world, and we completely understand why. Even though the market is shifting to online sales and social media, most galleries and artists still need a place for collectors and media to experience their work in person. Fairs provide a unique opportunity for exhibitors to show in a major city and share their collection with thousands of international visitors. We love attending these events because we inevitably discover great new artists. In addition, Kat has also previously exhibited her work at an artist-run fair.

Whether you are looking to visit your first event or considering exhibiting your work, we want to equip you with vital information that will help you have an enjoyable experience.

WHY ATTEND A FAIR?

Art fairs are mass gatherings of the various players in our industry: galleries, curators, consultants, collectors, press, and more. It's a chance to see and be seen and to potentially connect with important figures who could lead you to the next step in your art career. Equally important is the opportunity to view other artists' work. Art fairs allow you to see what artists are creating in your area, nationally, or around the world. You'll also be able to note what is selling, how certain works are being priced, and which galleries might be a good fit for your own art. Not to mention, there is usually a plethora of events surrounding the fair, including artist talks, book signings, or panel discussions, that you can use for networking, as well as learning about current news and trends related to the art market or the industry as a whole.

We love going to fairs to scout new artists for magazine or blog features, and we've been honored to serve as media partners for Art Miami, Moniker Art Fair, and PULSE Art Fair. After attending a record eleven fairs at Miami Art Week in 2018, we definitely understand that it can be an overwhelming and exhausting experience, but we do believe there is great value in doing it.

HOW TO MAKE THE MOST OF YOUR EXPERIENCE

Plan Ahead

First, look for the fairs that are closest to you, and then check to see if there are any additional events in the area that you would be willing to travel to or that you're already planning to travel to. Of course, the biggest fairs happen in major cities like Miami, New York, Los Angeles, London, Paris, Basel, and more—but new fairs are popping up every year, so there may be one closer than you think! If you're planning on networking with galleries, check out the fair website to see which ones are participating, and do a bit of research beforehand to locate any galleries that might align with the type of work you create.

If you're showing with a gallery for the first time at a fair, help promote it among your network and be proud of your accomplishment. Prepare all of your work in advance and make sure that everything is finished and framed or "ready to hang" so that you present yourself in the best light. For those who have paid to have their own stand, one of the best pieces of advice we can give is to have work available at a variety of price points. While you certainly hope to sell your most expensive pieces to recover the cost of your booth fee, selling several prints or smaller works can also add up. We'll go over more specifics on exhibiting at an artist-run fair later in this chapter.

Use Your Network

Especially if you have to travel to attend a fair, you likely won't want to dish out the extra cost of an admission ticket. Reach out to your network to see if by chance there is anyone you know who can provide you with a free pass. Otherwise, join the fair's email list, or one of its sponsors' lists, and they'll likely send out links to complimentary or discounted passes a few months prior to the opening.

Be Memorable

Dress nicely, but don't worry about being too formal. Since a ton of walking and standing is involved at fairs, you'll see many people wearing sneakers. If you're heading to the VIP preview, however, it might not be a bad idea to step it up a bit. This may also give you a little extra confidence boost when you're giving your elevator pitch to a new contact. Practice saying a few sentences about your art and what you do, so you are prepared for when you make a new connection. Don't forget to bring business cards, or something similar, that you can provide to a contact!

If you're showing at a fair for the first time, simply be polite and professional when others ask you about your work. Honestly, those are the interactions we remember the most from the fairs we've been to. We will give a special shoutout to artist Elisa Valenti here, who we met at Superfine! in New York in May 2019. Her work had already caught our attention, but she was also giving away chocolate-covered Oreos that had her images printed on them. How could we forget that?

Take Your Time & Remember That It Takes Time

Some fairs can have hundreds of exhibitors, so plan to spend at least a few hours at each fair you attend. Rushing to try to see everything won't give you the fullest experience and you might miss seeing an artwork or gallery that you really love.

Along the same lines, if you're participating in a fair and feeling discouraged that nobody has purchased anything from you yet, try to remain calm and positive. There are many pieces for potential collectors to look through, so give them time to find you. You've done so much work to present and promote your work, so now should be the fun part, when you get to meet and share your excitement about your art with collectors. Try to engage those entering your booth or your gallery's booth in a pleasant conversation, and if they express interest do your best to close that sale!

Grab a Drink

We love to use fairs as an excuse to splurge on a glass of champagne. It reminds us that this is a time to enjoy, celebrate, and find great new artists we might not have previously heard of. Also, a tiny bit of liquid courage never hurts when your mission is to network, but please stick to only one or two drinks.

Stopping at the bar for a bit also lets you take a much-needed break when you're in an environment where it's easy to overload on art. It is our job and our passion to see and discover amazing art for our readers, but even we get burned out after a while. You can only take in so much with fresh eyes, so when you start to get tired, it might be time for a cocktail or water in one of the seating areas.

Get Inspired & Dream Big

If it is your dream to eventually show at a major fair, this is your chance to start seeing how it works and to really visualize your art in this kind of space. Look at the artists around you and imagine yourself among them. Some artists hate fairs and get discouraged by seeing the dealing and exorbitant prices that certain works of art sell for, but this definitely isn't the time to play the comparison game. With so many fairs happening annually, we know that you can find the niche where your work would fit best and where you can connect with the right collectors. One of the best aspects of a fair for an artist is that it can put your work in front of potentially thousands of new people in the span of a weekend! Rarely do you have another opportunity to reach that many people in such a short amount of time.

Don't Get Run over by the Bar Cart

Yes, this almost happened to us. Those champagne promoters do not mess around when trying to navigate narrow aisles. Watch your feet! But in all seriousness, if you approach fairs with an open attitude about making connections and seeing new art for inspiration your time spent there will be worthwhile. We hope that with these tips in mind you'll begin to enjoy fairs as much as we do!

PARTICIPATING IN ARTIST-RUN ART FAIRS

If you live in a rural area without a major art scene or are looking to expand your network and meet new peers, collectors, and even press, participating in an art fair may be a worthy investment. Unless you are represented by a gallery that already takes your work to a fair, we suggest looking into quality artist-run art fairs that allow you to curate a booth and sell work for the duration of the event.

Several years ago, Kat was on a mission to upgrade her career. She noticed an open call for The Other Art Fair, which at the time had expanded their events into the United States. She signed up, received an acceptance letter, and started planning her first art fair experience. Overall, it was a success, but looking back, she could have made it even better. To save you time and effort, we want to share tips based on her experience, as well as feedback from other artists in our community who also have participated in fairs on their own.

If you are considering this type of event, we want to empower you with basic knowledge in terms of expenses and logistics so that you can make the most of your time. We hope that this information helps you get noticed, make sales, and enjoy being a stress-free exhibitor.

Consider the Cost

For those new to the art industry, the cost of a booth can come as a bit of a shock. Even the smallest rental costs can start anywhere from $1,500 and up. Aside from paying for your space at the event, there are a few other costs to consider before you sign up. If you create a plan and break down your budget, you can also prepare for unexpected expenses that may arise.

When Kat signed up for The Other Art Fair, she knew she didn't have a large budget, so she split the booth with her friend and fellow Philadelphia-based painter, Phyllis Gorsen. They coordinated the work they would each bring and curated a beautiful display. It helped that they were both interested in a similar color palette at the time.

To cut costs on lodging in New York City, a friend was kind enough to let Kat sleep on the couch. It was an exhausting week, and she would have been more comfortable in a private place of her own, but she made it work and was happy to save a bit of money on this particular expense.

If you don't have any connections and are participating in a new area, consider these hidden costs ahead of time. Here are some expenses to consider before you agree to participate in a fair:

- Travel costs (car rental or airfare)
- Art shipping
- Hanging supplies
- Marketing materials, such as postcards, prints, and merchandise
- Wall labels (if not provided), price lists, email signup sheet
- Hotel or Airbnb
- Food and drink
- Additional costs, such as lighting, a special paint color for the walls, or renting furniture for your booth, depending on the fair

Tip:

The most important thing to remember is that, while we hope you make sales and earn a profit, this is not guaranteed for anyone. Prepare your budget as if you won't have a single purchase, and focus on other aspects of the fair, such as networking with artists, curators, collectors, and press!

GETTING YOUR WORK THERE

To save money on art shipping, we recommend renting a car if the event is within driving distance. If you are flying and are a painter, you can roll your canvases and put them in a suitcase (same with works on paper). You can then assemble your work at a local framer or buy stretchers once you arrive.

WHAT TO BRING

You are probably wondering what kind of work to exhibit and what other items you may need to have. This is a critical question to ask yourself, even before you sign up for an event. Kat made a mistake by not having enough paintings ready before The Other Art Fair. Although she closed several sales and had a positive experience overall, she learned that she would need to bring a lot more work to make a profit.

If an artwork sells, it's a good idea to have another piece in a similar size and price point ready, so that you don't end up with an empty wall. Many buyers at fairs will want to take their purchases home with them right away to avoid having to return later, so plan for sales and have options ready.

Artwork
Small, Affordable Works or Prints
Most of your inventory should be works priced between $100 and $1,000. Pieces within this range are a great impulse-buy item for fair visitors and don't usually require much financial planning on their part. Collectors can easily justify spending money on a small work of art, even if it's unplanned. We're proof of this, as we ourselves often end up buying something when attending an art fair.

When Kat participated in The Other Art Fair, she sold most of her 9" x 12" paintings, which were around $200 apiece at the time. She also exhibited four medium-sized paintings priced around $1,200 each as her statement pieces.

Large Investment Pieces
While you want to try to appeal to those who thought they would only be browsing, many fair visitors do arrive with the intention of making a purchase. It's possible that they just moved into a new home and are looking for their living room or bedroom statement piece. When Kat showed at The Other Art Fair, she met interior designers who were scoping out new work for their clients, so you may connect with new collectors this way or via art consultants. Don't worry if the large-scale works you brought don't end up selling. You can use them to display the scope of your skills and potentially sell them in the future. Having a variety of work at your booth will create a powerful visual experience and may inspire commissioned work.

Kat ended up selling one of her larger paintings to new collectors, but months down the road, the other works she exhibited sold as well. Her art was featured by blogs and media that attended the fair, which helped bring attention to her work.

Mailing List Sign-Up
Some may express interest but not end up buying art during the fair, but keep in mind that numerous potential collectors may purchase from you down the line. You want to bring a sign-up sheet to collect emails from interested patrons, or use an iPad with an app for your email-marketing provider (e.g. Mailchimp or Constant Contact). Always ask for permission to add anyone to your list, and remember to send a thank-you email to new subscribers after the event is over to remind them of your work!

Postcards or Business Cards
During her fair experience, Kat had a stack of high-quality postcards featuring the paintings available in her booth. These were very popular with visitors and also served as a business card. We suggest that you bring beautiful marketing materials that will inspire your new contacts to follow your work online, long after the fair is over. It may even be a small, inexpensive print or sticker. For more ideas about best practices with business stationery, check out Creating Business Stationery (page 40).

Labels & Hanging Supplies
Before you arrive at the fair to install your work, make sure you bring correct labels for each piece of art you are exhibiting, and prepare a price sheet. You usually have to bring your own hanging equipment, such as a drill, hammer, nails, a level, spackle, ladder/step stool, and other items to ensure your work is hung professionally. Research what the event organizers offer in terms of lighting options and paint so you can order additional supplies if needed.

MAKING THE MOST OF YOUR EXPERIENCE

Plan for Comfort

Kat's booth partner, Phyllis Gorsen, brought two cube seats that opened up and also served as storage for extra supplies. Four full days is a very long time to stand on your feet, and most art fairs do not provide seating free of charge. If you want to be present at your booth and meet as many collectors and media partners as possible, we recommend preparing for your comfort ahead of time. Bring a small stool and definitely wear professional, but comfortable, shoes! You may also want to pack nuts, granola bars, fruit, and other easy-to-eat sneaks to help sustain you for the long fair hours. Food options at the fair might be limited and expensive.

Be Present at the Booth

We recommend being at your booth as much as possible, except for meals and other essential breaks. Some artists bring an assistant to help cover their booth, which is okay too, but remember that most visitors attending an artist-run fair are looking to connect directly with the creators. Collectors love to ask the artist about their process and inspiration, and get to know them on a level that's not possible online. When visitors enter your booth, be sure to welcome them with a friendly greeting and offer to answer any questions. If you are outgoing, you can approach them proactively and share a brief story behind the work they are looking at!

Tip:

Another reason why it is best to be in your booth is because when it is time to discuss closing a sale, you'll want to be the one doing the negotiating. The buyer may have questions or specific requests regarding shipping, framing, or discounts. Someone else likely won't know exactly how you want to handle these situations.

Promote the Fair

The fair will do a great job getting the word out about the event, but remember to do a full marketing campaign to your existing audience as well. If you are traveling to a new city, this is an excellent opportunity to notify your social media following and mailing list that you will be available to meet them at the fair. Send several reminders and include important information, such as dates, examples of work you are bringing, the venue location, and public opening hours. If your event offers complimentary passes, be sure to include a link to sign up or download them. When posting on social media, always tag the fair so they can repost your work and create excitement!

Fair Marketing Checklist

- Social media announcements
- Email blast
- Postcards
- Tell your close friends and family directly
- Pitch local media outlets about your participation and offer them a free pass to visit your booth to create even more buzz around your work!

We hope these tips will help you decide whether exhibiting at an artist-run fair is for you. This type of event is not necessary for your success in the industry, but it can certainly provide support in terms of publicity, building your collector base, and getting out of your comfort zone. You will learn a lot about yourself and your work when presenting it to a live audience for several days!

TAKE ACTION

- Research artist-run fairs in your area or in other locations you wouldn't mind traveling to and which might be a match for your art. You can start by looking into Superfine! Art Fair or The Other Art Fair.
- Create an estimated budget for exhibition costs, travel, lodging, and the other expenses listed in this chapter. Try to save a bit of extra money for any miscellaneous expenses that may come up!
- If you feel that you are ready, start applying to fairs and creating a plan for the work you will bring.
- To raise funding for the event, prepare a studio sale, start a crowdfunding campaign on Kickstarter or GoFundMe, or apply for a local artist grant.
- If you are accepted and commit to this experience, create a marketing plan for before, during, and after your big event!
- Curate a collection of your best work at a variety of price points and make sure all your work is ready to be displayed.

OVERCOMING CREATIVE BURNOUT

No matter how much we love what we do, inevitably, we all get tired and need time to recharge our human batteries. If, like us, you live in a culture that glorifies hustling and overworking, you probably have already experienced burnout at some point in your life. For Kat, it happened several times during college, and later when she started working for herself. It can be tricky to see the warning signs when you are in love with your work. Having invested hours of her time after working a day job to build a portfolio and creative business, it was difficult for Kat to stop working insane hours, even when she became her own boss. Rather than waiting until you reach your breaking point, we hope this chapter helps you prevent burnout—or guides you through the process if you're experiencing one right now.

THE SIGNS OF BURNOUT

Have you been struggling to start that new painting, or even show up to the studio? Does the thought of making new work drain you and fill you with dread? Kat once went through a very intense burnout that manifested itself as physical illness, an emotional breakdown, and a general inability to work. She was out of commission for nearly two weeks.

She had been running on empty for over two years without fully realizing it. From leaving her day job at a call center in 2016 to juggling her painting career and *Create! Magazine,* she unknowingly replaced breaks, fun, and time off with generating new ideas, networking, and more to-dos. She forgot what it meant to be truly inspired and enjoy the simple and free pleasures in life, whether or not they contributed to her art practice or career.

It's easy for creatives to feel guilty about taking breaks, because we either feel extremely lucky to be able to do it full time or are dying to make art after working a separate day job or part-time gig. Artmaking can be a great escape, but it can also become a burden when we put too much pressure on it. We need to give ourselves time to replenish our energy and creativity.

TIPS FOR BREAKING THROUGH

When art becomes an impossible task, it's time for a little intervention with yourself. Of course, we want to design our lives in a way that prevents these breakdowns altogether, but even when you're following a healthy schedule and know when to say no to an overload of commitments, burnout can still happen. Here are some steps to help you get back on your feet and return to your creative flow.

Schedule Your Breaks

Treat your time off like you would any crucial assignment or project. Try to incorporate at least one day a week where you indulge in guilt-free activities, such as reading, spending time with loved ones, or making art just for you (if you are up for it!). You will inevitably have new ideas, feel excited, and be motivated to get back to the studio after your break. Honor your deadlines whenever possible, but always put your mental and physical health first.

Check Your Engine

Sometimes we forget that we are living, breathing people and not machines pumping out ideas, art, and inspiration. Even if you exercise and eat well, stress and fatigue may have devastating effects on your overall health. When Kat was going through her burnout, she felt like she had the flu and could not stop sleeping, even though she may have looked fine from the outside.

Make sure you are conscious of whether you are getting enough sleep and drinking enough water, but also spend time laughing, smiling, taking a few deep breaths, and trying to enjoy your day whenever possible. Incorporate exercise into your schedule to give yourself mini breaks. For Kat, signing up for her first marathon in 2019 was a great experience. Even during her busiest times, she had to make sure to complete her training and was forced to be outdoors, which was incredibly therapeutic.

On an episode of our podcast Art & Cocktails, Kat interviewed one of her favorite painters, Andrew Salgado, an incredible and prolific figurative artist. Andrew shared that he takes a complete break after each exhibition and travels. Coming from such a successful role model, this made her realize how her nonstop schedule was probably hindering her growth in many ways.

We simply cannot expect to make good art if we continue to abuse our bodies and minds. We are all guilty of this from time to time, but as long as we strive to be more intuitive with ourselves, we are on track for a healthier, happier life and career.

Release the Pressure

The good news is, when we take care of ourselves and temporarily stop making art, no one is severely affected. When Kat worked at Macy's, her manager used to tell her on particularly bad sales days, "We are not saving lives—it's just lipstick," and that little saying stuck with her. No matter what's going on, your health and mental well-being are way more important than artwork. Plus, always remember that your gallery and collectors need you just as much as you need them. They will totally understand if you need a day, week, or month to take time away from your art. Only you know how much time you need, so if someone tries to convince you otherwise, think about whether they are really an important presence to have in your life.

There was an unpleasant moment in Kat's career when she decided to listen to her gut and refuse an exhibition opportunity. Though she was grateful for the show, she knew she desperately needed time off to prevent a severe burnout. Unfortunately, the person who was organizing the event did not take kindly to the news and tried to make her feel poorly about her decision. Though this situation was disappointing, it was also an indicator of what kind of intention this person had for Kat. If someone doesn't respect your physical and mental well-being, it doesn't matter what type of impact they can have on your art career. Pay attention when people show you who they really are, and avoid those whose motives don't align with your own. It's better to take care of your health and trust that other opportunities are on the way.

If you are generally a responsible, reliable, and pleasant person to work with, people will be understanding of your needs. Release the fear about asking so that you can recharge and remain the best artist and person you can be.

Prioritize

Sometimes we have projects and deadlines that determine the course of our career or if we are able to pay our bills that month. Highlight the immediate tasks at hand and complete them as well as you can, while saying no to anything that comes after. If you have things due in the future that are not pressing at the moment, you can use time now to recover fully. Don't look at, think about, or talk about upcoming deadlines that aren't an emergency, and focus on your health as much as possible. A great book we recommend on prioritizing is *Essentialism: The Disciplined Pursuit of Less* by Greg McKeown.

Say It Out Loud

We often get stuck in our own head and need someone to give us permission to take the break we know we need. Calling a friend or someone you trust and expressing your condition can help you view yourself from a third-party perspective. If you don't have someone to call, write it down on a piece of paper or in a journal. You are worthy of feeling your best, no matter how much time you need.

When you are ready to begin creating again, start slow, and shorten your workday from what you are used to so that you don't fall back into the trap of overwhelming yourself. Work on multiple projects at a time in bite-size pieces. Set a timer and take a five-minute break for every thirty you work. Make sure to step outside once in a while and breathe. If it helps, use little treats as motivation, like buying a new art book if you finish X-amount of work.

Continue ›

‹ Continued

Our art is about expressing our true selves, and if we are completely worn out, it is difficult to share our passion with others. We have to treat our life and career like a marathon, not a sprint, so we can continue to have fun and be prolific well into our old age.

Give yourself permission to rest. We promise you that your work will be better for it. We can't wait to see what you create when you come out on the other side!

WHEN BURNOUT IS SOMETHING MORE

Many of the signs of burnout cross over with those of depression. If you find that your feelings of exhaustion are coming from something deeper than working too hard, please seek help immediately.

Resources
• National Alliance on Mental Illness
• Anxiety and Depression Association of America
• American Foundation for Suicide Prevention: 1-800-273-TALK (8255) or text TALK to 741741
• World Health Organization

While our society as a whole has taken major strides toward bringing greater awareness to the importance of mental health and breaking down stigmas of the immense toll depression takes on the person affected, as well as those around them trying to help, we know there is still much work to be done.

TAKE ACTION

- Periodically check in with yourself. Are you in need of a day off, some fun, or time with loved ones? Schedule a day each week to do something just for you.
- Before saying yes to your next opportunity, be sure you are excited and feel capable of completing it without sabotaging your health.
- If you are currently in a state of burnout, practice self-compassion, and release the need to do work for others before taking care of your health first. Take time to sleep, go on a run, take a yoga class, or schedule a therapy session if needed. We promise you will come back stronger than ever!

HOW TO DEAL WITH IMPOSTER SYNDROME

ADVICE FROM KAT

When I first started putting myself out there, with both my artwork and in the early stages of *Create! Magazine*, I had to face fears and limiting beliefs about my place in the art world. Who did I think I was to begin sharing my work and starting a small business? After all, I didn't have an impressive education or even a background in publishing. I had so many doubts and insecurities about putting myself out there, as both an artist and an art-world professional, but eventually, I came to terms with my fears and realized that each of us has something valuable to contribute to the world. Our strength isn't necessarily in expertise, accolades, or prestigious degrees. We can make a big difference by sharing our story, being willing to learn the skills we lack, and serving our community in any way that we can. I embraced the fact that it simply takes time to get used to selling paintings and launching a creative business. It's uncomfortable at first and often feels unnatural, and you may even feel like a fraud in the process. But after your first few sales or other successes, you will start getting into the swing of things.

Though imposter syndrome may never entirely go away, we learn to build confidence by doing our work and sharing it with the world. The truth is, if you live with the mentality that humans are created as equals, then you will believe that we each have the absolute right to pursue our passion, put ourselves out there, and make a life and career we love. What often holds us back is not lack of time, credentials, money, or materials, but our feelings of unworthiness. Some of my biggest obstacles in the early stages of my career were being scared of silly, made-up problems: "What if this is the last good painting I make or sell?," "What if all this money goes away?" (spoiler alert: with that mentality, it definitely will), and, "What if something bad happens as a result of my success?" I even worried about not "looking like" an artist (what does that even mean?). I was seriously self-conscious and had a hard time forcing myself to show up to art exhibitions and networking events because I didn't feel thin or attractive enough.

Of course, I still have my share of anxieties and insecurities when taking risks and putting myself out there. By continuing to pursue my dreams despite my fears, I'm learning that it's usually much less scary than I initially imagined. There is more than enough room for all of us creatives to find success and our place in this industry. Each time you reach a new milestone, the universe will send a support system your way, so you will never be doing this alone.

The only way to fight fear, doubt, or disapproval is by staring it straight in the eye and doing it anyway. Share your artwork, submit that application, or write a grant proposal that terrifies you.

In so many instances, we're the only ones who think that an opportunity, show, job, or gallery is "out of our league" when it's actually not. Show up exactly as you are right now, not when a fancy critic approves of you, when you get signed by a gallery, or when someone buys your work. Show up exactly as you are at this moment in time and be proud of what you do and who you are.

When I first started selling my art, it was priced ridiculously low. It was almost embarrassing how cheap I made my paintings, but I kept going and pushing myself. With each sale, I slowly increased my prices, felt more like a professional, and upgraded my artist profile. Nobody can do this for you. Take your time and grow at a pace that feels natural, but I urge you to never wait for anyone's permission or approval. You are the only person responsible for elevating yourself and lifting yourself higher in your life and career. I had to learn this the hard way.

Several years ago, on a trip to Miami during the week when Art Basel is held, I had one of my favorite experiences that illustrates the lies of imposter syndrome. I was completely broke. At this point, I had already left my day job but was in the process of rebranding the magazine after a business partnership breakup. With about $80 to my name and a hefty credit card statement to top things off, I packed my bags and headed to the airport.

I was a part of an exciting exhibition at Art Miami Fairs during the annual Miami Art Week in early December. I was honored to be included, but had to scrape together every last penny I had to travel to the show. The exhibition was sponsored by a prestigious, philanthropic jewelry company called Unleashed World, and I was invited to come to their cocktail party before the fair. Insecurities about my outfit, a few extra pounds induced by stress, and my lack of money felt like rocks in the pit of my stomach. I mustered up the courage to go and used my last few dollars to Uber to the event. Even though I did not feel ready or good enough, I knew that for me to climb out of the pit that I was in, I had to start showing up for myself and become the person that I wanted to be.

Continue ›

When I arrived at the party, it was even more extravagant than I imagined. I surveyed the scene of this large, ocean-view apartment complete with white leather couches, an impressive collection of contemporary art, and trays of fancy champagne floating around the room. I was sure I didn't belong. Much to my relief, however, the attendees were some of the friendliest people I had ever met. I began chatting with designers, art dealers, artists, and art collectors who were all brought together through this organization for their love of art. Nobody cared that I wasn't wearing a designer dress or that I was an emerging artist trying to make things work. They just wanted to see my paintings and hear my story. I will never regret stepping out of my comfort zone to attend this event. I got so much confidence from the simple fact that I could hold a conversation with a famous art dealer that evening.

Of course, not every situation in life will go this smoothly. Still, it's important to remember that even intimidating individuals, who appear to have everything you don't, had to start somewhere too and would never have arrived at where they are now if they didn't face their demons head on. It's often our insecurities that prevent us from putting ourselves into the situations that can help us the most.

If you are worried about all the things you are not, or all the skills you don't yet have, I urge you to take a moment and see yourself for everything you are. Ask yourself: What have I accomplished so far?

> *"Say yes to showing up and sharing your gift, and watch the magic unfold in your life."*

What am I most proud of? Where do I want to go next? Please don't leave any room for doubts and negativity, especially when it comes to your art. Imagine the person who needs to experience what you create in yourself and don't deprive them of that joy. Say yes to showing up and sharing your gift, and watch the magic unfold in your life.

TAKE ACTION

- Examine areas of your life and career where you may be holding back. Journal and meditate about where you would like to see more growth and results. Be gentle with yourself during this process, but allow yourself to expand going forward.

Journal Prompts

- *If you were your most confident and successful self, what do you see yourself doing more of in your life, art, and business? Write about what you would like to see yourself doing more of, if fear wasn't holding you back.*
- *Why are you currently not taking action in the areas you listed above? Confront what's holding you back and list any fears and limiting beliefs.*
- *Rewrite your fears into positive statements and create affirmations to help you gain confidence in these areas.*

DEALING WITH "UN" FEELINGS

It's okay to not be okay. You've probably seen this phrase posted often on social media and heard it in reference to mental health awareness. We both agree that it's absolutely true and think that it is relevant for creatives in a big way. In a sense, you can think of this phrase as a reminder that your life and career will have high and low seasons. Some months or years will bring you sales, commissions, and an abundance of new opportunities, while at other times you'll hit a creative roadblock, lose a sale, receive multiple rejections, or simply hear back nothing at all. In addition, circumstances in your personal life will affect your work life too, both in good ways and, unfortunately, negative ways. Yet, you must try to accept these seasons as they come and keep pushing through.

Thinking more about this phrase, it also aligns with our advice to strive for authenticity in your practice and how you present yourself in person and online. We're so conditioned to saying, "I'm fine," or, "I'm good," as an automatic response to the question "How are you?," regardless of how we actually feel. The same holds true with your art and art career.

When we saw Jerry Saltz speak at Frieze Art Fair, one of the things we took away from his talk was his emphasis on "radical vulnerability" and how that is one of the things that makes great art. Your art is for you—there's no need to put up a facade. You don't have to keep posting on social media if you're not feeling inspired to, you don't have to paint if you're not motivated to at the moment, and you certainly don't have to keep making sculptures of figures just because they've been selling steadily. It's a good idea to get in the habit of really checking in with yourself to see if you're happy and excited about your work and what you're doing, rather than forcing yourself to keep going.

Don't be afraid to be honest with friends and peers. Of course, you'll only want to share what you're comfortable with among the right group of people who will be understanding and supportive, but we've both had powerful conversations with others when we openly admitted that we were struggling with a problem, disappointed that something didn't work out, or stuck creatively. People appreciate honesty, and they'll likely be able to commiserate or perhaps even offer a new perspective to help you feel better.

Let's explore some of the most common "un" feelings we experience—not just as artists, but as humans.

IDENTIFYING YOUR "UN" FEELINGS

Following are a few common "un" feelings and some tips and ideas for how to handle them.

Unwell

*We are specifically referring to feeling physically sick here. If you are dealing with any mental health issues, we urge you to seek professional help.

Alicia used to get colds very often and, never wanting to fall behind, she would continue working at full speed and even going to the gym. She kept this up for years, always wondering why her illnesses seemed to last much longer than everyone else's. If you are injured or get sick, that is a sign from your body that you need rest. Take it! Don't try to power through—you'll simply risk making yourself worse. You may think you have a deadline that you absolutely cannot miss, but it is only on very rare occasions that a quick note to the other party explaining your situation won't get you at least an extra day or two to complete your work. Always ask others for help if and when you need it. When we say take a break, we mean it. Working with your laptop in bed might help you feel productive, but you should try to unplug in order to let your body fully focus on healing.

Uninspired

You might feel worried looking at your blank sketchbook if you haven't had any new ideas for work in a while, but this is normal. We say this a lot: you're not a creative machine. Expecting that you'll have a constant stream of new works to execute is unrealistic, so the first step is to adjust your expectations.

Perhaps you were feverishly working on a new idea or series for months or years and now your momentum has slowed. Take a step back and think about whether you may be ready to move on to something different. There are also artists who place so much pressure on themselves that they immediately shoot down any new idea they have. This is based on an irrational fear that nothing will be good enough. If this is you, we encourage you to at least give these ideas a try before throwing them out completely, because even if it doesn't work, you'll likely learn from the process.

"You can't force inspiration—you just have to let it happen."

You can't force inspiration—you just have to let it happen. In the meantime, allow yourself to read, look at a lot of art, and participate in activities that you enjoy, in the hopes that one of these activities will help spark your imagination again.

Unmotivated

For most of us, periods of feeling unmotivated don't come because we are lazy. When you find yourself thinking this way, take time to think about and identify what is at the root of not wanting to do work that you previously enjoyed. First, did you actually previously enjoy your work? If not, what can you do to change that? Whether it is something in your studio space or the subject you're currently exploring, make adjustments when you need to in order to get back to being your best creative self.

After you've received a string of rejections or had a quiet spell, it can feel difficult to keep going. This is when you really have to pick yourself up, dust yourself off, and get back to work. Letting yourself succumb to feelings of unworthiness or falsely believing in a scarcity mindset will only dig you deeper into a hole. Instead, put faith into your manifestations, affirmations, and goals. Most importantly, after you have acknowledged that whatever opportunities didn't work out were simply not meant to be, put in the work.

With a major deadline or project coming up in the future, you may be tempted to procrastinate. While it could be that you work great under pressure and thrive on last-minute adrenaline to get the job done, more often than not we put off difficult tasks because we try to do too much at once. If you have twenty new drawings to complete for a show in a few months, that can be overwhelming! Break down the final result into smaller, more manageable tasks. Don't think about the twenty that you have to finish eventually—focus on the one you're working on today. Approaching big projects this way, with your own set of mini deadlines or target completion dates, helps you stay on target and feel less overwhelmed.

Unproductive

This "un" feeling can be similar to being unmotivated, but it can be caused by different factors. The first question we suggest you ask yourself when you feel this way is if you have identified how you work best. Are you the type of person who prefers to focus on and complete one task at a time or do you work on several projects at once, putting in short blocks of time daily on each? Do you prefer waking up early or working at night? Can you handle noise or do you need a quiet space? If you're forcing yourself into one method of working when you'd actually prefer another, that might be why you're not as productive as you could be.

Another way to boost your productivity might be to see if you can organize and streamline your studio practice. Make sure to check out our chapter Creating Systems to Stay Organized (page 46) to make sure that nothing about your creative space and process is hindering the efficiency of your workflow!

Finally—and this is an important one—being unproductive (and sometimes unmotivated too) can be an indicator that you've spread yourself too thin. When you're ambitious and want to please as many people as possible, you fall into the trap of not being able to say no. However, you may then start to lose track of deadlines or not complete work to your usual standards and ultimately, that isn't doing anyone any favors. Hopefully, you're in a place where the money doesn't outweigh the cost of the combined time and effort to make the extra commitment. Rather than get to the point of exhaustion, try to identify this as early as possible.

Tip:

To boost your productivity, try to get regular sleep, stay hydrated, eat well, and give your eyes a break from screens!

Unsuccessful

For us, it is always disappointing to hear other artists lament that they'll never "make it" and downplay what they've already accomplished. Just as we urge you to not define an artist in absolute terms, we want you to measure success in your own way, according to your own standards. You can set lofty goals — and we agree that in many instances you should — but what should drive you is the effort you constantly put in toward working to achieve them, not necessarily the end result.

Artists measure much of their success by the frequency of when they make a sale. However, this is not something that is easily comparable between people working in different mediums or in various stages of their careers. Other factors like how fast you work, how you market your art, and where you sell all play a role in your rate of sales. If you think you're not selling as much as you should, keep in mind that an unsold work usually only means that you haven't found that perfect client yet, not that you never will or that your art isn't good enough.

You may notice a slump in sales if you've just raised your prices and your collectors need to adjust to the new costs, or if you introduce a different style of work than what you've shown before. We've also had promotions, discounts, and flash sales completely flop. It's certainly not fun to have this happen, but we try to use these situations as opportunities to figure out if the timing wasn't right or if we didn't promote to the right audience. Going back to the idea that rejections can cause lack of motivation to work, they can also have a detrimental effect on how you see yourself as an artist — if you let them. However, the same antidote applies: stay in a positive mindset that sales, better opportunities, and more will come soon.

Likewise, be grateful and proud of what you have achieved, despite the fact that you may not have reached the exact goals you set for yourself. If you wanted to get into five shows and only were selected for two, that's still worthy of excitement and should be shared with your audience.

We hope that with this insight, you can turn these "un" words into their opposites and return to a state of positivity, productivity, and health!

TAKE ACTION

- Identify any of your own "un" feelings. Are they the ones we discussed in this chapter or something else? What can you do to address them?
- If you feel comfortable sharing how you feel with others, decide who you can reach out to.

COMING BACK TO YOUR ART
AFTER A BREAK

Maybe you suffered a bad case of artist block, or perhaps you experienced severe burnout. Whatever the case, we all step away from our work from time to time. We go through periods in which we are not as productive as we hope. It's okay to have times of reflection and to take a break for as long as you need. If you are ready to get back to your work, we encourage you to use the tips in this chapter to guide you.

Sometimes our breaks or dry spells are not about the art itself, but are meant to serve as a reminder or means of discovering the real motivation behind why we create. We have to be especially kind to ourselves about taking time away when we experience serious life changes, including having children, grieving the loss of a loved one, suffering health issues, moving, or dealing with other major life events. Regardless of the reason you stepped away from your beloved art practice, your work will always welcome you back with open arms and infinite possibilities, if you let it.

LET GO OF UNREALISTIC EXPECTATIONS OF YOURSELF

The year Kat was signed by her first gallery, she started experiencing immense pressure and anxiety. This result had nothing to do with the gallery and everything to do with her expectations and false assumptions about what would come next. Nothing was different, except that she had someone to help sell her paintings. This new experience brought up insecurities for her, and she immediately started to question every brushstroke, study, and idea that came into her head, analyzing it and worrying about whether it would sell or be well received. As a result of this panic, she overcommitted to unrealistic deadlines to please others. Even though no one was pressuring Kat, her work in the studio became heavy and burdened. She had a hard time enjoying her artmaking. Painting used to be her escape, but now thoughts of failure and disappointment loomed over her as she scrambled to finish her paintings.

She had a mini intervention with herself after several months of unsuccessfully fighting through it. After taking a break, she uncovered the beautiful reasons why she always wanted to be an artist, whether working with a gallery or hustling on her own. She started to journal and meditated about the type of work she hoped to create. She asked herself questions like "What keeps bringing me to the studio?" and "Why do I continue to make art, even when no one is paying attention?" Healing Kat's relationship with her work and protecting it from outside validation took time. After she fulfilled her commitments to the gallery, she asked them if she could have a few months to explore her work on her own terms and without planned exhibitions. They were beyond understanding, and this took the pressure off Kat's work almost immediately.

BE HONEST WITH HOW YOU SPEND YOUR TIME

After Kat reclaimed ownership of her work and studio practice, the wheels began to turn. The first step to healing for her was to detach from exterior validation and break the ties between the process of creation and the business and career side of her work. Kat enjoys sales and marketing, but these things have very little to do with her desire to make art or her willingness to put in hours in front of the canvas.

Kat decided that she would stop fueling her anxiety and get back to what lights her up at the most basic level of creation. She continued to meditate and journal to uncover what was causing her to be so distant from her work. Looking back now, she realizes that she wasn't spending as much time in the studio and was frequently distracted by checking emails or allowing other interruptions to disrupt her work. She desperately wanted to get back to the state of playfulness and flow, and in order for that to happen, she needed to make a few changes.

WHAT KIND OF ARTIST DO YOU WANT TO BE?

Kat had another revelation during her break. She realized that she wasn't fully expressing herself in her studio practice and was holding back due to fears of change or not being able to sell the type of work she wanted to create. Since we only get to live once, it's essential that we liberate ourselves and make room for experimentation, play, and frankly, just letting ourselves make bad work at times. We don't have to share it with anyone, but how will we know our next step if we are too scared to step out of a self-imposed box?

Are you subconsciously making the same painting (sculpture, photo, etc.) because you know it will sell to your collectors? Maybe you are worried that if you switch things up, you will lose your followers and people will judge you or stop buying from you. We all have these fears, and it's not a bad idea to check in with yourself once in a while to make sure these fears aren't ruling your creative process. Determine if you are creating out of genuine interest, love, and excitement, and not someone else's expectations. We invite you to be the most unapologetic, fearless, and genuine artist you dream of becoming. What do you want your legacy to be?

CREATE A SACRED ENVIRONMENT

Do you light up when you enter your workspace? If not, rearrange furniture or go thrifting to find a few objects that make you feel in the mood to create. Having a designated environment, or even a corner of your kitchen table, where you feel safe, inspired, and comfortable is vital to help you thrive as an artist.

Kat didn't get her own creative space until later in her career, so for her, renting a large studio space in a giant factory building in Philadelphia was a difficult adjustment. From painting on the floor of a studio apartment, to using a spare bedroom, to finally having a place of her own, she realized the importance of making the space as comfortable and beautiful as you can with whatever resources you have at the time. For Kat, adding touches that reflect her work, such as decorating with plants and flowers, painting a wall pink, and finding affordable, eccentric furniture, is important. She loves creating a sacred space that's filled with bright colors, seashells, plants, candles, and anything else that makes her feel like it's her sanctuary. Your studio or art area should feel like your creative home, even if you have never had one before. Readjust as often as you need to until you are happy to spend hours doing work there.

You may love a creative mess, but make sure you feel organized and comfortable enough to work. Even if your only available space is your kitchen table (we've both had to make do!), jazz it up with some flowers, a favorite magazine or two, textiles, or anything else that helps you feel creative and inspired. Then add to the ambience by making your favorite cup of tea or coffee and putting on some music, an audiobook, or a podcast. We both enjoy working while listening to specific Spotify playlists and podcasts that help put us into an artistic state. Condition yourself to respond to your environment and find positive triggers that help you settle into your creative mode.

WHEN YOUR BREAK IS LONGER THAN A FEW MONTHS...

Alicia once had an artwork selected by multiple juried exhibitions and then featured prominently in a blog feature online. This same piece was the reason she was contacted by a media source for an interview and by a band soon after asking to use it for a gig poster. People began to regularly reach out to see if she made any others like it. Sounds exciting, right? Like a turning point we all long for in our career when we feel we've been discovered. Yet, the work was a fluke—something she had made in a few hours as an experiment that she never even thought she would end up showing publicly. She didn't even really like it, but was curious enough to submit it and see what would happen (and was subsequently blown away when curators, writers, collectors, and more showed interest!). It was nothing like the series of paintings she had spent years developing—the ones she loved and was proud of.

Around this time, she also visited several graduate MFA programs in New York City. Looking through each of the open studios at four different universities, she just couldn't picture her paintings alongside the students' work. She felt like her artwork definitely didn't belong, and therefore, that neither did she. In small part affected by

Continue ›

the disillusionment from both of these experiences, but mostly pulled toward the new excitement she felt from working in galleries and writing about art, Alicia went on to pursue her master's in art history instead.

Early on, she was still diligent about making art, applying to new opportunities, and exhibiting, in addition to keeping up with her graduate studies. She participated in an art exchange with a group of printmakers, in which she had to produce a new limited edition of twenty, which was no small feat done from her kitchen table. But once she began working full time, with other part-time commitments on the side to generate extra income, life got in the way of making time for creating new art.

YOU'RE STILL AN ARTIST

A period of years passed before Alicia would make a more consistent and deliberate effort to make new work for herself. During this time, since she worked in the arts, Alicia was repeatedly asked, "Are you an artist?," and internally, she winced at the question. If she answered no, she would feel as if she was betraying her formerly active artistic self, and if she answered yes, she thought she was being untruthful. But thinking about this now, and having met so many artists who have taken one, five, or even ten or more years away from their work, there should have been no doubt in her mind about the response: yes, she was an artist and also is one today. Not just because she had earned a BFA (although this applies to those who are self-taught too!), but because it was a part of her and still is, whether she was regularly making traditional fine art or not.

You can define yourself as whatever you want to, and if you feel called to create then you are an artist. Remember that there is no one way to be an artist—and no right way either. If you've made a thousand paintings, it likely means you're more consistent and committed than someone who has made ten, but it's not an automatic indicator that you're the better artist. Everyone is on their own timeline, so your business should be to focus on your own journey.

POUR YOUR CREATIVITY INTO SOMETHING

As an artistically inclined person, you'll still probably crave being creative in some way when you're not able to spend time in a studio or make new artwork. If this is the case for you, try to find little ways to infuse creativity into the work that you're already doing. Alicia was able to do this with the marketing-related tasks in her various jobs and as a social media consultant. It's certainly not the same as pushing paint along a canvas or wiping ink from an etching plate, but shooting and editing beautiful images for Instagram, designing email newsletters, and writing catchy captions and campaigns helped keep her creative instincts alive.

You may be in a situation where the majority of your work, both at a job or at home, is non-art-related and that's okay too. Identify other instances or opportunities where you can express yourself. Perhaps it could be through the way that you cook, organize your house, or dress. Alicia enjoyed embracing photography while traveling and to capture special moments from her life and also started building her personal art collection. Although neither of these were directly related to making a new body of her own artwork, they still allowed her to flex her creative muscles.

Again, it's important to not let yourself or anyone else place limitations on what your creative practice should be. If you don't make any traditional art during your break or try creating work in a new medium, there is nothing wrong with that. You can take it a step further and share it if you are comfortable with the idea. Alicia decided to submit one of her photos for a project on the noted art blog *Boooooooom* and it ended up being featured on their Instagram profile and website as well as in an email newsletter.

CAPITALIZE ON INSPIRATION WHEN IT STRIKES

After moving to Amsterdam and before she found steady work, Alicia struggled to feel at home in the new apartment she had rented with her partner. They had only arrived with the essentials stuffed into four suitcases, so the modest art collection they had built between them was sent to be stored at her parents' house. Determined to add life to their new home, Alicia found inexpensive art supplies at a local store and created two large statement paintings for their living room area, finishing each piece within a few days. The pieces were never meant to be serious works of art, but just making them felt great and helped remind her of what she loved about the creative process. If you find that you have a bit of extra time or additional cash and a new idea, allow yourself to pursue it with passion and without any expectations. You never know if this is what will get you back to being a regular, practicing artist!

SLOW & STEADY

Those two paintings did not act as an immediate catalyst for Alicia to dive back into her art more fully, but they did help eventually lead her back to drawing (along with a friendly little push from Kat in the form of a beautiful new sketchpad and a workbook by Alli Koch on illustrating florals). In 2019, Alicia began sketching more frequently than she had in years. At one point, she thought it would be the right time to try a 100-day challenge, but only made it about 30 days in before becoming overwhelmed. After years away from art, it was a bit unrealistic to expect that she would suddenly be able to keep up with creative output on a daily basis. Instead of giving up completely, she recalibrated her expectations and decided to simply keep sketching and drawing on a more fluid schedule depending on when she felt inspired to do so, rather than trying to force a commitment. She has enjoyed being in the stage of research and sketching before deciding what idea or subjects to pursue next in her work. Not only has this helped her grow as an artist, but it also supports her creative process as a writer and aligns with her various roles as a businesswoman in the arts.

Sometimes it may feel like the longer you are away from your studio practice, the harder it will be to return. If you know that you ultimately want to be an artist, however, don't give up on that dream. Incorporate as many of our tips and pieces of advice as you can into your life. Baby steps will still move you forward and help you make progress. Trust in yourself and believe in the power of supportive family and friends who will continue to encourage you to meet your goals. It's never too late to start or start over again.

ADDITIONAL TIPS

Make Sure It's Still Fun

Pay attention to the work you are making and see if it's still exciting for you. Do you have more ideas than time to execute them and keep coming back to a subject, palette, or texture that you can't get enough of? What colors and objects are you naturally drawn to throughout your day? Sure, we have commitments, projects, and obligations to others, but are you taking the time to create work that makes hours go by unnoticed? Be honest with yourself and make changes if you need to. This is your life: make it fun!

Try Something New

If you are still in the midst of an artist block or having trouble getting started, it's not a bad idea to check local museums or other arts organizations for class or workshop listings. Kat has taken clay and textile classes and also connected with an artist on Instagram who was offering affordable embroidery classes. Alicia took workshops in jewelry making and crafting with concrete. Neither of us had much of a background with any of these mediums, but that was part of the point in choosing them. We allowed ourselves to get lost in the new processes, to learn, to make mistakes, to experiment, and to think of something else beyond our current work.

Tip:

You can use these experiences to focus on yourself and your creative practice, but sometimes it is also fun to invite a friend.

Just Show Up

Sometimes just showing up makes a big difference. Maybe you will fiddle with a painting, and then perhaps clean your studio. There are days when you will end the day after completing ten new pieces, and others when you'll barely put one new brushstroke on the canvas. It's all part of the process. Train yourself to honor your studio time, no matter the outcome. Consistency is how you will generate new ideas, resolve existing works, and gain more confidence that you are committed to being an artist.

Get Back to the Basics

Lastly, sometimes we are so caught up in creating epic new work that we forget why we even became artists. Keep a sketchbook for daily drawings or take your camera to the beach or on a hike. Doodle on an iPad or tablet while watching TV, or make a silly drawing of your pets just for fun. Ask yourself what the best version of you would be excited about at this moment and start from there. Don't be afraid to make something terrible in the process!

TAKE ACTION

- Examine your current body of work and practice. Journal and ask yourself if this is truly the type of art you want to spend your days creating. If it's not, what is your heart calling you to try? Is there a type of work you are jealous of in a good way? See what you can apply to your practice to freshen things up.

- Create an inspiring workspace, even if it's just a corner of your living room. Make it as comfortable and creative as you possibly can so that you are excited to come back time and time again.

- Make a folder (we love Pinterest for this) to collect visual fodder, even if it's not directly related to your art. Save photos of color palettes, textures, photographs, artwork, and anything else that visually makes your heart skip a beat. You never know how it may show up in your work later!

- Step outside of your comfort zone and try something new! Take a ceramics class, try weaving, or experiment with anything else that sounds fun to you. It doesn't have to be art-related. If you've wanted to learn more about cooking, gardening, or writing, go for it. Allowing yourself to be creative in another discipline can definitely help ignite new ideas and skills for you to use in the studio too!

- Create a flexible studio schedule. If you are getting back to your work, designate two to three days per week to be in the studio. Make a promise to yourself to sketch, make work, or research for a few hours on each of those days until you want to add more time. Ease back into making art without setting rigid timelines and, most importantly, enjoy the process.

YOU BELONG IN THE ART WORLD

Over the years, we have had the pleasure of attending numerous museum exhibitions, gallery openings, and art fairs. The one unifying factor across these events is the diverse range of work featured by galleries, museums, nonprofits, and other institutions around the world. The best opportunity to see this in action for yourself is to visit an international art fair. We challenge you to attend at least one in the coming year to see what we mean. There are paintings, sculptures, installations, prints, photography, mixed media, and more, all at varying price points depending on which fair you go to! If any of these artists can be exhibited at this scale, you can too, if that is your dream.

While artists are touted as some of the most adaptable and free-thinking people, it's surprising that so many of them still expect their careers to go smoothly from point A to point B. There is not one linear path to success as an artist. You have to first define what success means to you in order to accomplish what you want in your career. We hope that more artists do this, because once everyone realizes that their goals are different, we won't feel forced into competition with one another and will embrace the fact that there is a niche for everyone.

It's sometimes easy to get caught up in following artists online who work similarly to each other, unless you are actively looking for different styles and genres of art. We tend to get sucked into comparing ourselves on social media and trying to become a specific type of artist we think will be successful. But through a decade of making our way in this industry, we have learned that the art world is broad and has room for all types of work. There are no limits to what you can create and what you can achieve doing what you love with the skills you possess naturally. Therefore, our goal in this chapter, and throughout this book, is to convince you to embrace your unique creative superpower and truly get you to believe that you have a place in this market.

"There is not one linear path to success as an artist. You have to first define what success means to you in order to accomplish what you want in your career."

WHEN YOU'RE NOT ONE OF THE WHO'S WHO

There are certainly those who will have an easier time getting ahead in the art world, whether through family and business connections or where they live. But this is no reason to feel as though you'll never make it. Neither of us had strong ties (or any!) to the art world before we embarked on our careers. What is more important to focus on is hard work, presenting yourself professionally, and being clear about what your ultimate goals are. A person who is simply handed something will almost never appreciate it as much as someone who worked for it.

That being said, you really can't judge someone just from looking in as an outsider. You don't know what their experience has been like or what is going on in their life. Even if it looks like they've had it easy, it may have been anything but that. So much of your career in the art world is about making connections. Instead of criticism, we'd all do better to embrace compassion and empathy, as well as offer support when we're able to. Refusing to reinforce barriers between "haves" and "have nots" creates a more welcoming and transparent community where artists of all levels can feel accepted.

Create without Limitations

Artwork can be funny, political, romantic, tragic, or whatever you want it to be. You can use found materials or even trash, like contemporary artist Leo Sewell does with his "Junk Sculptures," to create impressive works. For other artists, perhaps it is science, history, or nature that inspires and informs their creative practice. If there are rules in the art world, they aren't about what type of work you should make, so there is no reason to try to fit into an existing category.

Once you embrace your aesthetic, background, interests, and passion, your distinct voice will shine through your work. We want you to understand and believe that there is enough room for everyone in the art world, as long as you are willing to accept and own who you are as an artist. The only advice we have is to be yourself. We promise it's a lot easier than trying to pass as a second-rate copy of someone else.

Follow Your Passion

When Kat graduated, she was very insecure about the type of work she was creating. She felt trapped by the comparison game and would spend hours obsessing over what kind of paintings she should make to be considered "contemporary enough." She started by painting interiors from her past and memories of growing up in Russia, and eventually created work inspired by her current environment. She experimented with different styles and subject matter to try to create something unique, but the harder she tried, the less authentic her paintings became and the worse she felt about them.

Over time, she realized that her audience responded the most when she simply painted what she loved, using her favorite color combinations, exploring the luscious texture of oil paint, and getting lost in the moment. Art can be a transfer of energy and experiences, and viewers can sense if you are trying to push something that you're not naturally excited about. Make sure you love at least one significant aspect of your practice and think about what keeps bringing you back to the studio over and over again. This is what should be driving you to create your best artwork!

One morning during one of Kat's daily painting challenges, she posted her work as usual while enjoying her morning coffee. That day, the simple painting of her bedroom went viral. It was similar to her other pieces but effortless to execute. Was it a fluke? Maybe. Or perhaps it was the result of consistently showing up every week and promoting the work she cared about until someone noticed. Moments like this don't happen often, but you can increase your chances of being seen by doing the work you truly have a passion for and sharing it with your audience.

"It's Been Done Before"

Just because a particular subject or technique has been explored before, doesn't mean that you can't put your spin on it and thrive as an artist. Even if you are passionate about work that has already been done by someone else, your voice, perspective, and personal background will make it unique. For example, there are hundreds of artists today and throughout history who have painted interior spaces, but there is still so much to explore even within this particular subject matter. To experience success, you must unapologetically use your creative voice and be consistent with your studio practice for your work to get noticed and be taken seriously. As you develop your artistic style and polish your skills, this will become easier over time.

Don't worry if your immediate community doesn't understand what you do just yet. Eventually, you will connect with like-minded individuals and find your tribe. Keep showing up, challenging yourself creatively and intellectually, and bravely taking risks as you follow your passion!

Right Place, Right Time

Alicia used to feel discouraged reading "30 under 30" lists, thinking that she'd never be as accomplished as the type of entrepreneurs often featured in those articles. Then she finally thought to herself, "Who actually cares about those lists?" Success is success, whether you are twenty-five or eighty-five, a self-taught artist or have an MFA, hold down a day job or maintain a full-time studio practice, have raised a family or are still single. Why put unnecessary pressure on yourself?

Not having a solo show at a major gallery by the time you are X-years old is not a failure. Again, we remind you that everyone's journey is different. Even if it takes longer than expected, you will find your place and all of the prosperity that comes with it.

TAKE ACTION

- Challenge yourself to visit exhibitions or art fairs that you usually wouldn't attend. Observe the artwork on display and write down your favorites. Try to find work that takes you out of your comfort zone!
- Find ten artists you admire who work with a similar subject matter or technique as you. Study their work, process, and career to see all that is possible.
- Create a list of things that makes your perspective and story unique as an artist, and think about how you can use that to describe your work to your audience.

FINDING YOUR TRIBE

Although the majority of your artmaking and business tasks will require solitary work, you'll also want to build a support system of clients, peers, and mentors as you navigate your career. In Networking 101 for Artists (page 182), we discuss how being able to connect with important figures in your local community or the larger art industry can lead you to new opportunities. You can also learn valuable advice and, as long as you leave a great impression, create a pool of people who would be willing to act as a reference for you when needed.

While we never recommend that you seek validation from outside sources, it's always nice to have others who encourage and help promote what you do. People will come and go throughout your life and career, but if you meet someone who brings out the best in you, make the extra effort to build and sustain that relationship over time. You really don't need to have hundreds or thousands of clients to be successful and feel supported. Even a handful of active collectors and loyal friends can make a significant difference. Read more specific information on connecting with your ideal clients in Finding & Building Relationships with Collectors (page 182).

YOUR PEERS

When you go through a BFA or MFA program, it's easy to meet other artists at your same level who have similar interests. Keep in touch with any students, or even professors, with whom you connected after graduating. Once you're out in the real world, reach out to artists online, introduce yourself to your studio neighbors, and attend art events in your area. You can invite new acquaintances to chat over coffee or to visit your studio—it should be evident fairly early on if you've made a valuable connection.

If we hadn't stayed in touch with each other after graduating from Kutztown University, who knows if what we're doing together today would exist! During the years of being peers and supporting each other in our respective art careers, we also built a friendship. Then, after almost a decade of knowing each other, we decided to work together on various business partnerships because we'd already established a foundation of trust. Looking back on our time as undergraduates, neither of us could have imagined that we'd be so close now or that we'd eventually run a magazine and gallery, as well as write books, record podcasts, teach workshops, and more, together.

In addition to our other undergrad peers that we check in with periodically on social media or via email, Kat makes it a point to have a yearly meetup with another of our fellow KU graduates. Alicia has maintained a very close relationship with a friend she met all the way back in her high school art classes and also has remained in contact with a small handful of people she knows from her time in grad school.

ACCOUNTABILITY ALLIES

One reason to seek out other artists you admire and would be interested to work with might be to have an accountability partner or group. You can ask one or a few other peers to join you and set up weekly or monthly meetings where you talk about your struggles, wins, and what you're working on, and give each other feedback and guidance. It will motivate you to keep pushing your work when you know that others are working hard too.

MASTERMIND GROUPS

You may also consider taking this to the next level by joining a mastermind group. In addition to accountability, these weekly or monthly sessions may also include lessons, mentoring, and talks with industry experts. If you are interested in a more intense program to develop as an artist, this may be right for you. Note that due to the serious nature and commitment of these groups, there is often a fee involved, and some may require an application and interview in order to join. You'll have to do research to find the right group for artists, or you may consider participating in a group focused on business if you want to improve your skills in marketing and sales.

It's important to remember that while staying in the art industry is excellent, you can also join masterminds and courses that help you gain skills in other aspects of your creative business, such as marketing, sales, and self-development. Sometimes having a fresh perspective from other industry leaders can inspire us to approach our work in new and exciting ways.

MENTORS

Having a great mentor is an invaluable resource, so you should definitely be on the lookout for a person who could act as one for you. Hopefully, this happens organically and someone who is already a favorite teacher or supportive boss has taken an interest in you and expressed a willingness to help you. We both had incredible high school art teachers who we have stayed in touch with over the years. We definitely feel indebted to these teachers for guiding us through our uncertain teenage years and for arming us with the skills and tools we would use later in college. Alicia was also very fortunate that a pair of dynamic, established women gallerists took a chance on her and allowed her to intern for them early in her career. Later, she went on to work for a talented printmaker and professor in Philadelphia, who was always willing to listen and give advice as she navigated her graduate studies and began working in galleries.

If a connection doesn't happen naturally, you can look into apps like Bumble Bizz or join a professional artist network to help match you with someone. This is especially useful if you want your mentorship relationship to be formal and to meet regularly. You can also reach out to someone you admire, such as another artist, curator, writer, gallerist, advisor, etc. The more high-level this professional is, the less likely they are to have the extra time to make a commitment to you, so do bear that in mind. However, if you present your request politely, they may at least be able to meet you, have a phone call, or keep in touch every once in a while. In Alicia's case, her relationships were a bit more casual and simply revolved around having consistent, open conversations about her life and career, where she was offered honest advice, feedback, and guidance.

If you haven't met your mentor yet, remember that this can be anyone you look up to, even if you never met them in person. Books you read, podcasts you listen to, conferences, and workshops that impact you can also all serve as "mentors." Though working directly with someone can help speed up your growth and offer you more immediate support, don't be discouraged if you haven't met your mentor in real life yet.

COACHES

Working with a coach is a premium next step to elevating your business. Though it is a significant financial investment, if you are looking to learn directly from someone who has achieved a specific result in their life or career for which you need support and guidance, this is certainly something to consider. One-on-one coaching can save you hours of trying to figure out your next move on your own. It also offers accountability and support that's probably not available to you on that level elsewhere.

The coaching industry has grown in popularity over the past few years and provides an in-depth support relationship between the coach and client. You can hire an individual to help you elevate your sales strategy, expand your knowledge of art marketing, come up with customized action plans for your goals, and more. Every coach typically has a niche area specific to them. Examples include: overcoming financial glass ceilings, business growth strategy, and increasing sales, among numerous other topics. Whatever area you want to see improvement in, there's likely a professional offering that specific information and advice on how to implement it in your career. In the art market, there may be individuals who specialize in helping you sell work or write grants. Some are experienced in licensing and can support you in finding companies to sell prints or products to create new revenue for your art business.

Continue ›

Remember that your coach should have a specific area of expertise, or at least a focus in which they pride themselves, for you to see a return on your investment. We see tons of people promoting their business as the "#1" or in the "Top ten of coaches on X topic," but like art agents, this industry has few regulations. Make sure you do research on who this person is, what their qualifications are, who they've worked with previously, and if they are really worth investing in. It's quite easy for others to dole out advice and collect money, even if they aren't actually living what they preach.

When Is It Time to Hire a Coach?

The right time for you to hire a coach is when you have done everything in your power and are simply not getting the results you want on your own in a specific area of your life or business. You should also be producing work, have a consistent income stream to support this financial investment, and feel ready for the next level in your career. You cannot expect that a coach will be able to solve your problems for you, but rather that they will be there to guide you, ask you questions, and help you come up with solutions to accelerate your growth. Kat worked with multiple coaches after she left her day job and wanted to scale her business. She received mentorship in both 1:1 and group settings. These experiences provided invaluable support and guidance, which she wasn't able to obtain from anyone else in her community. Experienced coaches will have the necessary tools and resources to help you succeed.

How Do You Find a Coach?

You can find a coach by attending workshops and conferences, listening to podcasts, or joining masterminds in your industry. It's normal for coaches to approach you, but make sure you get to know them, respect their work, and feel 100 percent ready to invest in the experience. Kat found her coaches through workshops, a Facebook ad, a podcast episode, and direct outreach on Instagram from someone she admired.

Identify Any Potential Red Flags

Sometimes well-meaning professionals can offer damaging advice that can hurt your art career and business. Whenever you work with anyone, always trust your expertise and intuition and only implement the information given to you if it feels right. No matter how experienced or high-level the individual may be, nothing trumps your knowledge of your own life, collectors, and resources.

Trust yourself, and don't agree to work with someone if they feel pushy, competitive, or overly assertive. Even if you have a decent experience with them at the time of your coaching period, if you have a bad feeling about their motives or approach, it may come back to haunt you at a different time. Keep in mind that the coaching industry does not always require licensing, and the advice you receive from your coach will be individual to his or her experience. Read customer testimonials, ask around to see if others have worked with this coach, and trust your gut above all.

Keep A Tight Circle

It's easy to know what kind of people you want in your art "tribe." You'll likely be looking for those who are either smart, accomplished, ambitious, friendly, and supportive—or a combination of these traits and similar ones. However, as we all know, what you see is not always what you get. Heed the warnings of any red flags, as mentioned previously. Definitely form your own opinions, but if many others have expressed a negative view of someone, they may have a valid reason for doing so and perhaps this is not a person you want to closely associate yourself with. Notice how a person speaks to you and others. Are they excessively sarcastic or harsh? Do they tend to speak with undertones of jealousy? Always pay attention to people's actions, as well as their words.

Unfortunately, we've both been burned in the past. It can feel heartbreaking to have someone who you considered a friend, partner, or mentor betray you. Yet, if we are being honest with ourselves, we could typically have identified warning signs that we should have paid more attention to beforehand. True professional relationships shouldn't cause jealousy in the other person or aggressive competition. Take note if you find yourself feeling stressed, drained, or fearful in any of your relationships. Sometimes it is hard not to brush away the mistakes of those close to you, but you should only give people so many chances. It will be difficult, but sometimes you have to cut ties completely with someone whose relationship is no longer serving you. We promise that this will be easier than having the constant threat of them hurting you in the future hanging over your head.

Luckily, our negative experiences have been few and far between, and we're now confident that we both have created our ideal art tribe. It may take time, but we know you'll eventually find great people to surround yourself with so that you can stay accountable, feel supported, and help others on your path to success.

TAKE ACTION

- Think about your current art tribe. Do you have a solid community of peers, clients, and a mentor or coach supporting you? Take action to stay in touch regularly and make sure you are supporting them in return however you can.

- If you don't yet have a mentor or coach, identify someone in your life who might be a fit, or do research online and by asking around in your community to see if you can be connected to one who would be right for you.

MAKING TIME FOR YOUR ART WHILE WORKING A DAY JOB

Whether we are fulfilled by our current employment or dragging ourselves to work every day to pay the bills, at some point in our lives, we will all probably have to work for someone else, or we'll have other commitments that keep us from making art. There is no wrong way of being an artist, and we want to help you eliminate any negative associations about having to earn money from multiple sources to support your lifestyle and creative practice. It shouldn't matter what else you do to get paid. You are an artist if you make art: it's that simple. Even if you are self-employed, you will inevitably have projects and obligations that yield financial results, but may not be as enjoyable as making your own pieces.

When you are working forty hours a week, have family obligations, and still want to be an artist, it's essential to commit to your practice as much as you can without sacrificing your health, well-being, or the quality of your life. This will look different for each individual, but putting in the hours is a requirement for anyone who wants to build a solid body of work, improve his or her skills, and eventually become a professional.

Before we share tips on how to best use your free time so that you can make great art and still find time for rest, we want to remind you how important it is to remember that you are in charge of designing your life. There is no formula, specific amount of hours, or absolute requirement for how much time you spend in the studio or marketing your work. We suggest that you take a moment to think about your final goals to make the most of your time. We find reverse engineering helpful in any aspect of our lives and businesses.

WHAT IS THE MOST IMPORTANT THING YOU WANT TO ACHIEVE RIGHT NOW?

Ask yourself what your ultimate goal is as an artist, as of this moment. It's okay if it changes. Knowing this will help you manage your current schedule. We want to equip you with as much helpful information as possible, yet that doesn't mean you need to be using it all at once. Channel your desires, biggest dreams, and fantasies about your ideal life as a profitable artist, and work backward from there.

Use the following questions to help you get clear on what you need to spend your free time on.

Do you want to be a full-time exhibiting artist living from your art sales, grants, and teaching?

Do you plan on leaving your day job and becoming self-employed?

What is the most important achievement for you right now? Is it creating a strong body of work, getting media recognition, coming up with additional income, or something else?

Depending on what your answers are, use the information to guide you. Take time to journal and get crystal clear on your goals, and plan your schedule accordingly. For example, if you are trying to have your first sale, devote a few hours of your free time after work to researching marketing podcasts, reading art business blogs, revisiting chapters in this book, and exploring any other resources to help you learn and succeed in this area. Instead of feeling like you HAVE to do something, ask yourself, "Is this serving my biggest goal of [insert your unique goal here]?"

YOU DON'T HAVE TO DO IT ALL AT ONCE

Being an artist, especially if you are interested in treating your work as a small business, requires an incredible amount of research and dedication to not only making the work but also documenting, promoting, submitting, and selling it. You may feel like you will never have enough time in the day, but that's simply not true. Many artists keep their day jobs and successful art practice for years. Kat painted after work and on days off for five years before she became self-employed, thanks to a combination of income streams.

Continue ›

‹ *Continued*

Yes, you have to dedicate time to any area in which you want to see results, but you don't have to rush into anything where you'll likely end up feeling overwhelmed. When Kat was working at her call center job, she created a schedule that enabled her to work four long days and have three days off instead of two. She dedicated one day off to painting, another to marketing, administrative tasks, or networking, and used the last one for rest. You can even commit to thirty minutes a day after work, one day a week for your business tasks, and design the other free time for artmaking or other projects. Try to separate your creative and administrative work when you only have limited amounts of time. Each type of work requires a different part of our brains, and it can interrupt the flow when we switch between tasks. For example, you'll get more done if you focus on sketching for an hour or applying to shows for an hour, rather than trying to do a half hour of each consecutively.

If you have been at your job for a while or have a great relationship with your manager, see if you can get a little more schedule flexibility to help support your art practice. If you are worried about jeopardizing your career path, ask what your options are without bringing up your passion. Use your intuition and have a polite, respectful conversation with your boss.

If you need help with navigating an unpredictable schedule, we are here to help. Kat used to work at Macy's in the cosmetic department. She did not have a set schedule, and her hours fluctuated weekly. For her to achieve results in her art business and stay on track with creating new work for an upcoming exhibition, she would create general goals for her week that were flexible and not time-sensitive. You don't have to keep a rigid schedule. You just have to keep moving forward to see results.

Kat's Example Retail Schedule + Studio Time

Monday: 10–5 shift. Read magazines about art on lunch break

Tuesday: 12–9 shift. Write ideas and research call for art sites on lunch break

Wednesday: Day off. Paint for 3–5 hours, visit a new local museum exhibition

Thursday: 11–7 shift. Write ideas and research call for art sites on lunch break

Friday: Day off. Paint for 1–3 hours, spend a few hours applying to exhibitions and grants

Saturday: 10–5 shift. Sketch on lunch break, work on social media marketing

Sunday: Day off. Relax!

One of the craziest schedules Alicia had was when she worked four different jobs to support herself and partner when they lived in Amsterdam. Saying that she had to be organized to manage it all is an understatement! Some days she would have a shift at a boutique fitness studio, starting very early in the morning, followed by a shift at a gallery, but she still had to make time for working on projects for her social media consulting clients or finishing up articles for *Create! Magazine* at night. Like Kat, she made time for the work that she truly enjoyed whenever she could and used small pockets of time during the day, like breaks, to finish quick tasks or do research. Equally important was that she balanced this intense workload with time off to travel.

No matter where you work or how demanding your job is, you will feel better if you dedicate at least a few hours each week to your passion. The best way to get started is to try spending thirty minutes per day five days a week on your art. There is a ton of research on how powerful this small time commitment can be. Set your alarm for a few minutes earlier, or use part of your lunch break to invest in your future. It can be exhausting, but it's worth it to see your dreams come to fruition. Take it from us!

"No matter where you work or how demanding your job is, you will feel better if you dedicate at least a few hours each week to your passion."

THERE IS A TIME FOR HUSTLE

While we are strong advocates for self-care, mental health, and balance, there are also times to work—and this will not be a consistent occurrence in your life unless you allow it to be.

There will be times when you are presented with an incredible opportunity, have a deadline to meet, or realize that you are super close to your goal—maybe even to leaving your day job! This means that sometimes you won't get enough sleep or you'll have to sacrifice your day off to finish work. As long as you are mindful of the fact that this is a temporary scenario, you should feel good about making progress and taking steps to live your dream. Reward any excessive work periods with time off as soon as you are able to.

MAXIMIZE RESULTS BY MINIMIZING DISTRACTIONS

We are all sometimes guilty of constantly checking our phones and scrolling through Instagram, but it takes a long time for the human brain to regain focus after it's been distracted from a task.

When you are creating art, writing, or researching opportunities, keep your Facebook, Instagram, and other distracting apps closed as much as you can. Ideally, you'd put your phone out of reach and facedown so that you can't see any notifications pop up. Of course, you can keep the sound on for emergency calls, but the reality is that the vast majority of the time it's fine to not respond to anything for an hour or two. Let your friends and family members learn to respect your sacred art time. You will be so much more fulfilled, and possibly even better at your day job, when you begin to carve out time to pursue your passions as an artist.

BANISHING THE GUILT MONSTER

For many artists, it may not be that they don't have the extra time to dedicate to their creative practice, but that they feel guilty for taking time for themselves. Remember that you have every right to be an artist if that is what you want, and you can be both an artist and a mother/father, an artist and a wife/husband, an artist and a business owner, an artist and [anything]! You shouldn't have to choose one or the other in the long run, even if you have to focus on one right now.

Ultimately, even if you have to take a little bit of time away from your children, family, or other work, you'll feel more fulfilled as you dedicate yourself to achieve your goals. Don't let the disappointment of not focusing on your studio practice transition into guilt about finally carving out this time for you. Enjoy it, and realize that when you use this time to develop your creative skills, you are growing as a person, and the happier, satisfied you will actually be able to give more to those around you.

Enlist the help of others, such as friends, family members, and your partner if you have one. Explain why it is so important to you to commit to your art, and come up with ways they can support you. Hopefully, they're on board and will urge you to keep going, while helping out in any way they can! We've both been fortunate to have many people like this in our lives.

TRANSITIONING TO SELF-EMPLOYMENT (IF THAT'S YOUR GOAL)

There is no rush to go solo and, if anything, we recommend that you stay with a steady paycheck for as long as you can until you have consistently tested your income streams and feel confident that you will get paid once you leave your day job. The hard part starts when you are 100 percent responsible for yourself, and potentially the rest of your household too.

Tip:

You can learn more about both of our experiences with transitioning to self-employment in the chapter Taking the Leap & Leaving Your Day Job (page 75), and Kat shares additional insight on various episodes of her Art & Cocktails podcast.

Artists can be their own bosses with hard work and dedication, so if that is your ultimate goal, we believe in you and can't wait to see you thrive! Surround yourself with encouraging people and dive into as many business and marketing books, podcasts, and workshops, as you can to empower you during this transition.

Remember to do your research beyond the tips we share in this book. We are not financial experts, and this advice is based on our individual experiences. Depending on where you live, you'll need to plan separately for health insurance, keeping up with the costs of running your art business, and any unexpected expenses that may arise. Read about the various aspects of working for yourself, and ask as many self-employed artists as you can about how they did it to gather information and feel empowered!

In the meantime, or if you enjoy your day job and wish to continue working there for now or indefinitely, we hope you'll be able to organize your schedule in a way that allows you more freedom and time to make your work. We don't want you to look back one, five, or ten years from now and wish you had given your passion more priority in your life. Find ways, even if small, to be the artist that you want to be!

TAKE ACTION

- Get clear on your ultimate goal: are you happy with your job and hoping to grow within your company, looking for another employer, or wanting to be your own boss? Be very honest and journal about what comes up for you.

- Create a flexible after-work schedule for your art and business tasks. If you can't commit to specific days or hours, create a general list of activities for each week.

- If all you can do is find fifteen to thirty minutes here and there when you're starting out, do that! Use pockets of time on your lunch break, while waiting at the doctor's office, or on your daily commute to do things related to your art career.

- Find an accountability buddy for your art hustle and studio practice, and keep each other on track to achieve your goals and dreams! (See more about this in the chapter Finding Your Tribe, beginning on page 289.)

Bonus
Material

LICENSING YOUR WORK

As you develop your portfolio, become a marketing pro, and build meaningful connections with your audience, you may attract the attention of large companies, including retailers, hotels, publications, and others that reproduce art and sell it to consumers. We know many artists who have landed successful, lasting brand partnerships, giving them an even bigger platform to showcase and promote their work. One of the specific ways that certain businesses work with artists is through licensing, a topic we first mentioned in Diversifying Income Streams (page 85).

Licensing your work means that reproductions or limited edition prints may be available for sale through companies such as Target, West Elm, or Anthropologie. If this sounds like something you envision for your career, you can start researching now on how to make these additional income opportunities a reality.

We asked two creatives from our community about their experiences with licensing, and while many of them were contacted directly by agents or brands themselves, it doesn't mean that you can't prepare for your dream opportunity right now and start pitching your portfolio. When you create a strong personal identity for your art by consistently producing quality art, maintaining a professional website, and having a strong social media presence, you will inevitably draw the attention of your dream clients.

You can also look into trade shows, licensing agents, and websites that partner with hotels, stores, or other public spaces to offer their artwork-placing services. We definitely recommend spending time learning about royalties, copyrights, and the types of contracts that are common between artists and companies. Though each situation will be unique, you want to have a general idea of what to expect and how to negotiate when the ideal opportunity arises. Since you'll likely be working with a business that has an entire legal team behind them, it's important to make sure you are 100 percent comfortable with all the terms of your contract before you sign anything. Artists have definitely been burned in the past, and we would never want this to happen to you.

Tip:

If you don't have a lawyer, or someone close to you who you trust to provide legal advice, do a search in your area to find an organization that provides free or discounted counsel to artists. You never know when you may need it, so it's better to have a contact ready as a precaution.

Continue ›

To provide more specific information about artwork licensing, we've interviewed artists Lisa Krannichfeld and Jenny Brown. They have both partnered with multiple brands over the years and have two unique perspectives that will help you decide if this is a viable avenue for you as well!

LISA KRANNICHFELD

www.lisakrannichfeld.com

How did you get into licensing?

Several years ago, I started selling reproductions of my own art. To come up with formats and prices, I just did some price matching to print reproductions I saw for sale elsewhere. It allowed me to get a feel for the demand out there for reproductions of my work, which pieces were most popular, and what sizes buyers preferred. The pros are you don't share commission fees with another company if you do all the printing and selling yourself. The cons are you have to do all the printing, selling, and marketing yourself, which is likely going to be to a smaller audience than if you partnered with a large print reproduction or art consultant company. I just thought a lower-priced print is a good way to introduce your work to a larger audience, some of whom will want to come back and get an original piece later.

What brands have you worked with so far?

Right now I license my work with Saatchi Art, Artfully Walls (Anthropologie via them), and Four Hands Furniture (West Elm, Perigold, and Pottery Barn via them). What I didn't realize at first is that major home decor giants usually work with print companies, as opposed to individual artists, so signing a contract with a company often leads to selling with other companies through them, in my experience. I also work with a few art consultant companies that place art in boutique hotels and corporate settings around the world.

What tips would you share with artists looking to get involved with major brands for the first time?

I would say it all starts with the work first. Your work needs to be high quality, with high-quality digital files accurately documenting the work. A lot of times the companies (especially art consultants) know exactly what they want, as for format and sizes, when they contact you and it's up to you to be ready to deliver. Sometimes time crunches are a thing and they only have a few days to pitch a project to a client using your work.

If you are the one reaching out to print reproduction companies, do your research about the kinds of art they represent and realize your art may not be a good fit. I know my art isn't for everyone and can be polarizing. If you get rejected, don't morph your art to match the market you got rejected from. Do your own thing, perfect it, and if it is high quality, eventually you will find the niche it fits into. Having an online presence is very essential too. My website has a pretty extensive portfolio of my work viewable, and sometimes I'll get an email from an art consultant or reproduction company that wants to license an artwork I did five years ago.

Share a few benefits of licensing your art through a major company.

You get to say your work was featured in Anthropologie! Ha! As a lifelong Anthro-lover, it was a pretty cool moment! More seriously though, it creates another revenue stream for a full-time artist. You can only make so many original pieces in a year and only have so many exhibitions. Oftentimes, licensing your work with companies is very little work, with little to no overhead cost to you, but brings in revenue. In some cases, if your work is placed in a very populated setting, you will get inquiries from collectors who saw your work, which is also great. They may want to purchase prints or commission original pieces from you.

How did you work out the pricing and royalties?

I honestly had to do a bit of Googling to figure this out. Sadly, there's no handbook on how to figure this out, but some factors can help you decide on a range: the quantity and size of the reproductions and if it's an open or limited edition printing are big ones. If it's a large quantity, royalties are smaller per print; if it's a smaller quantity then royalties are higher. If you're licensing to a band for album art, you factor in how big of a following the band has and how many times they want to print your work. Also, consider if you have to make new work for the project or use existing work. If it's more work for you, then pricing should be higher. Another thing not prompted by the questions but I think is important, is discussing limited versus open edition printing. If you choose to do a limited edition print run, it is important that you print only the amount you say you are going to print. So, if you say it's an edition of twenty, once those twenty are printed and sold, the edition is closed and never printed again. Even if a company wants to license that same artwork later, you have to decline. Buyers are purchasing limited editions because of their preciousness and limited quantity, and if you are not honest about that, it is not good for your reputation.

JENNY BROWN

www.jennybrownart.com

What was your first experience with licensing and how did it come about?

My very first experience with licensing was in 2013, when a magazine asked to use an image of my work as an illustration for an article in one of their upcoming issues. At the time, I had no idea what licensing or image use entailed. Fortunately in this case, the requestor was very professional (and also under a fast-approaching deadline) and basically told me everything I needed to do to make the deal happen: provide a hi-res file, send them an invoice for payment, etc. They also told me up front how much they could pay me ($200! I couldn't believe it!). I played off the whole deal like I'd done it a million times, but really I was jumping up and down in my house and rushing to my computer to Google instructions on how to send an electronic invoice.

What brands have you worked with so far?

In the past few years, I've worked with *Thames & Hudson Press, Ilex Press, Spirituality & Health Magazine,* and Anthropologie.

What tips would you share with artists looking to get involved with brands for the first time?

Follow and interact with the brand's social media. And try developing a few works that you think your targeted company would like, even if they don't see it. It sounds corny, but I found that when I had a clear vision of what a company might like and tried making that work (even though I had no contacts with them specifically) . . . other similar companies and opportunities approached me about it. And you never know where that can lead!

Share a few benefits of licensing your art through a major company.

The biggest benefit is that it allows your work to be seen by so many people—many people who may have never encountered your work otherwise.

How did you work out the pricing and royalties?

In most cases, publishers or printmakers approach me with their pricing structures already worked out. In cases where folks ask me what I charge for image use, my rates are (and will probably always be) a work in progress. I often create a pricing plan and run it by other artists to get their feedback. I would be lying if I said I had this part all worked out, and I know there have been a few cases where I sadly undercharged for my work. But I feel like these mistakes are part of the learning process. Now, with each project, I become more confident in my plans and need less support from others to create my pricing.

LICENSING RESOURCES

Websites

www.artlicensinginfo.com

Trade Shows

www.surtex.com
www.licensingexpo.com

Legal

www.legalzoom.com
www.copyright.gov

Books

Mind Your Business: A Workbook to Grow Your Creative Passion Into a Full-Time Gig by Ilana Griffo

Art, Inc.: The Essential Guide for Building Your Career as an Artist by Lisa Congdon

Art, Money, Success: Finally Make a Living Doing What You Love by Maria Brophy

TAKE ACTION

- Look over your website, social media, and overall online presence to make sure it is polished and professional. It should be appealing to licensing agents and brands that you dream of working with.
- Prepare top-notch photography for submissions so that you are ready in case your work is selected for a deal.
- Research and compile a list of agents, websites, and trade shows that may be a fit for your work.
- Start pitching your portfolio, always tailoring each submission and inquiry specifically to each organization you're applying to.
- Research common contract terms, royalties, and average payments so that you are prepared to negotiate, if needed.

CONSIDERING & ACQUIRING AN AGENCY OR ART REP

As a result of the rising costs of keeping a traditional brick-and-mortar gallery in business, those whose job it is to sell art on behalf of artists have evolved into new professional roles. In recent years, the number of independent dealers and curators, art advisors, consultants, and agents has grown rapidly. Rather than open or maintain a physical space with a large roster of represented artists, many decide to work with more focused groups of artists on niche projects. They may have a dedicated office, but sometimes they are able to do their work remotely and only need an established website as the anchor of their business.

Broadly speaking, galleries do fall under the category of agents, but for the purposes of this chapter, when we refer to an art agent (also called art rep) we specifically mean someone working independently or with an agency that represents artists. Art agents act in a similar way to galleries in that they can help artists sell work, reach new clients, promote their art and garner media attention, place pieces in important private and public collections, handle certain aspects of their business, and more. Just like with becoming a gallery owner, there is no formal license or educational requirement to start working as an agent (beyond the paperwork needed to set up a legal business). In fact, many may come from backgrounds outside of the arts, such as marketing, public relations, and sales.

One way agents often differ from galleries is that they tend to hone in on one or a few particular specializations. For example, they more commonly help artists secure mural projects, hang work in commercial spaces, sign a licensing deal, or land a major brand partnership. If these sorts of projects interest you and would be a fit for your work, working with an agent might be right for you!

SHOULD I SEEK AN AGENT?

As we advised with applying to galleries, you should not think of working with an agent as a savior for your art career. Any good agent should certainly give you a noticeable boost and push you to the next level, but there is never any guarantee that you'll suddenly be swimming in sales. You have to take charge of your art as a business first and set yourself up for success.

Continue ›

It is hard for an agent to work with you if you aren't already at least a bit established in the industry. They use your background, including media features, previous gallery relationships, significant exhibitions, and your sales records to build new relationships for you. Without any of these things, the agent would have to work much harder on your behalf. This means more time, perhaps more money spent, and likely fewer successes. Give it time and be patient until you are ready to make the most of this type of business partnership.

Besides having a solid foundation for your career, you definitely want to consider the costs. Luckily, most agents will work for a smaller percentage than the standard 50 percent commission taken by a gallery, but this is not always the case. Depending on how big the business is and what services they offer, they may require 10 to 25 percent, or more. Others may request a flat fee per month, quarter, or year, or ask you to pay per project they assist you with.[10] This is where some research will come in handy. Compare any offer with other artists you know who work with agents and make sure what someone is offering you sounds reasonable.

You've likely heard numerous artists lament about how many hours go into keeping up with email, social media, shipping, creating invoices, applying to juried shows or other opportunities, and performing other administrative work. Sure, you can hire studio assistants galore to help you with several of these tasks, but someone who is an expert at not only making your studio practice function more smoothly but also at developing your career may very well be worth the money. In addition to sales and sharing your work with their client list, working with an agent can help you carve out additional time in your studio.

This brings us to the next point, which is that even if you enjoy doing some administrative work, it may not be your area of expertise. It's never a bad idea to spend time developing your networking skills or reading about the best ways to market yourself (that's the point of this book after all!), but at a certain point in your career you may see great benefits and quicker progress when you invest in hiring a professional to help. Again, this gets you more time in the studio to focus on making great work and enjoying what you love to do most!

10 **Format Team,** *"Art Agents: Do You Need One?,"*
June 6, 2019, https://www.format.com/magazine/resources/art/art-agent-artist-agency.

WEIGHING YOUR OPTIONS

If it sounds like you're at the right stage of your career for an agent, there are still a few things to consider beyond how much you'll have to pay them. Again, we want to remind you that there is no license or other formal education required to become an agent. Beyond testimonials and vetting their business based on the quality of their website, social media channels, other marketing, and any previous projects you know of, you'll have to take them at their word that they are indeed as good as they say they are. If this makes you wary, artist coach Renée Phillips recommends building a relationship based on trust first, before entering into any sort of arrangement.[11] Meet in person, verify any credentials or reviews that you can, and make sure that they truly believe in you and your work!

Thinking that an agent is your best bet for getting a gallery to notice you? Well, perhaps not. Alicia worked in several galleries where agents reached out regularly to pitch a client's work, but she never saw any of them get accepted. Galleries prefer to work with artists directly, because they try to avoid sharing commission with more than one party whenever possible. It also creates more of a hassle if they always have to communicate with your agent rather than you, especially if a tight deadline comes up (which happens quite a lot!).

We also have mentioned previously that you should seek to create your own community of industry professionals. While one primary purpose of hiring an agent is for them to share your work with their contacts, establishing your own community is especially crucial if you decide to end the partnership for whatever reason. If they never allowed you to be in contact with any of their clients directly, you may lose access to them and it will take time to build up your network again.

The most important part of deciding whether you need an agent is finding the right person to work with. As you will be working very closely, you absolutely need to have someone who understands you and communicates well. If they are not already an expert in their field, do you admire how they run their business or respect their level of marketing skills? Trust your intuition if you aren't sure whether you should trust someone. Ask how much time they will be devoting to you alone, how many other clients they represent, and what their exclusivity policies are. The last thing you want to find out is that you've inadvertently given away your right to show with certain galleries, pursue other opportunities without your agent's involvement, or take full profit from a sale they didn't help broker. You may additionally want to suggest a trial period of six months to a year so that you can both test out the relationship and see if it is indeed a fit on both sides.[12]

Continue ›

11 **Renée, Phillips,** *"The Truth about Fine Art Agents," https://renee-phillips.com/fine-art-agents/.*
12 **Format Team,** *"Art Agents: Do You Need One?"*

Sort out all the details in advance and make sure to sign a contract. If they offer one first, read it very carefully and negotiate any terms that you are not 100 percent comfortable with. Always ask questions beforehand if you are not clear about something.

HOW DO I FIND THE RIGHT ART AGENT FOR ME?

Hopefully, if you've begun to establish your career and are putting your art out there, an agent will find you when you are ready. Since it is mutually beneficial for them to find exceptional new talent, they can often be found at art fairs and open studio events.[13] Search online to see if there are any agents based in your area, and ask around to collectors, curators, and artist peers to see if anyone works with or has heard of an agent they would recommend.

Alicia once knew of a couple where the wife acted as the agent for her husband's work. With her background in the hospitality industry, as well as marketing, and her savvy sales abilities, they made a formidable duo. Although they hired other sales assistants to help promote his work, none were ever as successful as she was with selling his art. People loved hearing the stories from her because she was so intimately involved with the work and the artist. He, on the other hand, loved and took advantage of the fact that he was able to spend the majority of his time in the studio.

More and more people today enjoy buying from artists directly because they want to learn about the work from the person who created it. Mimic that experience by finding someone who is as excited about your work as you are. While we don't necessarily recommend looking into family or friends to serve as an agent for you, since we all know that mixing business with pleasure can get complicated, you want someone who would be supportive in the way that those closest to you are.

Tip:

In a way, using your own network can be like having an agent. If you recommend others' work to various projects or opportunities that are a good match for them, they'll more often than not do the same for you. Remember: community over competition!

We hope that this overview has helped you decide whether seeking out an art agent would be beneficial for your practice. For a little additional insight, we've interviewed Elizaveta Zhurkovskaya, also known as @curatoronthego, who shares more about her role as an independent curator, art advisor, and agent.

ELIZAVETA ZHURKOVSKAYA

http://curatoronthego.com/

Elizaveta (Liza) Zhurkovskaya, the founder of Curator on the Go, is a Toronto-based independent art curator. She holds a BA in Art History & Human Geography from the University of Toronto and an MFA in Criticism & Curatorial Practice from OCAD University. Liza organizes exhibitions and art events around the city, and her research and curatorial interests include contemporary art, memory, storytelling, and community engagement.

Tell us a bit about what you do as an agent and independent curator.

Since 2015, I have been working with artists as an independent art agent and advisor. Through media opportunities, exhibitions, and curatorial advice, I help them thrive in the industry and establish themselves as entrepreneurs. Not being tied to any specific art institution provides me the freedom to work with a selection of local and international artists, and personalize the collaboration.

I find that the business side of the industry is often left out in art school and from the minds of artists, so I help shift the focus. I am trying to erase the "starving artist" trope and show artists that they can be successful without finding representation from an art gallery. As art entrepreneurs, they can showcase and sell their works at public spaces, art studios, and online, while establishing their brand identity through self-promotion and client outreach.

About how many artists do you work with and what kind of projects do you normally do?

I try to represent a maximum of five artists at once so I can ensure I am able to devote the proper amount of time and energy to each one. As a rule, I prefer to have a mix of media and artistic style on my roster so I can have a range to offer potential art collectors and minimize conflict of interest between the artists I represent. It also gives me the ability to create unique collections for clients by combining work from the different artists.

Another service I offer for artists is phone consultations that are catered to the artists' specific needs. Topics may include finding your artistic voice and niche, selling and pricing your art and services, and branding. I also curate exhibitions and art events in Toronto, working directly with artists or local art institutions to curate solo and group shows that are accessible for artists of any career level, and that unite the art community and the general public.

My goal is to encourage and construct a more inclusive and sustainable art community in Toronto and around the world. I recently launched the Curator on the Go podcast as a platform for artists, art professionals, and other creatives to share their stories and work, and to learn from each other on how to create a brand, self-promote, and most importantly, to be inspired to pursue their dreams.

What do you think is most different about working with an agent versus a gallery?

There are different names for the role of an agent—it can be a private dealer, an art consultant, a gallery, or a marketing consultant—essentially any professional who works on behalf of an artist to represent, promote, and sell their works.

Personally, I am not tied to any art institution or commercial art gallery, so the biggest difference between the two options is the commission percentage. Galleries average around 30 to 60 percent, while independent art agents, such as myself, range closer to 10 to 30 percent, based on the involvement of the project and experience.

Also, because of the more personalized experience of working with an art agent, more time is spent promoting the artist and searching for showcases and sale opportunities. Of course, it also depends on the independent agent, because the most important factor is how well he/she is connected to the circle of art collectors and potential buyers. For an agent to remain ahead of the game, they must be constantly on the go, networking at various events, investing time to meet potential clients, and be active in the art community.

In regards to galleries, especially established ones, they should have a contact list of regular clients that they invite to their shows and events. If you are interested in working with a gallery, you should make sure they are also spending time on marketing and promoting their venue and the artists, and reaching out to new clients, especially young collectors.

How should artists go about looking for an agent that is right for them if they are interested in working with one?

Some of the main reasons for having an agent are for their connections, to have more access to event and sale opportunities, and to help with business-related tasks so the artist can spend more time creating new work.

Of course, artists need to understand that there is a cost associated with hiring an agent. Many independent art professionals charge a salary or a fee for the representation, as selling art can be a challenging and time-consuming task. It is important to look at this expense as an investment in your career growth and as a way to get more exposure for your work.

Before signing with an agent, it is important to learn about their background, experience, and areas of expertise. Asking for references and names of artists they worked with before is a good way to get a sense of their career history. Most of all, it is important to make sure your potential agent has time to represent you properly.

TAKE ACTION

- Honestly think about whether you are at the right stage in your career that hiring an art agent makes sense.
- Do some research in your area and reach out to reps or agencies that you believe would be a good match for you and your artwork.
- Set up meetings and interview potential candidates. Be clear about your expectations and goals.
- Put together a contract and review it thoroughly before signing. Suggest an initial trial period to test out if you're a fit for each other.

FINDING YOUR VOICE AS AN ARTIST

KESTIN CORNWALL

www.kestincornwall.com

We discuss tips for how to define your style on page 211, but we also wanted to give you more in-depth content about why it's so important to find your creative voice. To that end, we're so excited to share an interview with Toronto-based figurative artist Kestin Cornwall.

Why do you think it is important to cultivate your own voice as an artist?

I think it's valuable. Fostering your voice as an artist will give you direction and a strong sense of self. You will need to form your voice to build and maintain a healthy level of confidence when creating and sharing your art. If you want to take it to the next level you will need a developed voice for marketing and branding. Having a voice allows you to ask questions and gain the understanding that you will make mistakes. Also, the understanding that calculated mistakes and, in some ways, assessed risk are the bedrock of creating.

You also have to be willing to accept criticism and welcome critique. Knowing that it's for your personal growth. This is valuable because as you develop your voice, aesthetics, some use the term 'style' and direction as an artist, you're more open to these steps, and you can use it to process your ideas and grow.

To improve and develop as an artist, and create interesting work, you also have to be willing to go into spaces you're not welcomed. You have to go into these spaces knowing you are aiming at developing a voice as an artist. This will allow you to feel more relaxed in these difficult spaces.

Keep in mind, I think to properly cultivate your voice as an artist you also must know you need support. To find this support, you'll need to first show up for places that want you, and love and fully support and welcome you. Spend time in these places. With these people.

I think it's also critical to push out the stereotype of an introverted artist, madman, locked in a room all day. This notion is contradictory in many ways. Artists want to show their work. Artists work in groups. Art brings people together. Cultivating your voice as an artist allows for a greater understanding of this and helps create community. Like most successful individuals, dedicated artists are well-rounded, hard-working, productive, and work to maintain a work-life balance, often focused around their work.

You want to give yourself the best chance; it's a tough industry. Many people can draw, a lot of people can draw and paint well, and even more people think they can. So with that rant out of the way, it comes down to the need to hone your skills and that includes crafting and forming your voice as an artist, with a willingness to change and adapt.

Why do many young and emerging artists struggle with this?

Upbringing. Human nature. Schooling. All of these things play a factor. Male artists struggle with school and expectations from modern society. From my perspective stereotypically because it teaches men they have to be the protectors and providers. This is a good thing. I agree with it on many levels but understand it raises some issues. Men are taught to accumulate wealth or symbols of wealth as soon as possible to gain status in their social circles. To attract or impress women. Art in some ways puts both of those responsibilities and wants in question. Stereotypically men are forced to decide very young on a profession that can successfully provide for a family: a trade, a well paying 9 - 5 task job, or a sport. Denying their inner artist, they choose a more proven, more stable, socially acceptable career path, often one that they have seen done by family members and friends in the past. This puts pressure on a young artist and in many ways distracts from the focus needed to develop their craft.

You also have to fully be comfortable and okay in knowing it will take time; you have to always create more work and you have to be willing to make mistakes.

The secondary school curriculum was designed to lower crime and to teach kids to be factory workers. Early school systems trained us to login or sign in, sit in rows, and wait for the bell. You sit while a larger, more dominant figure directs and is in control of when you speak, when you get up, and when you sit down. It's designed to take out part of your personality to control you and give you structure. In some ways this is good. But in many ways, early school systems push out creativity. Schools can hinder free thinking. Now those systems are slowly changing. Keep in mind, this is not to say the structure is not important; structure and consistency is unbelievably valuable. The point is that free-thinking is needed for an artist to form their ideas and voice.

It's also easy to choose low hanging fruit: it's there, minimum effort. Take whatever is there. Spend as little time as possible. Avoid being let down or the risk of failure: The safe choice. Follow the leader. It's easy to just draw a few pictures with a yellow Maxpen pencil. Maybe try some colour pencils your aunt gave you. Maybe you don't have the guidance as a young artist or confidence possibly to push to try other options. If you add gender, the want to have children, and racial stereotypes to the reasons why young artists struggle to find a voice, multiply the reasons not to work to craft a style and voice, or even time to do this by 10-1000.

What did you do to find your voice and develop your style? Did you look to certain sources for inspiration, practice and aspire to make a lot of work, or something else?

A friend told me this: write down a list of people you want to impress, girls, amigos that you grew up with, and your family. So I did. She then handed me a lighter; she told me to burn the fucking list. You can't do things to impress people. It's a weakness. It's a fault line. It won't allow you to focus. That was her point. Yes in a way when done right you can use it as fuel, but you have to be very careful with this. In some ways, it's better to just avoid it. I had to realize and accept that if I wanted to hone my craft, develop a more clear voice, I had to be willing to not look as good at first, sacrifice, look like I got it wrong, possibly even at some point look silly, or even foolish in the short term. When you do that, you're free in some ways. Free to take a calculated risk, free to grow without the feeling of other people looking over your shoulders; they are there, but you can focus on what's in front of you. This way you are free to make mistakes and find a voice. Find flow. Find a tribe. Find a path and grow as a young artist into a developed artist that can find a

Continue ›

way to thrive even in the worst of situations. This is your project. You are your project. You are working to be just a bit better, grow just a bit more than yesterday. You have to be willing to be wrong, maybe receive negative feedback, and have the composure and sense of purpose to zoom out, make small changes, and keep it moving. Nothing happens overnight. Again. Nothing happens overnight. Slow progress is still progress. That's what I did. That's what I'm doing. I have come to understand it's better to aim to create 20,000 paintings than to aim to sell one $20,000.00 painting. Put your ego aside and do the work. Don't always take the low hanging fruit, aim higher.

Yes. It's important to have people to compare your work with and steps to. If you don't, there's a missing goal, and you won't have the footprints they left behind to follow. With that in mind, you have to be careful with whom you compare yourself and not expect to start playing basketball tonight, as an example, and be as good as Scottie Pippen tomorrow. There are far too many factors, and you have to focus on the ones you can move and control in some ways. You must take the time to focus on those factors. They say life is short, I get that, but if you talk to someone who is 70 and successful at what they wanted to do, they say life is long. I took time to process the fact that when you look at the art industry, top-selling artists, the most developed artists, the artists selling prints and originals are grown ass women and grown ass men. It's the one industry that wants you more as you get older. There's no age cap, take your time, and craft your damn voice.

Finding a group of like-minded people to connect and grow with is of value to a young artist, looking to develop a voice, find a vibe, craft, and aesthetic. This will help you to articulate and understand your work, and once you can coherently explain and show it to those you trust and have an established relationship with, you can then more clearly tell and show others. In doing this you also should talk and debate with people who do not agree with your work or dislike what you're doing to help mold your ideas, your views, and your direction. I took and still continue to take the time to do all these things in some form or another.

Can you share some advice for artists still in the process of figuring out their style?

I come from the mud. I come from the mindset of, you got to just talk less and work all day and for some of us all night at times. Some people have a more stable base, more support. You have to be willing to put in the work regardless of your economic and social position at the time. Make your own odds, ball players say that all the time. Risk being wrong. Risk people not believing in you or your idea, in your process. Learn to be okay with people not liking or respecting the early results. Understand that what is old is new, and what's new is old. Take in information, process it, but also take time to yourself, take the time needed to reflect, and reprocess that information. I like the 50/30/20 rule for this: 50% of the time look for and digest information while making art. Then spend 30% of the time to process, develop new ideas, work to show the work, and get some responses and critiques. Spend the last 20% resting and recharging. Like those IG posts we see all the time that say, "you're basically a house plant, get some sun, drink some water."

I always give myself this advice. Talk less, and listen more. I would suggest to post less online and create more. Make a small list of people you value, add to it, change it, and put it away. Check back on it, during low points, remember to call them. Focus on your craft, fully enjoy it, and take a moment to appreciate the moments in time you get to work on your art.

Aim to be connected, always look for new inspiration. Always be open to trying new things to help mold your voice as an artist and shape your views correctly. As I mentioned early on, remind yourself to make more work.

Any other tips or advice you wish you knew when starting out as an artist?

I'd like to share my thoughts on the media. I want to point out to those reading this, artists on the come up, media romanticizes the steps toward success, making it seem easy, as if everything always works out in the end. But in real life, in real-time, everything worth doing is difficult. Cultivating your voice and finding a style or aesthetic is worth doing. So, it's hard.

There are countless hurdles, and when it gets difficult some young artists are unprepared and don't have the tools to be resilient. They risk giving up. I've seen it hundreds of times, from music to visual art to design. Not to say that I'm a rock star and I'm the perfect example, no, but I've endured many struggles and have managed to circumvent some huge difficulties that would have led me to stop painting or working as a creative. In my opinion making art for likes is poison, responding to or letting criticism affect you making more art is poison, the feeling of needing likes is poison. As creatives, specifically, we must be very mindful of how we respond to things. Be intentional in your response, and mindful of where you direct energy.

It takes time. Ten years is just the beginning. Most artists don't have their first solo show until they are 40+, even more people don't make their first million until they are over 60. Most people never make a million in a year or in five years. The best artists at some point had people they looked up to; they also made work that was not that good. I'm saying this because forming your voice as an artist requires some level of sustainability and reliability. You need to know that you have some art supplies, you need to know you have a space to work in, that you have a warm place to sleep at night, and some healthy food to eat. Everything else is extra; too much extra can be distracting.

Also, give people their flowers! If you admire someone, tell them. This will not take away from you or your shine. It will not hold you back. Them being great will not make you small. Put positive energy in the world and this allows you to move honestly through life. I try to do this, and it allows me to enjoy some success. But it's a learning curve and I'm still growing.

In the end, you get back the energy you put out, both positive and negative, but in countless different ways and never exactly how you want it. You have to choose to do the hard thing and then outwork everyone. If you choose to do these things, as a young artist over time you'll find and develop your voice and some form of success. You'll head in the direction of those you have admiration and respect for and for a small number of young artists, you will surpass those people you now look up to, and you will exceed expectations over time. Art is life.

EXPLORING OTHER SOCIAL MEDIA OUTLETS

We've discussed Facebook and Instagram in depth in previous chapters, and while those two social media platforms are the most popular for artists, there may be others that are relevant to your practice as well. From Alicia's previous experience in workshops on social media management and her time freelancing as a social media consultant and Kat's experience with growing her personal profile and the magazine's accounts, we recommend that you not focus on more than two platforms. Ultimately, you want to still be able to spend time making artwork and doing other administrative tasks.

Posting regularly on two channels already takes a fair bit of planning and effort, so four or five different channels will quickly add up. Perhaps you've heard of the quote "jack of all trades, master of none," which we believe applies to this situation. Would you rather spread yourself too thin across several platforms or get really good at one or two, keeping in mind that the better you are on those two platforms, the more likely your activity on these social media channels will translate to connections and sales? If you believe that it is necessary to be a part of more than two platforms, and that they relate to your work, then definitely consider using one of the scheduling apps we've mentioned previously to streamline your posting.

If you're still pretty new to social media, here is a quick breakdown of additional platforms that artists use and who we think they could be suitable for. Keep in mind that social media changes quickly and new platforms continue to be launched in the hopes that they become the next big thing to catch on. While these are the most relevant to artists today, the social media landscape could very well be different a year from now.

TWITTER

Even though Twitter expanded the text count allowed in posts back in 2017, it still is best for quick, snappy messages. If text plays an integral part in your work or you enjoy writing, this could be a great platform for you. You can also use a Twitter account to share events, news, and quotes. Hashtags are essential to using Twitter and help define which posts become the most popular, but don't forget to add photos at least periodically as well!

YOUTUBE & VIMEO

Facebook and Instagram encourage users to share video content through Facebook Live and IGTV, but YouTube still has a vast and dedicated audience, as does Vimeo, to a lesser degree. You may want to consider creating your own channel if you are a video or performance artist. Of course, you'll have recordings of your work on your website, but having them on these sites as well may help you reach a wider audience. Other reasons for launching a profile would be if you enjoy creating process videos of your art, recording installation walkthroughs, highlighting interviews with other artists, making tutorials about techniques you use, or giving general advice on art business and maintaining a studio practice.

PINTEREST

For those who primarily have been using Pinterest for recipes or home decor inspiration, think about how it may be an asset for your art career too, especially because it is a top destination for interior designers, decorators, and more—you may want to post about your art to get on their radar. It is also very popular for contemporary crafts, so if your work includes textiles, ceramics, embroidery, or something along those lines, this may be the perfect platform for you to share your work and find your peers. As we suggest with Instagram, your photos on Pinterest must be high quality to grab other users' attention. Instead of albums, you can create different boards on Pinterest of each series, medium you use, or the various sizes of work you make. You might also get creative and arrange boards based on a color palette or theme.

Kat often gets messages on social media from people who discovered her work on Pinterest. If a blogger or a big website featured you, your work might end up on this site. It's not a bad idea to search for your name periodically to see if you missed any media features. Don't overlook Pinterest—it may be the perfect way for collectors to discover new artists like you!

REDDIT

This is another platform that has an incredibly loyal fan base of users. It divides content into niche categories called subreddits, which you can then choose to follow based on your interests, like r/Art for example. You may certainly be able to share your work and find new followers of your work, but we're not familiar with artists who have used this successfully to make sales or connect to new opportunities. This is not to say that it isn't possible, however. If you already enjoy using Reddit, utilize it to your advantage!

LINKEDIN

We've mentioned LinkedIn previously in Networking 101 for Artists (page 142), but even if you don't use this social media outlet to post regularly, you should at least have a profile set up. Not only is it useful for job searching and having your resume listed online, but you can potentially find important gallery, museum, advisor, consultant, and designer contacts. Think of it like a professional search engine where you can find people working in your industry in any part of the world! It can be an invaluable resource for making new connections. Sometimes, if an institution or gallery does not list contact information on their website, you can still reach people through a message on LinkedIn. Alicia has been able to reach several significant interviewees for her articles by sending them a quick note this way.

If you would like to be more active on LinkedIn, you can post about accomplishments, article features, exhibitions, or simply share your work. The hashtag #art is fairly active and Alicia has noticed some artists receive a lot of attention when they post images of their work. LinkedIn also gives the option to upgrade your profile to get more attention, which can be useful if you're actively searching for work, and allows you to see everyone who views your page and boost your business posts in a similar way to other platforms.

OTHER PLATFORMS

There are still a number of artists who use Tumblr, Flickr, and other sites, but these platforms are much less popular than they once were. Most people have moved on to Facebook and Instagram instead. If your art is targeted to a younger demographic, you could think about joining and promoting your work through Snapchat or TikTok. Both platforms focus on short bursts of content (video and photos with Snapchat and quick mobile videos with TikTok). In order to be successful on these channels, you'll want to focus on creating content that immediately grabs the attention of a viewer in a matter of seconds and makes them want to share it. Think about your backdrops, any text or special effects to add, and getting clear audio when possible.

TAKE ACTION

- After reading this bonus section, is there another social media outlet that jumps out as one that would add value to your marketing efforts? If so, do thorough research online about how it works and then set up a profile to get started!

PLANNING YOUR SOCIAL MEDIA CONTENT

Before we get into tips on how to plan social media posts on whichever channels you choose to share and promote your artwork, we want to stress again that this should not be something that you worry about endlessly or that should take away time which could be better spent in your studio. Social media is a tool that can support your art career, but you should never solely rely on it for sales or to find new opportunities. It does not replace the fact that you must always strive to create your best work, do other traditional forms of networking in addition to marketing yourself online, and find spaces to exhibit your art where people can view it in person.

While there are many accounts online that stick to a specific formula of posting certain images or content on certain days, we like ours to feel a bit less curated. Not to mention, if you plan your ideas far in advance, other exciting news might come up in the meantime and you'll end up moving your posts around anyway. But it's really your decision on how much of a schedule you want to create for your social media accounts and how much time you want to dedicate to content planning. Either way, we recommend that you post a range of images and captions to keep it interesting for both you and your followers.

SOCIAL MEDIA NOTE:

You can get creative with how you choose to add variety to your social media feeds. We know artists who have garnered large followings from consistently posting the same type of images. Painter Erika Stearly enjoys sharing full, completed works and then viewers can swipe to see a series of photographs of how the piece progressed during its creation. Thus, the majority of her feed is finished artwork shots, but within each post you can often find work in progress images and even reference photos. She also adds personality through her captions. Find the routine that works for you and your audience!

Setting up posts in advance can be very useful in numerous situations and doesn't have to feel monotonous. If you are traveling, you may want to have two to three weeks planned in advance so that you can focus on packing, enjoying your trip, and getting back into your routine when you return. It is also helpful if you know that you have a big event or announcement coming up that you want to promote to your audience. You can even do a countdown starting a week to several days in advance to help build excitement. It helps to have your marketing efforts work together so try to coordinate your posts on Facebook, Instagram, or other channels, with your email blasts for a bigger impact.

When you have a business account, you may also want to check in on the analytics or insights section to see if each social media channel can give you ideas of which days and/or times you receive the most engagement from your posts. Once you have this information, you can then compare it to the type of content that you shared in order to see what has performed the best and how to maximize what and when you post going forward. But also, use your instincts too! You know which works and announcements you are most excited about so post those on high traffic days and during peak hours. Give them an extra boost to help spread the awareness of the post even further than your own group of followers and always set a target audience.

Generally speaking, we think about our posts on a weekly basis. For Kat's personal painting account, she mostly highlights full images of completed works and does so every few days at least. Each week, that could mean posting between two to four paintings, but if you don't have enough work to keep up as frequently as that you can either simply post less or alternate with other types of content. She also occasionally includes an older piece that she saw again recently, that was featured in the media, that has come back from a show, or that she is planning to offer for sale at a discount. Then she mixes in studio images, works in progress, and a selfie or two to add personality and diversity throughout her feed. In her stories, Kat likes to share inspirational quotes in her stories almost every day and she offers advice via short IGTV clips once a week or so. While this seems like a lot of content, she tends to post organically based on what is inspiring her that day or currently going on in her life.

Again, this should be a fun way to add insight into your work and connect with your audience. If it isn't enjoyable for you, think about why that is. Are you pushing yourself to post too frequently, bored of writing meaningless captions, or not yet comfortable with sharing your work? It's never too late to change to how you approach posting on your accounts, especially if it will benefit how you use it and therefore how successful your engagement with others will be!

Continue ›

On Create! Magazine's accounts, we share between 3 - 5 works of art daily (sometimes more or less depending on if we are busy) and we also find funny or motivational art-related posts to include on our feed about once or twice a week. We try to keep posts with text to a minimum unless we have an announcement to make about an open call for art, a new issue or product release, an exhibition, or a special offer. The one thing we definitely do on a weekly basis is share cat-themed artwork every Saturday for #caturday because our audience loves it (and so do we)!

On PxP Contemporary's account, Alicia likes to primarily share artwork that is currently available at the gallery and then she occasionally intersperses posts about gallery news, exhibitions, and installation views as well. She generally posts once a day, 5 - 7 days a week and likes to do a weekly highlight of one of the featured artists on 'Studio Sunday' if possible. Rather than use a scheduling app, she likes to email herself the ideas she came up with for content on a weekly basis. We've also mentioned before that we like to store blocks of hashtags in our notes app so that they can easily be copied and pasted after uploading an image to Instagram.

The best way to find what will work best for you is to look at other accounts and decide which styles you like. Look at how often these other artists post and decide if that is reasonable for you. Do they post one studio shot per every three full artwork images? Or do they share more works in progress and installation views? Try it out for one month and see if you can stick to it. If it works, keep going! If not, adjust how often you post or which types of content seem to work better for catching the attention of your audience.

Seven Day Sample (for one month):

Day 1: Finished artwork image (include details for how to purchase if it is available for sale)
Day 2: Install view (artwork in a gallery, hanging in your studio, client's home)
*this can be photoshopped if you don't have any in person images
Day 3: Finished artwork image
Day 4: Older finished artwork image
Day 5: Something that inspires you (quote, book, another artist, nature, traveling, etc)
Day 6: Finished artwork image
Day 7: Work in progress

Day 8: Finished artwork image
Day 9: Finished artwork image
Day 10: Photo of you working or selfie
Day 11: Work in progress
Day 12: Finished artwork image
Day 13: Detail of an artwork
Day 14: Install view

Day 15: Something that inspires you
Day 16: Finished artwork image
Day 17: Detail of an artwork
Day 18: Finished artwork image
Day 19: Install view
Day 20: Older finished artwork image
Day 21: Photo of you working or selfie

Day 22: Install view
Day 23: Finished artwork image
Day 24: Finished artwork image
Day 25: Detail of an artwork
Day 26: Finished artwork image
Day 27: Work in progress
Day 28: Finished artwork image

*Remember to add in important news about exhibitions and other events! Post multiple times so that people don't forget about them.

Five Day Sample:

Same as above minus one artwork image (current or older) and either install view, work in progress, or inspirational quote each week.

Resources:

We've mentioned in previous chapters that you can also use apps like Hootsuite and Buffer to schedule your posts in advance. Make sure to double check all of your spelling, links, and images so that everything is posted correctly! If you aren't ready for a full program for social media planning, you can try it out on your own within several platforms. Facebook, for example, will let you schedule posts directly within your profile and even backdate them if needed. If you want to get more involved with creating a very specific look for your feed, you can search for apps that will show you what your grid will look like based on your scheduled posts.

TAKE ACTION

- Decide if you want to try a social media scheduling app, set up your account, and link your profiles.
- Think about how far in advance you want to schedule your posts. You can try out one week first and then move on to planning by month.
- Plan out your grid on Instagram or simply choose how often you want to post various types of content. For example, three full artwork images per week, one quote, and one work in progress (or whatever mix of posts you'd like!).

ACKNOWLEDGMENTS

First, to our readers—thank you for letting us share our stories with you and for making the world a better place by adding beauty, creativity, and expression to our daily lives.

We never would have been able to create this book without the support of the generous community of creatives that has followed us through building the magazine, podcast, and gallery. It's hard to express how honored we are that several of you have been part of our journey from the beginning, and we're still humbled that people continue to join us today! We are also so grateful for the artists who were willing to share their experiences on these pages. Your valuable knowledge took this version of the book to the next level.

We cannot say enough how appreciative we are for the family members and friends who stood by us when we faced our biggest fears and challenges during the process of writing this book. Thank you to those who believed in us, even when we thought *The Complete Smartist Guide* wouldn't be published.

Of course, we are especially thankful for our friendship and business partnership (of over ten years!) that has only continued to grow stronger with time. Finally, we must give a special thank you to Alicia's cat, Zorro, for openly voicing his opinions on every call to make sure this project would turn out great (may he rest in peace). A big hug to Lourdes for her advice and for being one of our biggest cheerleaders. All our love to Grego and Sean for pushing us to be our best and always having our backs.